Comprehensive Inter

This book is a timely insight into the internationalization of higher education institutions. The internationalization of higher education is a global phenomenon, but with substantial variation in how it is made operational in individual institutions. *Comprehensive Internationalization* focuses on desirable practices in institutions and their actual approaches to implement a more integrated, strategic, or comprehensive global engagement across their core missions: teaching, research, and service.

Part I of the book investigates a wide range of issues governing the internationalization of institutions:

- outlining the origins, meaning and evolution toward more strategic and comprehensive forms of internationalization;
- building an understanding of the meanings of comprehensive internationalization, as well as common aspirations, when linked to different types of institutions;
- understanding the rationales and motivations for internationalization and intended results;
- creating an institutional vision and culture to support comprehensive internationalization; and
- implementing key strategies for successful internationalization in terms of practical actions and programs and results, including identifying and ameliorating barriers, engaging organizational change, assessing outcomes, and obtaining resources.

The writers in Part II of the book offer case stories from institutions across the globe which describe varying pathways toward more comprehensive internationalization. Institutions were chosen to reflect the diversity of higher education and approaches to internationalization. An analysis of the cases uncovers similarities and differences, as well as common lessons to be learned. With contributions from mainland Europe, Australia, the USA, the UK, Latin America, Singapore and South Africa, the global application of the book is unparalleled.

Comprehensive Internationalization will be of vital interest to a wide variety of higher education institutional leaders and managers as they address the problems and solutions for institutional internationalization available to them in a rapidly changing educational world and a 21st century global environment.

Professor John K. Hudzik of Michigan State University is past President and Chair of the Board of Directors of NAFSA, Association of International Educators, and also past President of the Association of International Education Administrators (AIEA). He was for nearly 15 years Dean and Vice President of International Programs and Global Engagement at MSU. He is the NAFSA Senior Scholar for Internationalization, recipient of the AIEA Charles Klasek Award, and recipient of the Transatlantic Leadership Award of the European Association for International Education.

Internationalization in Higher Education

Series Editor: Elspeth Jones

This series addresses key themes in the development of internationalization within higher education. Up to the minute and international in both appeal and scope, books in the series focus on delivering contributions from a wide range of contexts and provide both theoretical perspectives and practical examples. Written by some of the leading experts in the field, they are vital guides that discuss and build upon evidence-based practice and provide a clear evaluation of outcomes.

Titles in the series:

Comprehensive Internationalization

Institutional pathways to success

John K. Hudzik

Routledge
Taylor & Francis Group

LONDON AND NEW YORK

First published 2015
by Routledge
2 Park Square, Milton Park, Abingdon, Oxon OX14 4RN

and by Routledge
711 Third Avenue, New York, NY 10017

Routledge is an imprint of the Taylor & Francis Group, an informa business

British Library Cataloguing in Publication Data
A catalogue record for this book is available from the British Library

Library of Congress Cataloging in Publication Data
Hudzik, John K.
Comprehensive internationalization: institutional pathways to success / John Hudzik.
pages cm
Includes bibliographical references and index.
1. Education and globalization. 2. Education, Higher—International cooperation. 3. Universities and colleges—Administration.
4. International education—Case studies. 5. Education, Higher—International cooperation—Case studies.
6. Universities and colleges—Administration—Case studies. I. Title.
LB2322.2.H84 2015
378—dc23
2014021707

ISBN: 978-1-138-77853-5 (hbk)
ISBN: 978-1-138-77854-2 (pbk)
ISBN: 978-1-315-77188-5 (ebk)

Typeset in Galliard
by Book Now Ltd, London

Printed and bound in the United States of America by Publishers Graphics, LLC on sustainably sourced paper.

Contents

Illustrations

Figures

Tables

Contributors

Bertil Andersson is President of the Nanyang Technological University in Singapore and was previously Chief Executive of the European Science Foundation, Rector of Linköping University and Chairman of the Nobel Committee for Chemistry and a Trustee of the Nobel Foundation. A plant biochemist by training with a PhD from Lund University, he is the winner of the Wilhelm Exner Medal.

Melissa Banks is currently Director, Swinburne International, at Swinburne University of Technology in Australia. With over 25 years' experience Melissa has led major research projects and contributed to national and international forums and publications on a range of topics relevant to international education. In 2012 Melissa was the recipient of the prestigious IEAA award for Distinguished Contribution to the Field of International Education.

Elizabeth Brewer is Director of International Education at Beloit College, USA. Active in AIEA, the Forum on Education Abroad, and NAFSA, she has presented and written on campus internationalization, study abroad integration, and study abroad learning outcomes assessment. She currently is AIEA's editor and a member of the Forum's assessment committee.

Anna Ciccarelli held leadership roles in Australian international education over a twenty-five-year period with ten years as a Vice President of International in Australian universities. Institutional policy and practice in relation to holistic internationalization approaches has been a long-standing interest.

Rosa Marina de Brito Meyer is Associate Professor of Portuguese L2, PUC-Rio in Brazil and Associate VP for Academic Affairs, International Cooperation (1996–2014). She is an elected member of the Board of Directors, Forum on Education Abroad (since 2013) and a member of the GE4 Advisory Board (since 2012). She has written seven books and 35 chapters and advised 59 Master and PhD theses.

Christine Ennew is Provost and CEO of the University of Nottingham Malaysia Campus and Pro Vice Chancellor at the University of Nottingham. She is responsible for the University's first international campus which is home to almost 5,000 students and around 600 staff. Over the previous five years, she managed the University's ambitious international strategy, which attracted students and staff from almost 150 nations to campuses in both Britain and Asia.

Andreas Göthenberg, Executive Director of STINT in Sweden, received his PhD degree from KTH Royal Institute of Technology in 2003. He was previously a Science and Technology Attaché at the Embassy of Sweden in Tokyo. During 2004–2006 he set up joint research and education centers for KTH Royal Institute of Technology at Zhejiang University and Fudan University in China.

Nico Jooste has been the Senior Director in the Office for International Education at the Nelson Mandela Metropolitan University in South Africa since July 2000. He is responsible for the Strategic Leadership of Internationalization of the University. He is currently also Vice President of the International Education Association of South Africa. He holds a PhD in History.

Markus Laitinen is currently the Head of International Affairs at the University of Helsinki, Finland and has more than 20 years of experience in international higher education and research. He holds a Master's in Social Sciences from the same university and in Spring 2014 was elected to become vice-president and subsequently president of EAIE.

Tony Mayer is European representative for NTU. He is a geologist and specialist in research management and administration. He was a member of the European Science Foundation and Scientific Secretary of the European Research Advisory Board. Formerly Director of the COST Office in Brussels, and was previously with the UK Natural Environment Research Council. He was the co-Chair of the First and Second World Conferences on Research Integrity.

Hans Pohl is program director at the Swedish Foundation for International Cooperation in Research and Higher Education (STINT) and senior researcher at Viktoria Swedish ICT AB. Previous positions include analyst at Sweden's Innovation Agency (VINNOVA), science officer at the Swedish Office of Science and Technology in Bonn/Berlin and area manager at ABB Switchgear.

Dawn Thorndike Pysarchik is a professor in the Department of Advertising and Public Relations at Michigan State University (MSU) and is engaged in international education, research, and outreach. Currently, she is the MSU project director of the eleven-university FORUM-coordinated Beliefs, Events, and Values Inventory (BEVI) project to assess students' curricular, co-curricular, and extra-curricular international, global and multicultural learning. She is former Associate Dean of International Studies and Programs at Michigan State University.

Janey Saunders has worked in Australian international education for over 15 years, across multiple sectors, as a teacher and most recently as a senior administrator. As a member of the Office of the Deputy Vice Chancellor International at the University of Queensland, her role has included facilitating university wide internationalization initiatives.

Series editor's foreword

This series addresses the rapidly changing and highly topical field of internationalization in higher education. Arising from the notion of international education, which had essentially a curricular focus on international themes such as development studies and comparative education, use of the term "internationalization" began more recently, during the latter part of the twentieth century. Since that time attention to the international dimension of higher education has become increasingly visible in institutional strategies as well as national and international agendas. Early distinctions were established between, on the one hand, market-driven interests in the recruitment of fee-paying international students and, on an increasing number of practitioners who see transformational potential through internationalization activities as a means of enhancing personal and professional development.

While those themes continue to be of importance, the intervening years have seen a more nuanced range of interests bridging that divide. Informed by diverse disciplines including anthropology, languages & communication, business & marketing, environmental studies, strategic leadership, and pedagogy, internationalization is now high on the priority list for universities around the world. This is, in part, as a response to changing global environments but also in reaction to globalization itself with its potential for homogenization if taken to extremes. The many dimensions of contemporary internationalization require institutions to adjust and define the concept for their own purposes, adding to the richness of our understanding of the "meta-discipline" of internationalization in practice. This is perhaps most evident in countries where institutional and curricular internationalization is a more recent development, and traditional "western" internationalization practice requires further exploration for appropriacy in local contexts. Development and implementation of the concept in such new environments will add to our understanding of the benefits and challenges of internationalization practice over the coming years.

The answer to the question "What is internationalization?" will thus vary from one university to another and indeed by subject discipline within that institution. It will also change over time. Books in this series provide some guidance for those seeking to determine "What is internationalization for this university, in this particular context, and for this discipline within it?", reflecting the diversity and complexity of this growing field.

Today there are compelling drivers for university leaders to adopt an integrated rather than a unidimensional approach to internationalization. Intensifying competition for talent, changes in global student flows, international branch campuses and growing complexity in cross-border activity, along with the rising influence of institutional rankings, all provide economic impetus and reputational consequences of success or failure. Meanwhile additional incentive is provided by growing awareness that the intercultural competence required for global contexts is equally important for living and working in today's increasingly diverse and multicultural societies. Research indicates a rising demand by employers for university graduates with enhanced global perspectives and intercultural competence, and students themselves are showing increased interest in international and intercultural experience. Internationalization thus has both global and more local intercultural interests at its heart.

Internationalization can facilitate an inclusive, intercultural dimension to the teaching, research and service, dimensions of a contemporary university, including its commercial and entrepreneurial pursuits. It is most successful when seen as an enabling factor in the achievement of wider corporate goals rather than as an aim in itself. Embedding internationalization through changing institutional language, culture, and attitudes into standard university practice is more likely to achieve this than if seen as a separate goal in itself.

Internationalization as a powerful force for change is an underlying theme of this series, in contrast to economic or brand-enhancing aspects of international engagement. It seeks to address these complex topics as internationalization matures into its next phase. It aims to reflect contemporary concerns, with volumes geared to the major questions of our time. Written or edited by leading thinkers and authors from around the world, while giving a voice to emerging researchers, the series will offer theoretical perspectives with practical applications, focusing on some of the critical issues in this developing field for higher education leaders and practitioners alike.

The present volume addresses one of those critical issues. Focusing initially on the development of a comprehensive approach to internationalization, it places the contemporary university in a global and historical context to locate the drivers for and purpose of this key topic. Rationales and motivations for comprehensive internationalization are considered and its implementation explored through a range of pathways to delivery. Along with an important emphasis on funding such initiatives and measuring achievement along the way, potential barriers to success are also considered.

The book's emphasis on comprehensive internationalization from an institutional perspective is further developed through the case stories from a representative range of country and institutional contexts. The final chapter draws together the key themes of the book as represented through those case stories and offers further illustration of the pathways and routes for the journey towards comprehensive internationalization.

Key topics include:

- roots and evolution of a comprehensive approach to internationalization;
- trends and environments shaping the need for such an approach;
- institutional rationales and pathways to achieving goals;
- moving from rhetoric to reality in implementing a comprehensive approach, including how it can be resourced;
- measuring achievement and minimizing barriers to success;
- comprehensive internationalization in action: institutional case stories.

The book is aimed at those who wish a better understanding of comprehensive internationalization. It offers readers practical advice on implementing a comprehensive approach and pathways to success in achieving institutional aims. Its broad reach will make the book a valuable tool, regardless of where an individual institution may be in its own journey.

Elspeth Jones
Emerita Professor of the Internationalization of Higher Education,
Leeds Beckett University
Honorary Visiting Fellow
Centre for Higher Education Internationalisation
Università Cattolica del Sacro Cuore Milan

Acknowledgments

I am grateful to those who have read and commented on drafts of the manuscript. Their efforts and care in doing so greatly improved results.

John J. Wood was saddled with the extra burden of being first to review drafts. His diligence and the amount of time and thought he gave resulted in significant changes for the better, as well as providing the basis for reorganization of subsequent drafts. Elspeth Jones, series editor, brought crucial perspective to reviews of drafts and careful attention to detail. She made key recommendations for strengthening manuscript focus and clarity. And she kept me on schedule. My long-time friend, colleague, and collaborator on several internationalization writing projects, Robert Stableski, was a concluding reviewer on substance. I am indebted to him for his review of this manuscript and his involvement over several years on many other projects.

Anne Kelly Hudzik carefully read every word, sentence, and paragraph for clarity and provided numerous improvements. I am fortunate in so many ways to have her as my wife and also as a trusted sounding board.

Finally, I thank Lou Anna K. Simon for the many opportunities to gain experience and to be given roles shaping the internationalization of the higher education institution in concept and action.

John K. Hudzik, *Michigan State University*
E. Lansing, Michigan, USA

Introduction

This book is about the internationalization of higher education *institutions*. It is distinguished from many contemporary publications which focus attention on higher education internationalization as a concept, an organizing paradigm, and a value system. It is also different from publications which concentrate on government policy and funding to support internationalization, or to compare national and regional higher education systems. To concentrate on what happens in an institution as it engages internationalization is to focus on how abstract visions for the internationalization of teaching/learning, research/scholarship, and service/engagement play out.

Comprehensive internationalization is the means by which higher education institutions respond to widening and more complex expectations to connect globally across all missions to better serve students, clientele, and society in a twenty-first century context. In brief, comprehensive internationalization seeks to mainstream access of all institutional clientele to international, global, and comparative content and perspective. There is the accompanying expectation that everyone in the institution has a role to play in its delivery. The overarching intention is for the integration of internationalization into core institutional ethos, values, and missions.

Organization of the book

This book has two parts. Part I covers a wide range of strategies and practices that shape and govern the internationalization of an institution, with particular emphasis on the evolution toward more comprehensive forms. It examines the meanings, strategies, motivations, expectations, and challenges that arise from a comprehensive approach to internationalization. Part II is a series of case stories from institutions around the world which describe varying approaches to more comprehensive and strategic forms of internationalization.

Part I

The internationalization of higher education is a global phenomenon, but with substantial variation in how it is made comprehensive and operational across regions and institutions. The diversity in pathways toward comprehensive internationalization, even when pursuing common aspirations, is necessary and a strength because higher education institutions differ substantially in size, mission priorities, cultures, and modes of operation. A comprehensive approach to higher education internationalization must be fit to these diverse institutional and organizational realities.

Chapter 1 examines the origins, meanings, and development of the concept of internationalization and its evolution toward the comprehensive internationalization of higher education institutions in the twenty-first century. This evolution is partly in the form of moving from individual and laissez faire manifestations of the mobility of people and ideas in the search for knowledge toward an institutionalization of strategy and support—not just for mobility, but for "internationalization at home," and for building cross-border learning, research, and problem-solving collaborations. Higher education internationalization has evolved over centuries into a multi-faceted concept with very substantial ramifications for higher education orientations, priorities, and actions in the twenty-first century. Globalization is a powerful factor in this evolution. Comprehensive internationalization is an agent of organizational change.

Chapter 2 explores the external drivers of change inherent in the higher education environment and over-arching global and societal trends. The key issue is understanding how these shape the course of internationalization, particularly its evolution toward comprehensive internationalization. Relationships are reciprocal: Internationalization must play out in an environment of emerging higher education challenges and constraints and cannot be held separate from these; but internationalization and its companion globalization are also shaping higher education and its evolution and reform.

Chapter 3 considers how visions, rationales, and motivations for internationalization have become more complex and in turn drive a widening set of expectations for higher education's twenty-first century internationalization. Particular attention is paid to visions, rationales, and motivations emanating from within the higher education institution. The drivers of internationalization, particularly comprehensive internationalization follow from a complex array of rationales and motivations that have only partially overlapping and sometimes conflicting clientele and values associated with them. Institutions and policy are being challenged to sort and mediate these, particularly in terms of accountability. Together, Chapters 2 and 3 provide a basis not just for what comprehensive internationalization becomes operationally, but the factors involved in shaping action.

Chapter 4 shifts the focus from concept to action—or, how does the rhetoric surrounding the concept of comprehensive internationalization turn to action in higher education institutions. Comprehensive internationalization will assuredly activate organizational change, potentially fundamental changes. Broader forces of higher education organizational reform will also have an impact. Discussion focuses on the importance of action at the macro strategic level as well as at the program or operational level. Core components include, building an institutional support culture for internationalization, strategic inclusion of internationalization, and several key enabling strategies and tactics.

Chapter 5 continues the theme of moving from concept to action, but here the focus is on examining common institutionally based barriers to comprehensive internationalization, and their amelioration. Many barriers relate to views about internationalization itself but equally important are organization and personal barriers to change generally and to internationalization specifically.

Chapter 6 is about assessing the impacts and outcomes of comprehensive internationalization, and ultimately about accountability. It begins with a review of some of the generic research issues and models of organizational assessment and accountability, and then turns to applications for comprehensive institutional internationalization. The challenge is complicated by matters of research methodology (preferences vs. possibilities). Suggestions are offered for beginning to move forward the assessment of outcomes as essential to building the case for comprehensive internationalization.

Chapter 7 focuses on resources for comprehensive internationalization. Resources cannot be an afterthought but neither can the topic come first. A successful resource acquisition strategy is heavily dependent on building a campus culture of support as described in Chapter 4, bringing reality to other elements of action discussed in Chapters 4 and 5, and setting priorities within a longer range plan. The chapter builds heavily on the notion there are not enough new resources available to almost any institution to freshly fund comprehensive internationalization; rather, adequate resources will depend significantly on accessing existing institutional resources through strategies of integration and dual purposing, combined with some new resources. Another key point emphasized is that the multi-dimensional character of comprehensive internationalization requires diversification of sources of revenue and a matching of differing sources of revenue with particular program initiatives.

Part II

This part comprises a series of 10 case stories from institutions scattered across the globe. Institutions were chosen to reflect some of the diversity that constitutes the higher education institution. There are comparatively new institutions as well as those with hundreds of years' experience. There are comprehensive institutions and more specialized institutions. There are institutions long experienced in internationalization and those much less so.

Each has made strides in their own ways to engage more comprehensive and strategic forms of institutional internationalization. They demonstrate diversity in approach, but all highlight elements of a more comprehensive, robust and strategic engagement of higher education internationalization. As each institutional case story acknowledges, achieving a vision of comprehensiveness is a long-term undertaking and a road without end. Manageable steps forward means that institutions will prioritize the elements and actions of "moving forward" to fit their own circumstances, present position, and abilities. So, institutions will differ in how they have taken on both the vision and the challenges.

Included are case stories for: Beloit College, USA; the University of Helsinki, Finland; Lund University and Blekinge Institute of Technology, Sweden; Michigan State University, USA; Nanyang Technological University, Singapore; Nelson Mandela Metropolitan University, South Africa; University of Nottingham, United Kingdom; The Pontifical Catholic University of Rio de Janeiro, Brazil; University of Queensland, Australia; and Swinbourne University of Technology, Australia.

Chapter 18 connects materials in Parts I and II recalling key issues and strategies raised in Part I and connecting these to examples from the institutional case stories in Part II. Attention is called to two issues governing the organization and content of this chapter. First, reading this chapter is not a substitute for reading the flow of the institutional stories in the cases. Second, while this chapter seeks to identify how diverse organizations have attempted to implement key strategies and practices leading toward comprehensive internationalization, the institutional stories are also about diversity in how individual institutions approach comprehensive international in their own ways and to fit their institution's mission priorities, starting points and histories and capabilities.

Part I

Comprehensive internationalization of higher education institutions

Chapter 1

Comprehensive internationalization

Roots, aspects, and evolution

Higher education internationalization is not a new concept. Its roots and guiding principles can be traced back thousands of years to higher-learning idea centers which attracted scholars and students from diverse places. These centers, among them the Confucian Schools in China (sixth century BCE), the Platonic Academy of Athens (fifth century BCE), the Library of Alexandria (fourth century BCE), the Academy of Gunishapur in Persia (third century), Nalanda in India (fifth century), and Renaissance Italy (fourteenth century) were intellectual hubs drawing mobile scholars and the curious from afar.

The movement of people in search of new ideas and the movement of ideas to influence people in new places, as well as the blending of diverse cultures and epistemologies formed the inner core of early higher learning. These also provided the root stock (perhaps the *telos* in Aristotle's terms), for contemporary forms of internationalization of higher learning.

In ancient periods, as well as with more contemporary idea centers such as universities, cross-border and cross-cultural influences impact the core missions of higher learning. These missions center on knowledge creation and knowledge dissemination (the latter includes applications of new ideas).

Comprehensive internationalization is a relatively new term and is in part a response to the greater complexity and dimensions associated with an evolving notion of internationalization. Although mobility has been the most visible facet of higher education internationalization, much attention is now directed also to internationalization cutting across all key institutional missions and integrated into the ethos and key functions of higher education. In a contemporary and commonly cited definition, comprehensive internationalization is viewed as:

> Commitment confirmed through action to infuse international and comparative perspectives throughout the teaching, research and service missions of higher education. It shapes institutional ethos and values and touches the entire higher education enterprise .... It is an institutional imperative not just a desirable possibility .... [It] not only impacts all of campus life but the institution's external frames of reference, partnerships and relations.
>
> (Hudzik 2011: 6)

While the seed stock of higher education internationalization traces back thousands of years, its contemporary manifestations have evolved to become multifaceted. There are many reasons for this elaboration of dimensions and aspects, some aspects are controversial, and there is diversity in how internationalization plays out in practice across institutions and regions and evolves toward more institutionalized, strategic and comprehensive forms.

This chapter focuses on these issues to provide a foundation for successive chapters.

Evolving and diverse meanings and dimensions

Higher education internationalization is not a homogenous concept. It has many aspects. It is more akin to the idea of a "global concept" as the term is used in the philosophy of science—a concept formed of many interrelated dimensions, each given practical meaning by action and measurement. An analog is the "global concept" of intelligence. Intelligence has many aspects (observation, recall, analysis, synthesis, conclusions, forming generalizations, etc.) each defined by different means of measurement. The same has become true with the concept "higher education internationalization" as it applies across missions and the multi-dimensional meanings and measurements of learning, discover and service.

The "neatness" that might come with a simple uni-dimensional meaning for higher education internationalization would not reflect the reality of how people see it (Knight 2004: 6); they grow accustomed to the concept in terms relevant to them. More to the point, a homogeneous view of what internationalization is will not square with the reality of diverse facets, actions, and responsibilities that are now associated with it.

Numerous programs and activities fall within higher education internationalization: for example, the organized cross-border mobility of students and scholars, language learning, internationalization of curricula (e.g., internationalization at home (Waechter 2003) which is inclusive of cross-cultural learning and sensitivity and internationalization of the on-campus curriculum), cross-border institutional partnerships for learning, research, service and development (e.g., joint degrees, joint research, branch operations), and area or regional studies. In this sense the term "cross-border" as it relates to internationalization has both import and export dimensions, as well as joint multi-national undertakings.

Another aspect focuses on cross-border studies of thematic knowledge areas (e.g., international business, health, agriculture, international development, global environmental studies, peace studies, to name a few) to recognize that nearly everything today has local and global connections.

Other aspects shape ways of thinking about cross-border and cross-cultural similarities and differences, transitioning from the comparative exploration of diversity of culture and place toward critical thinking and learning through the several lenses of different cultures and world views. This means changing ways of thinking, adopting new methodologies, raising different epistemological questions, and developing critical consciousness and values awareness for a globally diverse environment.

Institutional diversity in priorities and actions

Hans de Wit pointed out as early as 2002 that as "the international dimension of higher education gains more attention and recognition, people tend to use it in the way that best suits their purpose" (de Wit 2002: 14). So do higher education institutions. Not all universities or knowledge centers emphasize or even pursue all types of actions associated with internationalization. Institutions are idiosyncratic in their priorities for action and will engage comprehensive internationalization in their own ways. Yet, what institutions share under the banner of internationalization is the idea that innovation and learning is not bound by place, but rather aided by connections to other places and cultures. Similarities and differences in approaches to internationalization are probed further in Chapters 2 and 3 and also in the institutional case studies.

Those involved in higher education internationalization also tend to focus on what is relevant to their experience. Individual and institutional experiences and priorities morph over time, so it shouldn't be said that higher education internationalization is a static concept. New behaviors, actions, and program approaches arise over time. Existing programs are renamed to reflect new visualizations (e.g., from international studies to global studies, or the focus of mobility redefined from students alone to incorporate faculty, or the emergence of branch campuses abroad as a redefinition of the meaning of "offshore" educational delivery) (de Wit 2013).

From national to international institutions?

As institutions internationalize, caution is advised not to assume "a change process transforming a national higher education institution into an international higher education institution" (Soderqvist 2002: 29). While internationalization drives an institution's vision outward toward a borderless frame of reference, it remains the case that institutions largely remain locally and nationally funded and influenced by national policies, as well as by local constituencies. There are examples of institutions with a global vision serving a global clientele (for example New York University under the presidency of John Sexton) (Loveland 2011b). Several have the clout and/or financial independence to carve themselves huge degrees of freedom to prioritize and envision as they see fit. However, national and local influences remain powerful factors for the great majority of institutions as well as global ones.

Local vs. global is a false dichotomy when thinking about higher education internationalization. Higher education in the twenty-first century can mediate the global impacting the local and the local mediating the global (Hudzik and Simon 2012). The diversity in how internationalization is made concrete by individual higher education institutions reflects in part the differing ways in which the local and global play out.

Is there a dark side to twenty-first century higher education internationalization?

There have been a number of significant concerns raised about the direction of internationalization by those long experienced in higher education internationalization, including Brandenburg and de Wit (2011a, 2011b, 2012); de Wit (2011a, 2011b, 2012); International Association of Universities (IAU 2012); Knight (2011a, 2011b); and Maringe and Foskett (2010). Such concerns are popular topics at recent international education conferences (e.g., NAFSA, EAIE, AIEA, and the British Council's Going Global in 2012; also see Elizabeth Redden's (2011) summary of a NAFSA panel session). The critiques and concerns are varied and not uniformly agreed on by commentators; the more common issues include:

- With marketing and commodification of higher education internationalization, we are moving away from assistance and aid to support the education of students from developing countries to revenue enhancing fee- and cost-based models, with many students priced out of access.
- There are fears that the emergence of a global higher education system will be one in which institutions are homogenized to a common standard or model (IAU 2012) and riding over local/national needs and priorities.
- The emergence of developed-country branch-campus and franchise operations represent a new form of market-driven colonialism, and a disincentive to high-quality indigenous capacity building.
- There remain strong concerns that the global competition for talent is moving higher education internationalization away from cooperation toward competition to attract the best with consequences including student and faculty brain drain and with concentrations of talent and resources in intellectual hubs, and little available for the rest.
- Ascendant neo-liberal values coupled to higher education commodification and marketization in its most virulent form deprioritizes actions and programs that don't have a readily recognizable revenue stream, affecting both quality and access.
- The rise of global ranking schemes puts a premium on the value of international engagement as a means of "becoming known" and building collaborations, resulting in building rank within the club of players. The additional concern is that cross-border institutional networks form around exclusive clubs of institutions with the "right" pedigree, and not necessarily around other criteria such as maximizing institutional capacity building and program excellence.
- There is the general critique that higher education institutions are moving from cooperation, partnership, exchange, and mutual capacity building to competition, commercialization, self-interest, and status building (Knight 2011a).

- Viewing higher education internationalization as an end instead of as a means focuses assessment on inputs (money, people, programs devoted to it), and outputs (e.g., numbers of study abroad programs or participants, numbers of international students, numbers of memoranda of understanding (MOUs)), instead of outcomes (measureable improvements in the objectives associated with core higher missions in teaching/learning, research/scholarship, service/problem solving).

The International Association of Universities' (IAU 2012) call to reaffirm academic values in the internationalization of higher education received input during its drafting phase from a distinguished global panel of higher education internationalists. Among the concerns listed in the IAU report are: (1) The prevalence of English as the common language for a global system leading to cultural homogenization; (2) global competition among higher education institutions; (3) acceleration of brain drain; (4) large-scale recruitment of international students producing domestic backlash and unethical recruitment practices; (5) transnational education threatening developments of indigenous higher education capacity development; (6) rise of development of exclusive clubs of partner institutions, fuelled by rankings and thereby restricting broader institutional partnership formation; (7) asymmetries in the power and position of cross-border partner institutions with unbalanced advantage for the powerful.

Perhaps of equal importance, the IAU began its statement of purpose with "This document acknowledges the substantial benefits of the internationalization of higher education" (IAU 2012: 1), although adding that "potentially adverse unintended consequences" as well as benefits are playing out under an evolving concept of internationalization, and a changing nature of internationalization in the context of globalization.

These areas of concern are taken up again in Chapter 2 under a consideration of the rationales and motivations for internationalization and in Chapter 3 when considering the changing higher education organizational dynamics which are potentially altering basic institutional governance structures and value systems with clear implications for the conduct of international engagement.

Blending key concepts leading to comprehensive internationalization[1]

In conversations about internationalization many terms are often used without clarity regarding their origins and meanings, or how they shape higher education internationalization—past, present and future. We sprinkle conversations with talk about, for example, globalization, internationalization, inter-cultural relations, comparative and cross-culture learning, mobility, cross border partnerships and networks, and other terms.

Has internationalization become a scatter shot of terms without an underlying coherency? Some hint that a few of the words are in opposition to one another, for example, "internationalization vs. globalization," or that one is dying and another taking its place (e.g., globalization for internationalization). Others view one as good (internationalization fuels cooperation) and the other as bad (globalization fuels competition) (van Vught *et al.* 2002: 17).

A better understanding is to see such terms as distinctive but complementary foundation blocks for an enriched evolution of higher education internationalization. Peter Scott (2003) sees overlap, intertwining, and possible symmetries involving internationalization and globalization, and Jane Knight hypothesizes "Globalization is changing the world of internationalization" (Knight 2008: 1).

Roots

The ancient intellectual hubs named at the start of this chapter drew mobile scholars and the curious from afar; they were magnets for new ideas and the new ideas themselves became mobile across regional and political boundaries. Some of these hubs later were proto-universities or began as universities as in France, Bologna, and England in the sixteenth and seventeenth centuries (and earlier) and later in the German research universities (Marginson and Rhoades 2002: 288). There are equivalents in twenty-first century knowledge communities that typically have a constellation of research universities as part of their core. Such hubs attract scholars and ideas from diverse places and cultures and typically intertwine multiple disciplines of thought and practice. Universities have a natural affinity for welcoming international perspective in their normal modes of operation because the unfettered and neutral (Barnett 2013) search for universal truth requires a borderless search for knowledge and ideas.

While mobility has always been a key aspect of higher education internationalization and an indicator of the degree of internationalization, it may have been higher 200–300 years ago in Europe. Perhaps as suggested by Teichler, the more recent internationalization of higher education may actually be a "re-internationalization." One also wonders about the role of a common language (Latin in the European academy in the past and English increasingly today).

> Historians … inform us that the strong national focus of higher education, coupled with relatively low levels of mobility, might have been a temporary phenomena, i.e., prevailing through the two hundred years of the dominance of the nation state, the 19th and 20th centuries. For example, there are estimates that intra-European mobility, now possibly on the level of about three percent, stood around ten percent in the 17th century (Neave 2002: 181). Thus, "re-internationalization" might be a more appropriate term to describe recent developments.
>
> (Teichler 2004: 8–9)

The "original idea" for higher education internationalization is the borderless and mobile search for learning and knowledge, but it was not an institutionally organized and supported cross-border flow. Innovation and learning is not bound by place, nor does it necessarily require institutionalized support, because connections to other places and cultures can be by individuals.

The borderless search for learning and knowledge is the "seed gene" for higher education internationalization, but it may be lost when other motivations intervene (e.g., the revenue potential of international students or the desire to play the institutional ranking game). Some suggest that these other motivations have "changed the meaning of higher education being dedicated primarily to knowledge creation, truth, and reason, to an activity that is increasingly viewed as a commodity and a credential" (Brandenburg *et al.* 2013: 68). There is no doubt that the rationales and motivations for internationalization have expanded (the subject of Chapter 3), but it is too strong a statement to say that knowledge creation, truth, and reason don't remain front and center as core motivations. Indeed, what is the commodity being sold or the credential being defined without these things?

Idea mobility and receptivity

Internationalization is not simply peoples' travel to far-away places—Leif Ericson to North America, Marco Polo to China, the Chinese admiral Zeng He throughout Asia and East Africa, or Magellan's circumnavigation expedition. Although physical travel of people (mobility) is often involved, the core notion is in the mobility of ideas. Ideas spread not only by travel of people but by other means, too—clearly the internet has accelerated the spread of ideas through a global electronic net. There are campus parallels: While not everyone can study abroad, the massification of international learning can take place "at home" through internationalization of the on-campus curriculum and via the internet.

Another part of the original idea is that if the mobility of ideas is to have impact, a companion need is receptivity to their arrival. Partly this is the domain of inter-cultural learning and sensitivity and partly it is the requirement of open mindedness to the new and different. Internationalizing learning and the curriculum has to deal not only with barriers to new ideas ("we don't do it that way") but also barriers imposed if the source of new ideas is from a different culture ("they aren't like us; what could we possibly learn from them"). The success of earlier as well as contemporary cross-border and cross-cultural idea flow is a reciprocal receptivity between senders and receivers.

Individualistic, laissez faire, or institutionalized

There is fairly convincing evidence that institutionalized support for internationalization has a fairly recent origin and was not a core element of universities of the Middle Ages (Neave 1997; Scott 1998a, b; de Wit and Merkx 2012). Certainly the concept "wandering scholar" does not lend itself to features of formal organization and institutional structure. The dominant models for contemporary universities originated in the eighteenth and nineteenth centuries and paralleled growth in power of the concept of the nation state; universities were creatures of their national settings. Tension could be found between national interests to be served by universities and the free flow of ideas and scholars across borders in search of universal knowledge. Internationalization as an individualistic phenomenon was in tension with political, institutional and culture resistance to it.

> Today, the new forms of internationalisation may be said to bear only a distant resemblance to the old community of scholars and to a growing extent to be transforming the institutions of higher education and contributing to redefinition of the relationships between the state, society and higher education …. Traditionally, the international activities in higher education consisted of international contacts between individual academics, students, universities and states, and individual aspirations for international experience and knowledge. International co-operation took place between individual countries, rather than being based on wider networks or shared policies, and there were hardly any competitive factors. The traditional internationalisation was not institutionalized in the practices at the organizational level, but, rather, it was based on the voluntary activities of individual actors. Thus the autonomy of the nation-state or the higher education institutions was not touched by this type of internationalisation.
> (Nokkala 2007: 14, also noting Trondal *et al.* 2001)

It is only well into the twentieth century, and then perhaps significantly only after World War II, that an institutionalized approach to internationalization became more a reality. Even so, vestiges of political, culture, and institutional resistance persist. They can be found in restrictive immigration policies, export controls of research findings, debates within institutions that both domestic and international agendas cannot be afforded, and suspicions among those parochially oriented that cultural purity will be subverted by ideas and practices from the outside.

The ancient root stock of the internationalization of higher learning is found in its individualistic manifestations, while its institutionalized organizational support in universities and other forms of higher education is a recent modification.

The twenty-first century environment

Globalization is reconfiguring, not replacing, older conceptions of "international" engagement. The paradigm-reshaping practice involves four distinct concepts: "international, global, comparative, and networks."

Historically, the term *international* references bi- and multi-lateral relations among sovereign states, some through formal treaties, others no less powerfully through trade patterns. Higher education parallels exist in the expanding global free-market mobility of student and scholars, as well as more formally in bilateral student exchange agreements and in cross-border inter-institutional collaborative research, degree programs, and branch campuses. Often these involve two institutions (occasionally a few more) each maintaining their own identities and "sovereignty."

More recently, some of these bilateral (and multilateral arrangements) have begun to mediate aspects of institutional sovereignty (Nokkala 2007: 15) such as may be the case with the University of Warwick (UK) and Monash University's (Australia) collaboration where joint strategic and operational inter-institutional priority-setting and decision-making occur. There are parallels with the EU broadly and with "Bologna" more specifically where individual institutions have had to reshape their curricular and related decisions and policies in response. Of course, higher education institutions are never really sovereign as they are responsible to others (e.g., government regulations, accreditation standards, general legal requirements), but one institution can rarely "make" another do something. The collaboration emerging in a few of the more recent partnerships mediate institutional independence by forging joint cross-border and cross-institutional steering groups with significant decision making influence.

Globalization emerges from world-spanning forces and factors that transcend borders, ignoring sovereignty. This reflects, while not perfectly, Ulrich Teichler's (2004: 22–23) view that globalization is a term used for any supra-regional phenomenon. Instantaneous global communication and easier mobility of people, ideas, and commodities exponentially accelerate and diversify the borderless flow of just about everything, both good and bad. It is impossible to control access to ideas originating anywhere on the planet, which in turn expands knowledge and reduces local advantage across the globe for learning, research and applications. It is difficult to imagine a single discipline of inquiry that isn't better informed by a cross-border perspective, or unable to make a useful contribution to the global idea network. Globalization is clearly seen as a major driving force not only for internationalization of higher education, but in government policy and strategy focusing on higher education internationalization as a productive societal response to the broader aspects of globalization (Daquila and Huang 2013).

The border-ignoring features of globalization have consequences for how institutions organize their cross-border learning and discovery activities (Marginson and Rhoades 2002; Marginson and van der Wende 2007). In the United States, for example, Title VI of the National Defense Education Act passed in the aftermath of Sputnik initially funded creation of area centers to study various world regions. Centers were regionally compartmentalized. Moving toward and into the twenty-first century, thematic centers in international business, health, agriculture, international development, global environmental studies, and peace studies, among others, emerged to recognize that nearly everything today has local and global connections. The global impacts the local, but the local also mediates and shapes the global; local prosperity and global co-prosperities are increasingly interdependent (Hudzik and Simon 2012).

Theme-focused centers not only recognize the globalization of opportunities, problems, and solutions, but the proliferation of and sources of each. Global context modifies geographic compartmentalization. Because globalization affects localities differently (Knight and de Wit 1997: 6), thematic and cross-regional studies provide a window for the comparative analysis of the impacts of globalization.

Comparative methodologies are central to any inquiry; they identify similarities and differences across entities and seek to explain causes. Comparative methodology is core to building cross-cultural understanding, widening appreciation for diversity, and building mutual understanding. Comparative methodologies offer means to look not only across borders in bi- and multi-lateral terms, but in global terms. The danger to avoid is letting "us vs. them," "good vs. bad," dominate rather than to learn from the differences. There is a long-established application of the term "comparative" to understanding why educational systems vary, particularly in relation to social factors (Epstein 1994).

There has been a maturing of how comparative studies manifest themselves in higher education internationalization, particularly internationalizing the curriculum. Internationalization of the curriculum aims to prepare learners for life, work, and careers in a global and multi-cultural context. It recognizes the importance of such preparation for all students and not just the few. It can involve different levels of outcomes from comparative components in curricula: "A graduate of our institution will ..."; "Our general education curriculum provides ..."; "The curriculum of our majors offers ...."

There are at least three stages and levels of sophistication in thinking "comparatively" in a twenty-first century global environment about curriculum internationalization:

1   adding cross-border content, concepts, themes, and perspectives to the curriculum without engaging a real comparative analysis;
2   infusing the curriculum with course content that reflects diverse perspectives to provide knowledge of differences and similarities in practices or ideas;
3   transitioning from the comparative exploration of diversity in culture and place toward critical thinking and learning through the several lenses of different cultures and world views.

The third stage requires changing ways of thinking, adopting new methodologies, raising different epistemological questions, and developing critical consciousness and values awareness for a globally diverse environment. There is a very strong "inter-cultural" basis for the third level of internationalizing the curriculum. That is, it is hard to learn from other cultures if there is no skill in inter-cultural relations and communication. Communication is understood here not just in terms of language but also in terms of ways of thinking and epistemology.

Hubs, clubs, networks, and matrices

Historically and contemporarily, intellectual hubs get much of the attention, but it is the network that makes the hub as much as the hub the network. Cross-road hubs require roads connecting numerous idea satellites. The emergence of a global higher education system and the flattening of instructional and research capacity (in Thomas Friedman's terms) are proliferating the number of hubs and networks shaping the sources and flow of ideas. In Ben Wildavsky's (2010) terms it is global brain circulation rather than a unidirectional "brain drain" from one part of the world to another. The multi-hub higher education network is ascendant.

The global leveling of capacity for innovation aided by the emergence of the internet superhighway system and the resulting near elimination of effective gatekeepers of ideas serves to greatly proliferate and elaborate cross-border relationships. Today, the more numerous intellectual hubs exist as parts of idea networks that run through multidimensional idea and talent trade routes. Patterns of flow frequently shift or reroute depending on issues, interests, and needs, such as mangrove ecology in Vietnam and Louisiana; stem-cell research in the United States, Singapore, and Europe; and software development in the US Silicon Valley and India. The issues and network combinations are endless.

With growth and spread in the world's higher education capacity (students, faculty, and institutions) over the last half century, there is a more diverse global base to support multi-directional cross-border interactions among higher education institutions. The OECD and others project a continued global "flattening" of capacity and advantage.

The unidirectional learning and assistance of older development networks ("we are here to save you") are being replaced with collaborative models. In transitioning from assistance to partnership, one partner does not engage others with the view of having all the right answers or even know which questions to ask. Instead, a non-judgmental comparative perspective provides insight into how others are approaching similar challenges in other parts of the world and cultures. This means, among other things, giving up parts of institutional "sovereignty" in setting research priorities, defining research questions, institution building abroad, and the content and design of courses, curricula, and degree requirements.

Comprehensive internationalization

The idea of higher education internationalization is evolving and filling out. It is a multi-faceted concept with many ideas beginning to coalesce to interconnect its dimensions. To think and act "comprehensively" about higher education internationalization benefits from sorting through the various ideas and concepts as well as understanding their place in the larger evolving picture.

The term "comprehensive internationalization" was popularized when the American Council on Education (ACE) used it in the title of several of its publications, for example, *Promising Practices: Spotlighting Excellence in Comprehensive Internationalization* (Engberg and Green 2002); *Building a Strategic Framework for Comprehensive Internationalization* (Olson et al. 2005), and *A Handbook for Advancing Comprehensive Internationalization* (Olson et al. 2006). Focusing heavily on internationalization of curricula and undergraduate learning, these publications highlighted a range of campus policies and programs that would lay the basis for a deep and integrative practice enabling full internationalization. ACE's focus at the institutional or campus level is of particular note.

The term was further publicized starting in 2003 when NAFSA created the Senator Paul Simon Award for Comprehensive Internationalization. In the early years of the award, there was a tendency to focus on awardees significantly engaged in education abroad and internationalization of the on-campus curriculum. More recently, from about 2010 onward, following a refinement of award criteria, selections are recognizing broader campus internationalization efforts including other institutional missions and types of cross-border activity (e.g., research, development, public service). In 2008, a NAFSA taskforce on internationalization focused attention on thinking and behaving comprehensively about institutional internationalization (NAFSA 2008). A 2011 NAFSA publication (Hudzik 2011) focused expressly on the comprehensive internationalization of higher education institutions (emphasizing US institutions, but with implications for higher education institutions worldwide). The definition used at the start of this chapter is from that publication. The 2012 sequel NAFSA publication (Hudzik and McCarthy 2012) added that comprehensive internationalization is "A means to advance the core learning, discovery and engagement *objectives* of higher education in a twenty-first century context" (emphasis added).

Since the release of these publications there has been a growing use of the term as reflected in conference proceedings and institutions' strategic international planning activities in several world regions. The 2012 NAFSA Conference and Expo theme was "comprehensive internationalization." It was the theme of a plenary in the British Council's Going Global in 2011. In late 2013, The European Commission released *European Higher Education in the World*. The largest section of that release focused on priorities for higher education institutions to engage comprehensive internationalization and specifically drew attention to:

> A comprehensive internationalisation strategy should cover key areas grouped into the following three categories: international student and staff mobility; the internationalisation and improvement of curricula and digital learning; and strategic cooperation, partnerships and capacity building. These categories should not be seen as isolated but as integrated elements of a comprehensive strategy.
>
> (2013: 8)

In later portions of the Commission document, it is clear that strategic cooperation, partnerships, and capacity building—as elements of comprehensive internationalization—included research and innovation.

Although student mobility has been the most visible facet of higher education internationalization, much wider attention is now being given to the dimensions of internationalization as noted by the OECD in answering the question, "Why focus on internationalization?"

Student mobility is simply the most visible part of the greater topic, namely, internationalisation, is more complex and multifaceted. One aspect, sometimes referred to as internationalization at home, consists of incorporating intercultural and international dimensions into the curriculum, teaching, research, and extracurricular activities .... Other fast growing forms of internationalization are emerging (e.g., transnational education sometimes delivered through off-shore campuses, joint programmes, distance learning, etc.) and suggest a more far reaching approach, especially where higher education is now seen as an integral part of the growing knowledge economy.

(Hénard *et al.* 2012: 7)

While not using the term "comprehensive," the intended comprehensiveness of internationalization as cutting across all key institutional missions and integrated into the key functions of higher education in a knowledge economy is clear in the OECD document.

Important groundwork for thinking comprehensively about higher education internationalization was provided by Jane Knight (1994), who wrote of internationalization as "The process of integrating international or intercultural dimensions into the *teaching, research and service functions of the institution*" (7; emphasis added). Knight later updated this to "The process of integrating an international, intercultural or global dimension into the *purpose, functions or delivery of postsecondary education*" (Knight 2003: 2, also 2004: 11; emphasis added). The updated definition was meant to make the notion of internationalization less higher-education-institution centric to allow room for the importance of national policies, and that a number of diverse educational providers "have different interests and approaches" to internationalization. In a minor reflection one might ask about the use of "or" in both definitions. Does "international, intercultural or global" mean one "or" another, or is it to imply that they are the same? If one accepts the multi-faceted meaning of internationalization, the use of "and" might have been preferred.

Earlier, Arum and Van de Water (1992: 202) saw internationalization as "Multiple activities, programs and services that fall within international studies, international education, international educational exchange and technical cooperation." The Knight and Arum and Van de Water views of internationalization are not necessarily at odds, but there are two striking features of the Knight definition that set the foundation for twenty-first century notions of internationalization, particularly comprehensive internationalization. One is that internationalization is intended to touch all higher education missions (teaching, research, and service). The second is explicit preference for the integration of internationalization into existing institutional missions rather than for it to be seen as something apart from or in addition to what higher education institutions do.

In light of the implications of Jane Knight's definition there has been commentary that questions the need for the term "comprehensive"—isn't "internationalization" sufficient and, by adding "comprehensive," a redundancy? (de Wit

2013.) Yet, an accurate characterization of the recent history of internationalization is replete with examples of higher education institutional internationalization behaviors being far short of anything "comprehensive." Internationalization has been used at various institutions to focus (in some cases exclusively) on mobility, language learning, internationalization of the curriculum, research and service engagement abroad, building cross-border inter-institutional partnerships, *or* internationalizing the campus living and learning extra-curricular environments.

Thus, there is substantial variation in practical and behavioral terms in what "internationalization" means or involves in actions and programs from institution to institution. Only a few institutions have orchestrated their internationalization efforts to systematically link the various components. A robust orchestration of internationalization was implied by Jane Knight's 1994 definition. While such breadth and orchestration may have been the intent of earlier definitions of internationalization such as Jane Knight's, actual practice did not routinely follow. The word "comprehensive" is meant not only to call attention to this disparity, but to flag the important changes in scale, scope, and inter-connected behaviors that a twenty-first century global environment is pressing upon higher education internationalization.

The more recent highlighting of comprehensive internationalization coupled to the widening debate over the meanings, directions, and consequences of higher education internationalization, has generated some debate, particularly in 2011. A short piece by Brandenburg and de Wit (2011a) emerged with the provocative title "The end of internationalization"; then, commentary by Jane Knight (2011b) asking "Is internationalisation having an identity crisis?;" again from de Wit (2011b) "Naming internationalisation will not revive it;" from Elspeth Jones (2011), "Internationalisation—aid, trade, pervade"; and again from Brandenburg and de Wit (2011b), "Has international education lost its way?"

While these commentaries are provocative, there are some conclusions to be drawn in the light of day: (1) Internationalization is not dead, or coming to an end, but rather continuing to evolve. (2) It is not a topic peculiar to one world region but rather is coming of age in a global context as we see from regional conference themes and presentations worldwide over the last several years. (3) It may or may not be having an identity crisis, but clearly it is being viewed now and shaped through the lens of a globalized twenty-first century reality. (4) Rapid expansion of teaching demand and higher education capacity (Hudzik and Simon 2012) and research capacity worldwide (NSB 2010), with high growth curves outside North America and Europe, particularly in Asia, is broadening the base for cross-border collaboration and sources of cutting edge knowledge. (5) It is not internationalization *or* globalization, and it is not local *versus* global in how higher education responds; rather a blending of all these concepts now drives not a piecemeal approach to higher education international engagement but a more comprehensive one.

That said, the concerns and critiques of possible consequences of internationalization noted earlier should not be dismissed; rather, if higher education institutions are to be vigilant about protecting their core values, such consequences need to be consciously minimized.

There is also another matter requiring attention, and that is whether behaving "comprehensively" when it comes to internationalization will enforce a kind of homogeneity across institutional engagement of internationalization—in effect everyone doing the same thing by virtue of a "comprehensive" approach. Given institutional diversity and varying institutional motivations to engage internationally (discussed in Chapter 2) a comprehensive approach does not seem likely to force homogenization on its own.

Homogeneity or heterogeneity in the practice of comprehensive internationalization?

The reality is that higher education institutions are idiosyncratic. Even in highly centralized national systems of higher education, institutions develop individual cultures and individualized formal and informal systems to shape and govern their behaviors based partly on traditions and personalities at each institution. While it can be argued that all higher education institutions engage the three core missions of teaching/learning, research/scholarship, and service/problem solving, they do so with differing priorities and weight assigned to each and through widely differing ways and programs. It is folly to suggest that a concept such as comprehensive internationalization should even try, let alone will be successful in over-riding this diversity. So, if comprehensive internationalization isn't doing everything (e.g., covering all of the facets of internationalization), what is it?

The answer is twofold: On the one hand, comprehensive internationalization must fit the institution, resulting in differences across institutions; on the other hand, comprehensive internationalization is a commitment to pursue a set of common aspirations (see Figure 1.1). These common aspirations emanate from a widening set of twenty-first-century rationales and motivations for higher education internationalization discussed in Chapter 2. Therefore, in answer to the question about homogeneity vs. heterogeneity, it is both.

- **Mainstream**: Expand faculty and student engagement
- **Integrate** CI into core institutional missions
- **Expand who supports and contributes**: Beyond the international office to academic and support units
- **Interconnect** CI activities to produce synergies

Figure 1.1 Common aspirations for CI.

Institutional fit

If internationalization is to find a friendly home, it must fit an institution's mission, priorities, values, and modes of operating (see Figure 1.2). Some institutions emphasize undergraduate (or first degree) education; others give special status and priority to graduate education and research; in the United States and in some other countries, community-style colleges provide the first two years in undergraduate education or specialty degrees. In Europe and elsewhere some institutions emphasize technical and craft education. At large comprehensive and research institutions the mix of foci is wide and deep and resulting engagements of internationalization are likely to be complex. It is really more complicated and diverse than this, but, regardless, it is nonsense to expect an institution to engage in international activity outside its sphere of emphasis. The first principle of "fit," therefore, is fit to mission and institutional programmatic priorities.

- **Institutions are idiosyncratic**—as will be their CI
- **Differences shaped by an institution's**

    ☐ Missions, values, and priorities
    ☐ Starting points
    ☐ What is possible at a point in time
    ☐ Modes of operation

- **There is no "best" model**

    ☐ The *best* model for any institution is the one that *fits **its** missions and circumstances*

Figure 1.2 Factors shaping CI diversity across institutions.

Some institutions quite appropriately will focus their international engagement activity on undergraduate education (on-campus curriculum, education abroad opportunities, and so forth). Others with a strong service component to their missions may engage development activity abroad. Those with strong research and graduate education foci may emphasize research partnerships and collaborations abroad as well as support for faculty and graduate student mobility, cross-border joint publications, and so forth. The combinations of mission and program fit are nearly endless so that it would be hard to find any two institutions engaging internationalization in exactly the same way—even among similar kinds of institutions.

A second principle of fit focuses on institutional process and modes of operation in making decisions, setting priorities, and taking action. It is axiomatic in human resource administration that management is far more likely to lose a grievance based on violation of process than substance. Put more generally, even ideas for internationalization with good substantive fit to the institution may be dashed if people feel that institutional procedures have been violated in advancing them. Fit in this case concerns how the internationalization agenda for the institution is formed, adopted, and implemented. Is the process for internationalization in synch with established institutional orientations toward centralized vs. decentralized decision making, roles, and prerogatives of faculty, governance structures, and procedures?

A third principle of fit focuses on capacity and what is possible at any given point in time. Institutions vary in size, scale, and scope of support structures, financial wherewithal, the skill and experience of personnel (particularly faculty), and leadership. It is difficult to imagine a successful strategic and comprehensive approach to internationalization without an experienced and engaged faculty supporting it. The same might be said for the nature of leadership, resources, breadth of an institutional culture supporting internationalization, etc. The institutional plan for internationalization will, for these reasons, have different starting points, scale, and speeds.

With such diversity in practice what can comprehensive internationalization mean in any helpful sense?

The glue of common aspirations

It has been argued that comprehensive internationalization is aspirational, a road without end. It is a long-term commitment to staying the journey (Hudzik and McCarthy 2012). In this sense, the common meaning behind diverse approaches is in the aspirations toward which action is directed. These aspirations are better understood in the context of contemporary rationales and motivations for more strategic and comprehensive internationalization (which is the subject of Chapter 2). In brief and for a start, the common aspirations include:

- *Mainstream* by expanding faculty and student engagement beyond the few to the many, driven in part by the ubiquitous influences of globalization breaking down barriers between local and global and impacting nearly everyone where they live and work.
- *Integrate* comprehensive internationalization into core institutional missions—not adding internationalization as a fourth mission but rather infusing it within existing missions. This aspiration is driven by several considerations including that in a resource challenged higher education environment, a free-standing fourth mission cannot be afforded either in terms of new money or personnel. Rather, internationalization must be significantly supported by tapping into existing resources via a strategy of "dual purposing," which is one of the topics of Chapter 6.
- *Expand who supports and contributes* beyond the international office to academic and support units. By definition and conditions put forth in the first two aspirations, comprehensive internationalization cannot be successful if it is the responsibility of the international office alone. Mainstreaming and integrating/infusing into existing missions requires the active participation of a constellation of institutional assets from top, middle, and lower level leadership, to all academic units and staff and all support and service unit staffs. This is discussed in greater detail in Chapters 3 and 4.
- *Interconnect* comprehensive internationalization activities to produce synergies. The desire for efficient and effective resource management as well as inevitable budget constraints prompt interest in investments that produce multiple payoffs. For example in forming cross-border inter-institutional partnerships, the choice of institutional partners may not simply be a matter of finding a good study abroad site, but one which might serve institutional research and outreach missions as well.

We will return periodically in this book to the interplay between programming diversity and common aspirations that drive us toward a commonality with respect to comprehensive internationalization. It will become a theme in the last chapter when drawing conclusions about similarities and differences from the institutional case studies.

The notion that comprehensive internationalization is a road without end draws relevance from both internal and external institutional factors. The external environment for institutional internationalization is in constant evolution. Think, for example, of the impact of globalization on earlier conceptualizations of internationalization and how the two now blend to reshape cross-border relations, competition, and collaboration. Global higher education development and the resultant movement toward "flattening" (equalizing?) institutional capacities globally re-engineers the opportunities for cross-border institutional collaborations from among those with uneven capabilities to those more evenly matched and with complementary capacities. As the world is in a state of constant change with an ebb and flow of challenges and opportunities, so higher education institutions and their internationalization need to be constantly adaptive in response. In part, therefore, the road is without end because the end of the road is a shifting target along a shifting route.

Internal factors also constantly reshape the meaning of institutional internationalization. As institutional internationalization links to broader institutional missions, values, and priorities, and as aspects of these are also constantly evolving, the programming priorities of institutional internationalization will change also. The adaptation of what institutional internationalization means operationally and programmatically in response to both internal and external factors is never ending.

Long-range commitment to comprehensive internationalization and manageable bites

Many of the most highly successful institutions have pursued internationalization over the long run and building on prior work and successes. In almost all cases, while certain programmatic thrusts may have stability and a degree of permanence in successful institutions, the programmatic thrusts evolve over time such that while, for example, an institution may have a long history and commitment to, say, study abroad or international development activity, the nature of actual programming associated with each constantly evolves in response to both opportunities and challenges.

In sum

While higher education internationalization is not a new idea, and neither is it a homogenous concept, the emergence of comprehensive internationalization (CI) as a concept begins to identify an approach and set of strategic, institutionalized and integrated higher education behaviors in response to changing higher education and twenty-first century environments. Subsequent chapters identify environmental trends, expanding rationales and motivations for CI, change-agent aspects of CI, and organizational behaviors needed to move from concept to action.

Note

1 This section is based on the commentary by the author in Hudzik (2014).

Chapter 2

Trends, environments, and organization shaping comprehensive internationalization

This chapter explores how internationalization is shaped by wider trends in higher education and its environment, and in turn how internationalization shapes higher education organizations. Some trends impact the higher education enterprise generally while others have particular impact on how higher education institutions engage cross-border and operationalize internationalization. Trends of both types interact to shape twenty-first century higher education internationalization.

Environmental factors are powerful change agents. A contemporary example is the on-going and widespread softening of public support for higher education, reflecting in part a shift from higher education viewed primarily as a public good to one of private gain as well. There are resulting implications for not only how higher education is funded but for how internationalization can be supported. Another example comes in the form of calls from regulatory bodies and various associations for greater higher education accountability (US examples include Miller 2006; McPherson *et al.* 2009; APLU 2011. In Europe, examples are given by Sporn 2003; Nokkala 2007; Estermann *et al.* 2013; and more broadly by Hénard *et al.* 2012).

Higher education institutions respond to a host of external stimuli, including government and quasi-governmental policies (e.g., Bologna and Erasmus in Europe, Colombo 2 in Australia, or Title VI legislation in the United States which funded language and area studies). The periodic work of faculty within institutions to revise curricula to reflect new pedagogy and content for teaching and learning are influenced by intellectual considerations of the faculty, and also by powerful influences from the outside shaping their discussions (accreditation or quality control bodies, governments, cutting edge knowledge, employers, stakeholders, funding opportunities, etc.).

Internationalization of higher education cannot absent itself from being cognizant of and responsive to wider forces of change in higher education because such forces also shape internationalization. Regular monitoring and assessment of evolving trends for impacts on internationalization are a responsibility of internationalization leaders. It can be argued that the intermingling of wider social and higher education trends with internationalization leads toward more strategic and comprehensive forms of internationalization.

Higher education environments and trends

As Rumbley *et al.* (2012) point out, "Internationalization is increasingly understood as a transformative phenomenon, moving institutions—and even national and supranational actors—to adjust everything from administrative policies to entire frames of reference." Internationalization mixes with the many consequences of globalization, and further mingles with wider forces of challenge and change within the higher education enterprise.

Internationalization causing institutional change is not a new thought, nor is it bound to a single region such as Europe or North America. Writing in 1995, de Wit saw the internationalization of teaching, research, and service as a positive institutional change agent. More recently, James Jowi (2009), writing about the internationalization of higher education in Africa, is quoted by colleagues at MOI University in Kenya that "the most significant global change in the institutions of higher learning has been manifested in [the] form of internationalization" (Jeptoo and Razia 2012).

Higher education supply, demand, capacity, money, and seats

There are a number of reciprocal impacts between higher education internationalization and challenges within higher education. On the higher education side are rising demographic- and knowledge-society demands for higher education, declining public support (at least declining on a per capita head count basis), and a growing middle class in numerous developing countries and regions now able to privately fund higher education for their children (see, for example, Kearney and Yelland 2010).

The short supply of seats, particularly high quality education, and the greater ability of families to support higher education for their sons and daughters have increased student mobility away from systems with short supply toward ones with capacity and which welcome fee-paying mobile students (e.g., Indian and Pakistani students enrolling in western branch-campus operations in the UAE). One of Australia's largest export earners is its higher education system. Some "indigenous" capacity is artificially enhanced through transnational and branch-campus efforts such has been the case in the UAE. Singapore attracts students from the region not only through its own institutions, but through branch campuses of institutions from abroad; and numerous efforts elsewhere to create "education hubs or capitals" (Lane and Kinser 2012, 2013). Of course it can be asked what impact off-shore operations have on enhancing indigenous capacity, or whether they are a form of higher education *institutional* mobility with a tinge of neo-colonialism.

The rising costs of higher education (both because of declining public support and rising costs above inflation in many countries) have heightened the cost consciousness of students and families, as well as their willingness to "shop around," including across borders (see Figure 2.1). Also a few figures may help set the stage for further thinking about such trends:

> - Spreading public disinvestment in higher education funding and rising costs to the individual buyer
> - Growing "private like" forces in public higher education and a growing private higher education sector
> - A more cost-conscious, "demanding" and globally mobile consumer. Strong demand, short supply of seats
> - Increased cross-border higher education trade and competition, collaboration and stratification promulgated by rankings
> - More comprehensive and strategic forms of internationalization and global engagement by institutions

Figure 2.1 Overarching variables of change in higher education.

- It has been projected that the demand for higher education seats will increase from approximately 100 million globally in 2000 to 250 million in 2025 (Ruby 2010), along with large increases in entry rates.
- Mobility has been projected to increase from about 3.1 million to approximately 7.2 million during roughly the same period (Banks *et al.* 2007; Van Damme 2014). From data provided by the OECD (2013b: 308), and using traditional mobility counting categories, there has been a steady and recently increasing growth in mobility to 4.3 million in 2011, more than tripling since 1990. Even if unlikely that increases would continue at this pace, Bernd Waechter (2013) emphasizes that the purposes and types of mobility are differentiating to include not just degree-seeking study, but also traineeships, not-for-credit, and "self organized." A more complete counting of mobility would take these other models into consideration, and as a result, the numbers for all forms of mobility are "under counted," as well as forecasts for them. The implication is that the global higher education system will not only have to respond to growing numbers of mobile students (as well as scholars), but will have to do so accommodating a diverse set of models and motivations for mobility.
- The OECD data show that the share of private expenditure for higher education rose to 32 percent by 2010 (Van Damme 2014) and is projected to continue to increase throughout much of the world. Privately funded individual consumers with their own expectations and motivations will become a more potent force in the higher education market place.
- Growth in global higher education demand and capacity is not limited to seats for teaching and learning, but in research as well. The National Science Board (NSB 2010) in the United States has conducted global surveys and analyses over the last several years to assess global growth in R&D and in science and engineering publications, particularly looking for changing global patterns of capacity. Among the main conclusions in its 2010 release of data and analysis are a global "flattening" of R&D investment and research activity (mainly fueled by growth in Asia and increased scholarly activity in the form of publications with similar growth trends (data based on science and engineering articles). A telling further statistic

is the large increase in the incidence of co-authored publications, with the largest percentage growth by several multiples in articles co-authored by scholars from different countries. The National Science Board also notes a rise in publication quality (particularly outside North America and Europe) as measured by citation incidence. "International" co-authorship increases frequency of citation and presumably has a positive impact on individual and institutional reputations.

- Middle-class growth is a global phenomenon with increasing economic and other forms of clout (Malik 2013). The middle class shapes a wide range of societal spending behaviors, including family funds for higher education. The definition of middle class is open to debate, and differs substantially country to country because of purchasing power differences. The World Bank uses an income figure of $10–$100 per day to define middle class. While such amounts may seem inadequate in much of the developed west, they can in purchasing power terms (PPP$) begin to elicit middle-class buying behaviors in many world regions, including for education. Global growth in the world's middle class is underway, the vast majority in Asia and not in the developed West. Ernst and Young (2013), based on World Bank data, assesses the global middle-class population will be about 3.2 billion by 2020 and 4.9 billion by 2030. The upper middle class will have its own substantial global growth, particularly in China, but also in Africa and Lation America.
- While research supports the obvious that "economic development has a positive effect on higher education enrollments," other factors are also involved (Schofer and Meyer 2005: 916). With rising private costs and growth in private education (PROPHE 2010), the private sector becomes demand absorbing (Teixera 2009). Both for-profit and not-for-profit private provisioning of higher education are important trends. More individuals and families and options in the market place are likely to support a differentiated demand and product stream in both the private and public higher-education sectors as well as in models and patterns of mobility.

In sum, these data suggest that global higher education instructional and research capacity are growth industries (albeit not in all countries—those with aging populations and negative population growth). Country and regional supply-demand capacities won't equalize quickly, but capacity will continue to grow overall, with major new growth being outside N. America, Europe, and the Antipodes. One can expect major shifts in global patterns of student, scholar and idea flows, as well as in global higher education patterns of competition and collaboration involving new regional trade patterns, flows, networks and partnerships.

A panoply of predictions about higher education itself and internationalization

There is almost no end to predictions about the future of higher education and universities, some apocalyptic. Predictions include "the end of the university as we know it" (Harden 2012); with technology a movement from "bricks to clicks"—from physical and face-to-face infrastructure to electronic and virtual infrastructure (Anderson *et al*. 2012); or that "the dominant university model—a teaching and research institution supported by a large asset base and a large predominantly in-house back office—will prove unviable in all but a few cases over the next 10–15 years (Srivastava *et al*. 2012).

Although the British Council in its 2013 Horizon Scan quotes from such studies, it puts them into perspective, noting that

> The accelerated pace of change in the world is taken for granted but it does not follow that the rate of change in human relations will be as fast .... Change is driven, and held back, by people, institutions and countries with political and economic interests.
>
> (OBHE 2013: 7)

It seems more reasonable to ground forecasts in non-apocalyptic terms. The world could come to an end, but that still seems somewhat unlikely. The university "as we know it" could come to an end, but that too seems unlikely. More likely is a continuous reshaping of the world, higher education institutions, and higher education internationalization in response to globalization and other factors such as those already discussed.

To celebrate its twenty-fifth anniversary, the European Association for International Education published a compendium of short essays by noted professionals in the field of higher education internationalization, entitled *Possible Futures: The Next 25 Years of the Internationalisation of Higher Education* (de Wit *et al*. 2013). Numerous trends were cited and predictions made. The non-apocalyptic future was championed by Eric Beerkens (2013: 45–46) in which he recounted the causes of dire predictions about the future of the university, as well as the counter argument.

> Three main drivers have been and still are fuelling these [apocalyptic] predictions: the world-wide massification of higher education, the increasing use of information and communication technology (ICT) in teaching and delivery of education, and the on-going globalization of higher education .... Despite its continuous change and adaptation, the model of the university as we know it has changed very little. The organization of faculties, schools and departments around discipline accountability in the form of peer review, comparable tenure and promotions systems, the connection between education and research, the responsibility of academic staff in both education and research and both graduate and undergraduate education, the primacy of face-to-face instructions, etc.; these are all characteristics that can be found in universities throughout the world, and which have existed for many, many decades—if not centuries. My bet is they will still be there is 2038.

Assuming Beerkens is right, and it would be a good bet that he is, the basic foundations of the university and the continuing internationalization of higher education will be preserved, but equally we can predict that there will be continuing change and adaptation of institutions and practices.

In the same EAIE volume, Lesley Wilson (2013: 29) foresees internationalization as "an increasingly important strategic priority for institutions but also for governments." Wilson predicts further that the difficult issues faced by an internationalizing higher education will include:

> Challenges of diversity (balancing home and international students); overseas operations that have to be set in different cultures and be sustainable in spite of high initial costs; developing partnerships (who to choose, what criteria, which networks, or perhaps international mergers); language policies (how to preserve linguistic identify and add to it); ensuring critical mass in research and dealing with intellectual property rights and publications; and the appropriate balance between research and education. Institutions are also faced with common questions: How to work within the framework of new government policies about international engagement? Are HEIs in the international arena to gain resources or are they committed to scholarly and intercultural exchange.
>
> (Ibid.: 32)

Wilson's challenges (and others) will force change and adaptation in ways we can only partially imagine, but the change is also likely to be bounded by Beerken's non-apocalyptic future.

In the same volume, Simon Marginson (2013: 49) observes that "in higher education and knowledge we can detect a continuing long-term trend to global convergence and integration. This long-term trend will increasingly shape not just international education but the national systems that are joined together." Peter Scott (2013: 53) is a bit more ambivalent in his core prediction that "under the impact of accelerating globalization, the world could become a radically different place; a new paradigm of international education might emerge that is both more threatening and more hopeful." One scenario is for existing and emerging economic and higher education systems to accommodate to one another; the other scenario is for emerging systems to become dominant, replacing the dominance of existing. Another possible alternative laid out by Scott comes closer to, if not at the apocalyptic edge.

> Education will cease to be a discrete category, rooted in recognizable institutions, processes and values. Viewed negatively, international higher education might be categorically absorbed into the global 'info-tainment' industry. More Apple and less Harvard. Viewed more positively, it could mean that international higher education might be one component of a complex web of wider global exchanges.
>
> (Ibid.: 56)

In *Horizon Scanning: What will Higher Education Look Like in 2020?*, the British Council (OBHE 2013) includes among its predictions that the demand for higher education worldwide will continue to grow to 2020 but at a slower rate. If right, then Peter Scott's notion that mobility has grown largely as a factor of overall growth in higher education enrollments will also slow (Scott 2013: 54).

The British Council projects that: the current major "export" providers for higher education will retain their appeal and positions, although others such as China and Malaysia will grow; the increase in domestic higher education capacity in many sending countries will mean that growth in mobility will not keep pace with higher education enrollment growth overall; the growth of transnational education will be greater than the growth in student mobility; there will be greater intra-regional mobility and cooperation as students stay closer to home. There will be a continued "unbundling" of degree requirements permitting courses to count from many institutions (OBHE 2013: 7–8). This latter point suggests facilitating for-credit, non-degree study abroad enrollments. This in itself could have a major impact on redefining what is tracked by various countries and therefore counts as mobility, especially if also counting students enrolled on short courses using their home institution's credit system.

In a research report the British Council (2012: 8) identified variables important to making higher education institutions competitive in the global higher education market place. Included, but not limited to, were an institution's: transnational education activities, academic and business collaborations, ability to attract top students and scholars from around the world, strongly internationalized course content, and opportunities for educational mobility. Also, competitive position requires linking international learning to employment and future labor market needs (British Council 2013a). Cumulatively, these variables build a case in institutional self-interest for comprehensive internationalization.

In a report by Srivastava *et al.* (2012: 4) regarding the future of the Australian higher education, a number of sweeping predictions were made that would fundamentally transform the higher education enterprise there, and perhaps globally: (a) "Democratisation of knowledge access" because of the internet and expansion of higher education capacity will change the "role of universities as originators and keepers of knowledge." (b) "Contestability of markets and funding" for the best in students and scholars but with a diminished government funding base will raise competition among higher education institutions. (c) "Digital technologies" will massively "transform the way education in delivered and accessed" and alter and perhaps bound the roles of traditional higher education institutions. (d) "Global mobility" will intensify the opportunities for competition and collaboration on a global scale. (e) "Integration with Industry" will be an essential requirement to "reinforcing the role of universities as drivers of innovation."

While there is probably little serious argument about the importance of these five factors, it is contestable how quickly such factors will produce change. Of greater importance, it isn't clear the ways in which higher education institutions will respond. If the past is an indicator, change will be excruciatingly slow for some and adaptions are likely to be quite diverse across types of higher education institutions. The same is probably true with respect to how such factors will impact the internationalization of higher education.

Democratization of access to international content in the curriculum is diversifying and expanding as a result of efforts to internationalize on-campus curricula, use of technology, and expanded mobility. Beyond the curriculum, diverse changes are certain in cross-border research and capacity and in ways institutional missions, core values, and institutional priorities come to be internationalization. Just as internationalization is not a homogeneous concept, neither will be its changing directions in response to overarching social changes and in higher education.

The OECD report *Trends Shaping Education 2013* (OECD 2013a) raises a number of issues. One is "that increased immigration and travel to OECD countries, along with trade and openness to global markets has led to a trend away from nationalized decision making" (Alexander, 2013). Higher education institutions will likely need to be increasingly cognizant of relevant policies and decisions of regional or supra-national bodies. Another issue requiring response is the aging population in OECD countries and also the need for more robust continuing education opportunities for knowledge society needs. Will higher education internationalization accommodate part-time adult learners, particularly those needing skills upgrading or in different areas of learning?

The European Commission (2013) communicated to the European Parliament on the topic of European Higher Education in the World. Although the purpose was not forecasting per se, conclusions can be drawn from the report and its recommendations for actions and matters of change to be addressed in the future. A sample of these include that member states and HEIs need to develop: (a) comprehensive internationalization strategies; (b) transparency in and recognition of learning acquired elsewhere; (c) immigration regulations that reduce obstacles to HEIs improving their international profiles; (d) digital learning and internationalization at home; and (e) substantial cross-border collaborations in research and innovation.

Results of a discussion at the World Economic Forum (Ivarsson and Petochi 2012) highlighted a number of challenges for the university of the future, including: (a) the need for institutions to differentiate their unique appeal in a global environment; (b) justifying high tuition fees; (c) developing effective on-line components; and (d) dealing with global institutional stratification with a few high-status, usually high-cost, elite institutions being well positioned in the global market place and others less so. Three implications follow. First, institutions need to build and market niche high quality brand identities. Second, cost control and price will be a competitive issue. Third, in forming partnerships, not everyone can or should try to "match up" with the same 50–80 global elite institutions. They should look for partner institutions where there is sufficient fit in inter-institutional mission, values, and stature (Hudzik and Simon 2012).

Lane and Kinser (2013) call attention to the increasing diversification in branch campus models and branch campuses which also engage in high-quality research and not just education. They also predict shifts in branch-campus trends from expansion to quality, from competition to education hubs (which may simply alter the nature of competition), and increased attention to economic development and diversity of programs (Lane and Kinser 2013). The focus on economic development is consistent with expanding expectations of higher education generally to play such a role and to improve quality.

Demographics and mobility

Roger Chao (2014) predicts that while the globalization of higher education has matured, regionalization of higher education networks is expanding and will likely continue to do so, with the implication that "closer to home" cross-border partnerships will gain strength in the coming years. A recent study of Hong Kong students suggests "closer and at home" parallels may be developing in students' attitudes because of employer recognition of qualifications and proximity to thriving East Asian Economies (British Council 2013b: 9) The near-future reality is an overlaying of both global and intra-regional mobility.

While the world's population overall is projected to age, significantly in many developed countries, including a 20 percent decrease in China in its tertiary education age bracket, growth in the 18–22 year-old bracket will occur in Africa and India (British Council November 2013b). With growing Chinese higher education capacity and a decline in the key tertiary age group, questions emerge about the sustainability of the proportion of Chinese students in global mobility patterns and whether there is a chance for excess capacity to develop in China so that it becomes a receiving country as a matter of national policy. Indian demand for higher education seats is likely to increase but unless there is substantial indigenous capacity development, Indian outbound mobility is also likely to increase. Even so, four countries will account for over 50 percent of the tertiary age population in 2024—India, China, Indonesia, and the United States (British Council 2013b: 4). While there is a growing number of US students degree mobile (IIE 2012), US capacity is more than ample to meet indigenous demand as well as absorb demand from elsewhere. The sufficiency of indigenous capacity is most in doubt in India, questionable in Indonesia and portions of Africa.

Economics and higher education trade

Predicting economic trends and their impacts is more difficult, perhaps the world's largest game of chance. Attention to the BRIC economies (Brazil, Russia, India, and China), is shifting according to the British Council (2013b: 5) to the CIVETS (Colombia, Indonesia, Vietnam, Egypt, Turkey, and South Africa). While there are ample data supporting economic strengthening in all of these countries generally, short- and medium-term ups and downs are also a reality affecting indigenous enrollments as well as outbound mobility. It has been known for some time that growth in GDP helps to drive trade, tertiary enrollments, and mobility (outbound mobility being greatest from countries where quality higher education capacity significantly lags demand and GDP growth). The directions and places of mobility are influenced not only by trade patterns and exchange agreements, but also by the cultural influence of the receiving country among mobile students—put simply, "is this a country where I want to send my son or daughter for living and an education?"

The relationship between knowledge economy needs and the future of higher education and its internationalization are a theme either implicit or explicit in a number of studies and forecasts. A study commissioned by the Austrian Federal Ministry for Education, Science and Culture (Pasternack *et al.* 2006) emphasized the importance of knowledge societies and economies under globalization as drivers of change and internationalization of higher education: "Having a knowledge lead is becoming a primary production factor in international competition of locations" (5). Key competencies and skills allow students to "cope with different settings and cultures ..." and "internationalization strategies are designed to promote international mobility and convey intercultural skills" (7).

Higher education change, reform, and accountability

As costs of higher education increase, there have been rising calls for greater accountability, quality assessment, and outcome assessment relating to the needs of students, employers, and governments. Examples include: The US Spelling Commission Report (Miller 2006); the Voluntary System of Accountability Program of The Association of Public and Land-grant Universities (APLU 2011); the European Commission's (2013) report on improving the quality of teaching and learning in Europe's higher education institutions; and discussions about the shifting fundamentals in European higher education governance, specifically "competition, ranking, autonomy and accountability" (Erkkilä and Piironen 2013). See Figure 2.2 for a sample of environmental factors and change trends in higher education.

- Global "flattening" of educational and research capacity

    ☐ "Seat" growth globally, mainly outside N. America and Europe
    ☐ Mobility growth (but changing patterns)
    ☐ Research capacity growth globally

- Multi-directional talent flows and collaborations
- Global ranking systems and stratification

    ☐ Focus on the global top 500 (and top 50 super elites)
    ☐ Affecting talent flow and network formation (pedigree)

- Competition and collaboration are shifting from the local/national to a global reference frame

    ☐ Increasingly in ideas and talent

Figure 2.2 A sample of changes in global higher education capacities and patterns.

The European University Association's interim report for the "Define" Project (Estermann *et al.* 2013) focuses on the necessity of higher education change prompted by financial shortfalls and the inadequacy of traditional funding patterns. Recommendations emphasize the importance of greater efficiencies in higher education. The section on criteria for funding formulae not only identify output measures such as funding based on numbers of students and scientific activities but also outcome measures such as research evaluations, successful patent applications, graduate employment rate, and national and international rankings.

Higher education internationalization cannot escape overarching forms of accountability that are being imposed on or accepted by higher education more generally. Among those that come readily to mind as having implications for internationalization are the following:

1 *Funding, accountability, and stature based on outcomes.* The growing pressure to measure outcomes will spread to internationalization (see Chapter 6 for a wider discussion of issues relating to outcome assessments).

2 *Time and cost to degree.* Students not completing degree requirements within standard time frames impose extra individual and system costs. Will internationalizing the curriculum delay time to a degree by adding requirements (rather than integrating them)?

3 *Growing use of strategic financial and cost/benefit analysis.* Can the benefits of internationalization survive its full cost modeling?

4 *Pressure to spread cost by establishing inter-institutional partnerships/collaborations.* What role will internationalization advocates have in prioritizing and defining cross-border collaborations and for which dimensions of internationalization activity?

5 *Pressure for innovation (modernization?) in practices.* Can campus internationalization leaders be innovative in expanding access and delivery of international programming? As discussed later in this chapter, merely scaling-up existing methods is not a practical solution.

6 *The pressure to build cost-saving cross-mission synergies.* Budget constraints prioritize investments that produce synergies across institutional missions. The internationalization of learning, research, and outreach will require their interconnection (further discussed in Chapter 7).

7 *Responding to nontraditional students who are now the "usual."* How will internationalization facilitate access and mobility for a more diverse client pool and for the many, not just the few? A diverse student population with more attending part time, working while attending, with their own families, and older is the spreading norm.

8 *Review of curricula, the academic core and governance models.* Will advocates of internationalization be in these deliberations?

9 *From expertise for the few to cost-effective access by the many.* The forces propelling internationalization require widening access to all. Can access be mainstreamed in a cost effective manner?

10 *Broadening internationalization beyond teaching and learning.* The "globalization" of information and research will expand internationalization beyond a curricular focus. This will remap the campus leadership of and participation in internationalization.

11 *From "add on" to integration into the core.* If internationalization is seen as an "add on," it can be "subtracted off" under financial stress. Integration into the academic core is essential to avoid the "tall poppy" syndrome.

12 *Global competition for the best faculty and students.* Research capacity is critical in a knowledge economy as well as in response to the decreasing half-life of useful knowledge. Will institutional recruitment expand globally to obtain the best talent?

These twelve issues are not small matters. With expansion of internationalization and its concomitant rising costs and higher visibility, there are concerns being expressed whether the benefits of internationalization can be demonstrated commensurate with its scale and cost (Ota 2012). Various items in the list are not uniformly relevant across all national higher education systems, and will vary in how they are operationally defined. However, the items relate to a fairly common set of global trends in higher education relating to cost, accountability, innovation, value, and competition.

While "accountability" issues will play out differently across regions and countries, the list begins to identify environmental issues to which higher education internationalization will need to be responsive.

Comprehensive internationalization as change agent in higher education

The OECD's *Education Today 2013* (63–64) notes four main challenges in managing higher education's expanding internationalization efforts: (1) "teaching and learning within different [cultural] contexts and conditions"; (2) an expanding breadth and depth of internationalization activities and components raise the level of management complexity associated with internationalization and call for "a specific strategy on internationalisation"; (3) contractual, legal and regulatory matters become more difficult across institutions, countries and legal systems in matters such as "intellectual property and the ethics of research, or quality standards . . ."; and (4) internationalization costs and "countries and institutions are not on an equal footing" in the availability of funds.

As comprehensive internationalization expands breadth and scope of effort, it will need to be accountable to deal effectively with resulting challenges in, for example, accommodating diverse clientele, managing the more complex internationalization enterprise, satisfying multiple and sometimes conflicting legal and regulatory environments, and ameliorating problems of unequal access. It will also be challenged by more complex regulatory and quality-control environments. So, too, one can expect significant challenges to institutional policies and procedures, invoking the need and rising pressure for organizational change. Institutional identity, core values and mission may undergo significant alteration.

Comprehensive internationalization and organizational change

For institutions moving toward comprehensive and strategic internationalization in ways consistent with meanings presented in Chapter 1, substantial organizational change is pre-ordained for most if not all. Changes may be institution-wide, or in practices and regulations associated with specific areas of programming (e.g., visa processing), or in something as broad as organizational identity. Institutional identity may shift from being seen as a local or national resource to also being viewed as a global resource. With more complex motivations and actions associated with internationalization, clientele and customer mix will change, as will the need for internal partnerships and external collaborations.

Some of the criteria for assessing impact, accountability, and application of standards will shift from local to globally recognized criteria (see Chapter 6). The implications are not only for teaching and degree quality standards but for research and publication standards as well. As Sporn (2003: 37) points out, the rise in cross-border research, publication, and cross-border joint authorship has required the lifting of some domestically focused journals to international standards regarding language and referee systems.

The *institutionalization* of internationalization at both organizational and national policy levels has begun to have fundamental impacts on higher education organizations. Tehri Nokkala has summarized the nature of these organizational change dynamics:

> During the last decade or so, a new phase of internationalisation has emerged, a result partly of these programs [e.g., mobility and information sharing] and more structured cooperation, partly of the changing context of closer international cooperation and interdependencies in all sections of society. International activities have 'institutionalised' into the organizational as well as national education system level reality to such an extent, that it changes national administrative, judicial and financial sovereignty over higher education and institutionalizing into the organizational cultures, structures and policies of higher education institutions.
>
> (Nokkala 2007: 15)

Even institutions which have experience and a history of activity in one or a few of the dimensions of internationalization (e.g., study abroad) may confront significantly changing organizational dynamics when moving toward more comprehensive internationalization.

Organizational change may be more complex if existing international practices will be replaced or at least substantially revised. For example, when establishing partnerships with institutions abroad to support student exchanges or other forms of study abroad, the search for partners is typically managed by the campus office of study abroad (sometimes with the involvement of a particular academic department or two). But when the objectives behind forming inter-institutional partnerships expand to include faculty exchange, joint research projects or joint development projects abroad, other powerful campus interests and criteria become involved in partner selection and site development; study abroad will play a far less dominant role in partner selection decision-making and management.

Managing the interplay of the diverse interests and priorities of a comprehensive internationalization strategy becomes an organizational challenge, often requiring the establishment of institutional governance mechanisms to guide the process and mediate across interests (e.g., establishing an overarching international program review and approval committee). Organizational change in the form of increased bureaucracy may be a consequence of attempts to encourage and coordinate more complex and larger-scale forms of internationalization. At the more specific level the types of changes forced are almost endless in possibilities. Here are just a few:

- Travel regulations if developed largely with domestic travel in mind or "western" cultures will undergo modification to accommodate swelling numbers of institutional travelers abroad to very diverse locations, and for employees living and working abroad.
- As institutions send greater numbers of students abroad and as concerns expand over their safety, site assessment for study abroad safety and security expands; often shortly thereafter similar kinds of considerations arise for faculty placements abroad.
- As numbers of international students from diverse cultures are attracted to the campus, residence hall food service choices and policies need to be changed, and other accommodations made for diverse religious practices.
- When increased international activity requires active and expanded faculty engagement, there are implications for faculty assessment, compensation, promotion criteria, and achieving job security (e.g., tenure, long-term contracts).
- A full-blown institutional commitment to internationalization is likely to impact basic hiring criteria and procedures, perhaps reorienting to hire individuals with experience and interest working professionally and personally across cultures and in settings abroad.
- When cross-border partnerships and collaborations are formed, business and contractual regulations and practices established under domestic legal and regulatory systems will undergo modification and compromise to accommodate different legal, regulatory, and cultural systems of "doing business."
- Personnel practices designed under domestic laws and procedures will have to accommodate personnel requirements in other countries and cultures for employees based there (e.g., hiring and termination practices, due process, and compensation to name a few).

Perhaps the biggest organization change under a steady march toward comprehensive internationalization is modification in the institution's perception of "who we are." The issue is, "Do we see ourselves as local and national resources, or also as a global resource." What are the implications for institutional visions, values, missions and priorities if viewing itself as a global entity, and for how it behaves abroad as well as at home?

Globalization, higher education reform, and internationalization

There are two overarching sources of organizational change. One is globalization and its impact on higher education organizations (Vaira 2004) and its impact on internationalization, as well as on "national legislated frameworks that define conditions under which universities operate" (Hunter 2012). The second is the widespread call for higher education reform and its greater accountability generally. The reform dynamic is global, placing pressure on established and developed systems in North America, Europe, and the Antipodes, and in the massive recalibrations of higher education taking place on virtually every other continent, particularly in developing countries and regions.

Globalization

Internationalization in a globalized environment, when combined with the requirements of knowledge economies has in the view of some led to an environment that is inherently competitive across institutions, regions and among countries (van der Wende 2001). In consequence, higher education institutions are seen to exist for the purpose of finding and engaging internationally in ways to create social and economic advantage in a global market place for their localities and clientele. As described in Chapter 1, this development is hardly universally regarded positively in that it is seen to override earlier objectives behind internationalization which focused on building cooperation and cross-culture learning and understanding. One implication of competition replacing cooperation is that models of international interaction can easily become more legalistic and self-protective compared to building mutual benefits and understanding in more collaborative environments.

A compounding factor inflating competition arises from declining and more uncertain sources of revenues to support higher education. This puts pressure on institutions to diversify their revenue streams and to become entrepreneurial institutions (e.g., Clark 1998, Slaughter and Leslie 1999; Marginson and Considine 2000). Slaughter and Leslie see emergence of the entrepreneurial institution in the United States as the biggest change in US higher education since introduction of the land grant institution over 150 years ago. The goals and missions comparing the US land grant to the entrepreneurial institution are easily divergent in terms of maintaining access and providing broad-based community service, regardless of its entrepreneurial potential.

The entrepreneurial institution can engender a range of reactions from queasiness to fear to derision over its impact on the academy. Many faculty shudder at the thought of having to become more market and entrepreneurially successful, selling service and advantage (to those who can afford to pay), or concentrating on revenue-producing activities (reallocating time spent away from teaching toward research having income potential). Institutional cost- or profit-centered budgeting is a natural extension of the entrepreneurial institution. Departments that can't produce sufficient tuition or research dollars are marginalized even though their intellectual contribution is core to a *university* learning and research environment including liberal education (e.g., a philosophy department?).

In an environment dominated by entrepreneurial objectives, priorities for international engagements including departments and programs that get to play internationally will be shaped by revenue and other clear contributions to institutional advantage. Institutional advantage may incorporate choosing international partners based on their pedigree in order to climb toward a higher "social level" (ranking) and come to take precedence over collaborations that will maximize intellectual and applications gains.

Higher education reform

Reforms agendas can be found throughout the globe, particularly in developing systems where the emphasis tends in the direction of adopting aspects of western higher education models and practices (including elements of the "German Humboldt" model). But there are many efforts underway to varying degrees in western systems as well, particularly in parts of Europe, the United States, and Australia. These reforms of higher education produce changes in higher education practice and culture and alter the environment within which internationalization can be implementation.

Barbara Sporn (2003) has described a wide range of European institutional reforms and organizational changes, many of which reflect earlier changes in North America, particularly in the United States. Among them:

> Privatization, increased managerialism and marketization, attempts to establish quasi-markets, the rise of cost-consciousness (i.e., providing "value for Money," or doing more with less), the use of performance indicators, auditing systems and central monitoring, and the management of change by high-profile executive officers in charge of public institutions.
>
> (32)

In Europe "harmonization" in relation to the internationalization of European higher education (Teichler 1998) has not only forced some homogenization across national systems, but has opened new avenues of competition in the flow of students in particular. So, the drive for greater internationalization is clearly a driving force behind not only increased international competition but change in institutional organization (Hunter 2012; Vaira 2004) and in national policy (Dale 1999).

Sporn (2003: 34) also notes changes in institutional governance. In Europe, on the one hand, the strengthening of institutional boards is a result of devolution of decision making processes from ministerial to institutional levels. On the other hand, the increased power of the institutional executive under aspects of managerialism and corporate governance models have weakened and otherwise altered faculty roles in the institutional and academic governance structures in both the US and European systems (see, for example, Kezar and Eckel 2004; Middlehurst 2004; McMaster 2007). Under the growing influence of the entrepreneurial university and the apparent movement away from the "Oxbridge" and the "shared" governance models toward the "corporate governance" model, one wonders about impacts on values in general (Kerr 1987; Vaira 2004) as well as those values driving internationalization. These are hot issues of change and dialog.

Terri Nokkala (2007) identifies three "discourses" relating to the "scope" of the university: (1) the science and knowledge discourse; (2) the civilization and well-being discourse; and (3) the competition and competiveness discourse. The first two focus on the more traditional purposes underlying the university, which although remaining viable, are being overtaken in her view by the competition and competiveness discourse which is arising out of globalization and revenue challenges and emergence of the entrepreneurial institution.

Interactions producing a changing internationalization paradigm

The kinds of broad-gauged organization reforms referenced by Sporn and issues being raised by Nokkala lead not only to wondering further about changing rationales for internationalization, but also how both might interact to produce change. For example, it is argued that emergence of the entrepreneurial university along with other change phenomena such as managerialism are moving higher education and its internationalization toward a corporate model and away from its more traditional and unique model (Scott 2003) which emphasized cross-cultural understanding and impartial knowledge creation and knowledge dissemination—all of which formerly occurred under the umbrella of academic freedom to set priorities and to conduct inquiries. The potential weakening of academic governance structures involving genuine faculty influence in favor of corporate executives is another issue not just for institutional governance but for how values and priorities for faculty international engagements are set.

These changes in institutional purpose, modelling, and practice have implications for the conduct of international engagement, which in its starkest realities can be visualized with a few examples such as:

- international development activity designed to achieve short-term government-sponsored diplomacy goals rather than long-term sustainable development;

- not engaging international activity unless it has a business plan that at least covers cost and preferably generates surplus;
- a requirement that mobility programs be self-financing; or, the recruitment of international students and scholars for entrepreneurial motivations.

Summarizing a few implications: managing a clash of values

In these changes and efforts at reform, there is a clash of values inherent in a wider array of motivations for international engagement (discussed next in Chapter 3). One consequence of a widening set of motivations is dissonance among diverse stakeholders of internationalization (both internal and external) which may weaken a cohesive internationalization culture in support of it.

In a complex organizational setting such as higher education, false dichotomies of all kinds need to be avoided: e.g., be entrepreneurial vs. reject entrepreneurialism in favor of traditional intellectual values and purposes. The reality of a complex organization with multiple stakeholders is diverse motivations, rationales, and preferred outcomes requiring development of organizational structures and processes that effectively mediate them.

In moving CI from concept to reality, the central issue is how will the journey from concept to reality play out in interaction with higher education organizational change. Traditionalists may have a strong distaste for the entrepreneurial institution. In a twenty-first century environment, though, ignoring such aspects of change is not a realistic strategy. The real issue is one of finding the right balance or co-existence among competing objectives.

The key to implementation of more comprehensive and strategic forms of higher education internationalization, in moving it from concept to reality, is to recognize the diversity of motivations, interests, measures of success and accountability, and methods that will draw together a critical mass of institutional leadership and participation necessary to make it possible. Ingredients and steps toward building a critical mass to move from concept to action is the focus of Chapter 4. Understanding the diversity of motivations that have grown around internationalization (Chapter 3) sets the stage for understanding the dimensions of action needed.

Action will play out under differing conceptualization of organizational reform and change, reflecting in part differences across higher education institutions as well as the varying ways in which local and national cultures mediate global forces affecting higher education organizational change (Vaira 2004). Internationalization has and probably always will play out under the dominant model of higher education of any particular era. But even when one model appears to dominate there are in Nokkala's terms, "not a single dominating discourse, [but rather] several discourses co-exist," in complementary fashion (2007: 236).

Chapter 3

Motivations and rationales for comprehensive internationalization

The theme of this chapter is that comprehensive higher education internationalization is shaped by widely ranging motivations and rationales, including institutional motivations and those of sundry stakeholders. A related theme is that as the motivations and rationales for internationalization diversify, they collectively encourage a comprehensive and strategic institutional approach to internationalization. As Chapter 2 noted, environments and overarching trends will do much to shape motivations and rationales for action, but motivations and rationales can take on lives of their own.

Motivations can be simple and singular (e.g., international engagement as an institutional revenue source) or they can be far more numerous and complex extending beyond revenue to intellectual outcomes associated with teaching/learning, research/scholarship and service, and beyond that to motivations relating to institutional global responsibility, institutional reputation, capacity building, and meeting needs of constituents.

The numerous constituents and stakeholders of higher education internationalization will vary in their expectations for internationalization. How a higher education institution attends to and mediates these varied and sometimes conflicting expectations will define what internationalization means for it in practice.

We are a long way from the individual motivations of the "wandering scholar" as the principal driver of internationalization. Now, there is great diversity in actions, priorities, and rationales which arise from the proliferation of stakeholders, each viewing the meaning of internationalization through different filtering lenses. Some lenses prioritize internationalization to serve the needs of clientele, society, and nations; others filter in the interest of the general search for knowledge, student learning, or cross-cultural relations; others are more organizationally focused on enhancing institutional funding, capacity, reputation, and mission outcomes. Diversity in purposes, motivations, and rationales leads to diversity in priorities and models of higher education internationalization.

From laissez faire to institutionalized motivations and rationales

A wider array of rationales and motivations are driving institutionally sponsored approaches to a more comprehensive internationalization. This is happening in part because of the growing scale and diversity of constituent expectations. As internationalization becomes institutionally organized, laissez faire aspects of it become more constrained by institutional procedure as well as by external regulations. For example, the curricular integration of mobility imposes constraints to achieve fit, so do institutional safety and security criteria regulating permissible destinations and modalities. Recent calls for improved quality control and assurance within and across higher education institutions in delivering services across borders (e.g., IAU 2012; AIRC 2014; NACAC 2013) are oriented at least in part to minimizing consequences of inadequate regulation of the industry delivering or selling product across borders.

Motivations and rationales driving comprehensive internationalization

Rationales and motivations are related concepts, often used interchangeably, but are not quite the same. Rationales help to explain, understand, or justify the reasons for actions. Motivations suggest prompting action; individuals may agree with rationales as to why CI should be advanced, but still not take action. There are hundreds, perhaps thousands of examples of institutional leadership touting the importance of internationalization and the reasons for it, but no follow through. However, compelling rationales can lay the intellectual foundation for the motivation to follow through.

Understanding motivations and rationales for CI are important because of its costs in money and effort to individuals and organizations. The benefits of incurring these costs must be assessed against purpose, motivations, and rationales and ultimately outcomes and benefits.

Purpose, goals, motivations, and rationales are aspirational; outcomes and benefits are the measurement of what happened or what was actually achieved. Goals provide the basis for later assessment and accountability—"Did we achieve what we hoped or were aspiring toward?"

This chapter focuses on the aspirations driving internationalization; Chapter 6 will focus on assessing outcomes and results. Evidence for the outcomes and impacts of internationalization runs a continuum from hope and belief, to anecdotal results, to systematic data collection to support conclusions. While the practice of assessment still tends to lean toward the belief/hope end of the continuum rather than the objective data end, it remains that aspirations and accompanying rationales motivate people and institutions to engage internationalization regardless of hard evidence of outcomes.

The question has been raised as to whether CI or any form of internationalization is an end or a means (e.g., de Wit 2013: 25). Imagining it as an end is limiting because logically as an end, the purpose of internationalization is internationalization—a tautology? Realistically, the cost and effort associated with internationalization are for further purposes. Just as higher education internationalization is not a homogeneous concept, neither are the rationales and motivations (ends) for doing it.

Expanding types of motivations and rationales for CI

When rationales expand, motivations can broaden and strengthen in part because the purposes and stakeholders being served widen—for example, when rationales and motivations expand beyond the search for knowledge, truth, and understanding to include global institutional credentialing (Brandenburg *et al.* 2013) or an array of political, economic, socio-cultural, and academic outcomes (de Wit 1998; Knight and de Wit 1999; Knight 2012). Motivations and clientele can widen and strengthen further if adding purposes related to: "expanding cross-cultural understanding; ... strengthening higher education institutional stature; ... enhancing national and global security; ... improving labor force and economic competitiveness; ... and enhancing knowledge, skills, attributes and careers for graduates ..." (Hudzik 2011: 16).

As Jane Knight (2012: 28) rightly points out, "vocabulary reflects priorities and phases" in defining internationalization. The operational meanings of internationalization are expressed through its actions, and types of actions are given labels. The popular vocabulary changes over time to reflect dominant realities and practices of the age. A sampling by Knight (2012: 29) of some of the dominant vocabulary included:

- *Fifty years ago:* "international education, foreign students, international development, student exchange."
- *Thirty years ago:* "intercultural education, international students, distance education, areas studies."
- *Ten years ago:* "globalization, global rankings, regional education hubs, international competencies."

With some exceptions (e.g., "international" replacing "foreign"), the vocabulary appears additive or cumulative. More recently we can see new terms being added such as comprehensive internationalization and allied concepts such as strategic and embedded internationalization. These new terms, particularly CI, provide a very wide umbrella under which to accumulate not only an array of motivations and rationales but numerous types of programs and activities.

The vocabulary of motivations and rationales for internationalization reflects the aspirational values for internationalization at points in time. Over time, we can detect an accumulation of motivations for internationalization; the list of motivations itself becomes more comprehensive and diverse. And there are value judgments assigned by some to certain of the motivations—for example, the "goodness" of CI if advancing cooperation and intercultural understanding, and its potential wrongness if emphasizing competition, commercialization, profits, etc. The problem may not be whether there are values behind the motivations for CI but whether if they are the "right values" as various people see them (Brandenburg *et al.* 2013). As rationales and motivations proliferate for internationalization in a twenty-first century context, so do underlying values, and hence the opportunity for value disputes.

Categorizing motivations chronologically

If vocabulary reflects priorities and phases in defining internationalization, so does it with respect to an evolution of motivations and rationales and for an accumulation of purposes. Several categories of motivation and rationales come to mind connected to historical periods:

1   the search for knowledge;
2   a "finishing touch" in the process of education and learning;
3   advancing local and national interests and needs;
4   cooperation and mutual understanding in promotion of peace and justice;
5   national security;
6   strengthening the higher education institution.

The order implies a chronology of their appearance, and not a "development" from simple to more sophisticated, and not a hierarchy. Some of the categories are implied by de Wit and Merkx (2012) in their able portrayal of the history of higher education internationalization. The six can also be seen as cumulative and as a driver of CI.

1 Knowledge

The notion that higher education internationalization has its roots far back in the mobile search for knowledge, innovation, and ideas, and that such intellectual purposes still underlie higher education today (Kerr 1994) has already been discussed at some length in Chapter 1. To the extent that the "business" of higher education and that one of its core values concerns the search for truth and knowledge (Barnett 2013) wherever it can be found, there is a certain stability to this rationale and subsequently as a motivation to internationalize higher education.

2 The finishing touch on learning and education

There is a long record of mobility for learning as a "finishing" touch to education—in the Renaissance as "a culmination of humanist education" for the elite, or the sixteenth century "wandering scholar" and the grand tour of the seventeenth and eighteenth centuries relating to the degree (de Ridder-Symoens 1996: 417–444). While there was periodic and documentable opposition to mobility and learning abroad from the sixteenth to twentieth centuries in Europe as a force of "contamination," as well as in the United States (Halpern 1969), scholars have generally agreed to a persistence in the notion that mobility was an important ingredient in higher learning, particularly for the elite.

3 Meeting national needs

The rise of the nation-state and the concomitant development and protection of national identity and position, coupled to the emergence of national funding systems for higher education reoriented higher education toward providing national advantage. As nation-states engaged others in commerce as well as in war, international education acquired the more specific motivation to develop advantage for the nation by acquiring cross-border, cutting-edge knowledge and intelligence. These are particularly strong developments and implications from the nineteenth century forward, continuing in the present day. Nokkala (2007: 209–210), writing about the impact of globalization, notes the rising dominance of contributions to competitiveness as a major rational and motivation. Competitiveness not only requires high-quality education but cutting-edge research, both strengthened through internationalization.

4 Advancing peace and justice

Following World War I for a brief period and then reinforced by World War II, a nascent motivation for international education and internationalization arose to serve the interests of peace through intellectual cooperation and cross-border and cross-cultural understanding. The formation following World War I of DAAD in Germany and IIE in the United States were strongly oriented to promoting international understanding in the interest of peace.

5 National security

In the United States, national security has been a powerful motivation for international education and internationalization. There is probably no better example than passage of the National Defense Education Act (NDEA) in 1958, a year after Sputnik (Hudzik 2011). Higher education internationalization is seen by a widening array of governments as playing a key role in "soft diplomacy" objectives. While it is probably unlikely that national defense rationales and motivations are as manifestly obvious in all countries and regions (e.g., Europe), de Wit (2002) believes that internationalization in Europe is motivated primarily by EC aspirations for economic and perhaps political integration, and as further reflected in institutional networking. Presumably, however, someone must believe that an economically and politically integrated Europe is a more secure Europe.

The 2012 US Department of Education International Strategy (labeled by the Department as the "First-ever, fully articulated international strategy") outlined four objectives for US international education and engagement (USDE 2012). While the USDE document is short on detail, the fact that it is claimed to be the United States's first-ever international strategy is noteworthy given its 2012 publication. The motivations for internationalization listed in the document—economic competitiveness and jobs and national security and diplomacy are a reinforcement of well-established rationales in the United States for internationalization. It is refreshing that one of the implied motivations of the international strategy acknowledges that lessons can be learned from abroad.

6 In service of institutional needs

In Scott's view it is a myth that universities were intentionally international from the Middle Ages onward (Scott 1998a). Indeed, international engagement and mobility were not core elements of institutional missions and values. In the United States, inbound mobility was more an artifact of "We built it, and they came." Communities and societies of scholars, and cross-border intellectual collaborations arose more from private and individual undertakings. Not until the twentieth century and until government policies encouraged mobility as a form of foreign policy and diplomacy were institutions awakened in any real sense to their international roles. Examples include the Colombo plan in Australia, the USAID long-term training and education program in the United States, and later Bologna in Europe, and then offshoots of these such as the degree "twinning" programs encouraged by Malaysia. For a good summary of the major events of this period, see de Wit and Merkx (2012: 47–57).

The academy's rising awareness of its legitimate purposes and roles relating to international engagement, as well as government policies, programs, and assistance to support it encourages *conscious* institutional attention to more strategic and comprehensive forms of higher education internationalization.

Motivations and rationales change over time

The chronology of motivations outlined above reinforces a sense of changing rationales over time which depend on internal organizational dynamics as well as environmental factors. For example, the rising importance of institutional global reputation as a motivation for international engagement was far less relevant prior to the emergence of global ranking schemes; it was also less relevant prior to the spread of institutions trading and competing globally (Altbach 2010). The ranking schemes have probably motivated a more strategic and comprehensive attention to international engagement because of their weighing of research reputation, mobility, global competitiveness in attracting the best in students and scholars, and reputation-building cross-border collaboration.

Before development and massive expansion of cutting-edge research capacity abroad, the motivations and rationales behind forming cross-border institutional research partnerships weighed heavily toward mobility rather than internationalization of research missions. It is probably also the case that without visible inclusion of international engagement in institutional mission and value statements, the saliency of internationalization as a matter of institutionalized attention was muted.

In sum, motivations and rationales driving internationalization, and particularly the relative weight assigned to a number of them will undergo elaboration and reprioritization over time. As motivations and rationales change, so will action priorities for internationalization.

Tensions across motivations

There is a tension between and among motivations, and perhaps none more obvious than the motivation to meet national competitiveness needs and those to lay the groundwork for pursuing cooperation and peace through mutual understanding. This tension can be seen in some of the critiques and concerns about internationalization discussed in Chapter 1 and in the IAU declaration referenced there, e.g., improving national competitive edge exacerbates the gap between rich and poor, thereby sowing seeds for international tensions. Globalization in the form of unregulated free trade (including particularly in mobility) is seen to greatly advantage the powerful while disadvantaging the rest, thereby further sowing the seeds for violence (e.g., domestic unrest, wars, and terrorism).

As motivations for internationalization multiply, they will conflict and CI leadership within institutions has to mediate the conflicts. While CI can be motivated by a desire to produce local and national advantage (e.g., global market knowledge for local industries), it can be mediated by a motivation to protect the conditions and balances necessary for international peace and justice and reducing economic and cultural dislocations at home and abroad. The aspiration to find a balance is the subject of an Austrian ministry study: "[While] … having a knowledge lead is becoming a primary production factor in the international competition of locations, … [t]he resultant challenge consists in organizing human co-existence on a global level by cooperation rather that competition" (Pasternack *et al.* 2006: 5). Whether or not such an aim is possible, the reality is that local prosperity is increasingly dependent on global co-prosperity in a myriad of ways (e.g., the economy, controlling communicable disease, safe and sustainable food supply).

Institutional and government motivations for CI

Increasing scale in cost and effort causes more attention to motivations, rationales and documenting benefits from CI. Knight (2004, 2012) separates institutional from national levels of rationales. At the institutional level she sees focus on "Institutional branding and profile, income generation, student and staff development, strategic alliances, and knowledge production." At the national level she sees the focus on "human resource development, strategic alliances, commercial trade, nation building and social/cultural development" dominate. There are similarities and crosswalks between these two lists; apparent differences may be in part a matter of scale and aggregation.

The OECD also distinguishes between institutional and government motivations for CI in order to explain "Why internationalisation matters" (Hénard *et al.* 2012: 9). In their view:

> Internationalisation enables higher education institutions to: increase national and international visibility; leverage institutional strengths through strategic partnerships; enlarge the academic community within which

to benchmark their activities; mobilise internal intellectual resources; add important, contemporary learning outcomes to student experience; develop stronger research groups.

Internationalisation enables governments to: develop national university systems within a broader, global framework; produce a skilled workforce with global awareness and multi-cultural competencies; use public higher education funds to promote national participation in the global knowledge economy; benefit from trade in education.

(Ibid.)

The Hénard *et al.* distinction is similar to Knight's. Policy is an important force in moving national or government aspirations forward and for shaping institutional possibilities and priorities. It can be policies in the form of immigration regulations that ease or impede the flow of students and scholars. It is policies linking internationalization to diplomacy priorities that can shape the form and destinations of mobility and establishment of partnerships (the same being true with respect to national security interests). Even in the United States where the Federal government has comparatively weak roles in education, programs like Title VI of the NDEA have had a huge impact on the more comprehensive internationalization of institutions as well as in reference to national interests. Also, policies may seek to enhance supra-national or pan-regional relationships which was a prime rationale and motivation force behind Erasmus (de Wit 2013).

The *institutionalization* of higher education internationalization has become one of the most potent recent developments in internationalization, carrying with it another list of motivations and rationales serving institutional needs. Some of these are noted or implied in the Knight and the Hénard *et al.* lists. The impacts of this development on higher education organizations and the motivations for them to move CI from concept to action and from piecemeal to something more comprehensive and strategic is dealt with more fully in Chapters 4 and 5.

Institutional motivations driving toward CI

It is arguable that four causes motivated the march toward building institutionally based motivations for higher education internationalization: funding; a changing clientele; globalization and global higher education capacity development. Together, these are also drivers of more strategic and comprehensive engagements of internationalization.

- *Funding.* Access to funding is one substantial motivation and enabler of internationalization. Tuition and fees from international students is an obvious attraction to many institutions. In the United States and later in Europe and elsewhere, governmentally well-funded international development agencies were sources of grant funds (often with very attractive overhead allowances). These not only funded institutional engagement abroad but in the process contributed to developing faculty cross-cultural and international skills through their participation on these projects. They probably also satisfied institutional motivations to "do good." (For a list of such development agencies, see http://en.wikipedia.org/wiki/List_of_development_aid_agencies.) Also, there are significant private donors with interests to funding international activity (Pratt *et al.* 2012).

- *Clientele needs.* Educating a populace to understand the "outside" world and to change viewpoints from parochial to outward looking was given significant public and policy attention from the latter half of the twentieth century forward. The upshot was a growing awareness that a country's education system, including particularly tertiary education, had a central role to play in preparing students for life and work in an international and global environment. By the twenty-first century, the breadth and scale in preparing students expanded: from preparing the few (e.g., those majoring in international "X") to mainstreaming such preparation for all graduates. Mainstreaming is one of the essential elements of CI. One recent manifestation of this sweeping re-orientation is the project of the Association of American Colleges and Universities to integrate substantial international and global dimensions into US higher education's liberal learning goals (Bennett *et al.* 2012).
- *Globalization.* The border-transcending forces of globalization impact all aspects of life including the "business" of higher education through the flow of students and scholars, access to cutting-edge knowledge, and institutional competitive position. Not to be globally engaged risks being globally marginalized, and shut off from the emergence of a global higher education system.

Robert J. Samuelson (2013) penned an intriguing opinion piece in the *Washington Post,* entitled "The New Globalization." It begins, "Globalization isn't what it used to be." Speaking mainly to the matter of global capital flows, Samuelson's view is that "globalization hasn't been repealed, but it has entered a more cautious and regulated phase. We are creating a 'gated globe,' argues Greg Ip [2013], U.S. economics editor of the *Economist* in a masterful analysis."

The question for higher education CI is how much of its expansion over the last decade or two is tied to largely unfettered economic globalization, as well as easier travel, communication, and border-crossing technology. Does further expansion in higher education internationalization require continuing expansion of global cross-border markets? Ip notes the cyclical nature of capital flows, but the potentially more significant factor, as he describes it, is "deliberate policy, . . . hidden protectionism is flourishing." The motivations behind recent actions by India to restrict entry of off-shore higher education branch operations or to constrain spaces for international students coming into India may have elements of protectionism, or just simple parochialism, or protecting insufficient indigenous capacity for Indian students. As China's indigenous higher education capacity and quality develops, how might its incentives change from continuing to support education abroad for its students? Perhaps, too, might China become a more significant net exporter of higher education through inbound programs?

Rising interest in quality control mechanisms for cross-border higher education collaborations and trans-national ventures will not only increase regulation but perhaps "ring-fence" internationalization methods as well as growth. Ip and Samuelson both cite increased regulation and ring-fencing with respect to global economic flows.

While there is evidence that trade and mobility patterns are coupled (British Council 2012), it is most unlikely that higher education internationalization and CI "will be repealed," or not continue a forward march. Rates of growth in areas such as mobility may pull back from the halcyon years of the mid 1990s through much of the first decade of 2000, just as economic trends are cyclical. But the motivations and rationalizations for higher education have broadened enough to begin providing their own momentum and do not appear to be heavily dependent on unbridled economic globalization.

Access to expanding global research capacity

High-quality and high-capacity higher education systems are developing throughout the world. Development initially emphasized educational capacity, but with the emergence of research hubs and research universities within them and in research network development, scores of non-western centers of discovery have emerged and are being planned in an array of locations such as Singapore, China, India, and Brazil). Stephen Toope, President of the University of British Columbia, notes that as the capacity of any single institution to afford the operational and infrastructure costs of cutting-edge research diminishes in the face of research scale and complexity, institutions look increasingly for inter-institutional partnerships. Further, as cutting-edge knowledge can be found in many places around the world, increasingly those partnerships are with institutions abroad (Toope 2010).

Institutional self-declared motivations

The most recent IAU survey and published results (Egron-Polak and Hudson 2014) updates institutional and regional patterns of motivations for internationalization. The IAU survey question was framed in terms of "benefits to the institution" to which motivations and rationales can be inferred. Respondents were asked to rank their top three benefits from internationalization. Results were summarized in a variety of ways, the list below represents the percentages of respondents who ranked an item first, second or third in a list of ten (ibid.: 50):

- 52 percent: international awareness of students;
- 44 percent: improved quality of teaching and learning;
- 41 percent: enhanced international cooperation and capacity building;
- 37 percent: increased international networking by faculty/researchers;

- 34 percent: strengthened research and knowledge production capacity;
- 31 percent: enhanced prestige/profile for the institution;
- 28 percent: benchmarking institutional performance according to international practice;
- 10 percent: increased/diversified revenue generation.

A breakdown of the first three ranks across regions tended to cluster around "international awareness of students, quality of teaching and learning, institutional cooperation and capacity building, and strengthened research and knowledge production capacity" (ibid.: 53).

Thinking systemically about rationales and motivations

Hans de Wit and Jane Knight, separately and together, have written numerous times over the last two decades on the issue of rationales for internationalization. The two chronological bookends for these several publications focused on four key rationales for internationalization (de Wit 1998; Knight and de Wit 1999; Knight 2012). They are: social/cultural, political, economic, and academic. Knight's (2004) rendition, based on a de Wit (2002) update, and repeated with some variation by Knight in 2012, includes the following more detailed elements for the four rationalizations:

- *Social/cultural:* national cultural diversity; intercultural understanding; citizenship development; social and community development.
- *Political:* foreign policy; national security; technical assistance; peace and mutual understanding; national identity; regional identity.
- *Economic:* economic growth and competitiveness; labor market; financial incentives.
- *Academic:* international dimension to research and teaching; extension of academic horizon; institution building; profile and status; enhancement of quality; international academic standards.

What can be made of these categories and associated detail by de Wit and Knight? The first and obvious conclusion is that the list of motivations, rationales, and purposes are multi-faceted; any institution pursuing all would have to be engaged strategically and comprehensively in the act of internationalization. While the list is itself fairly comprehensive, neither de Wit nor Knight suggest that institutions will or should necessarily pursue all of these rationales.

It is also possible to see many of these categories and sub-categories as both the means and the ends of internationalization. For example, internationalization of learning produces knowledge for its own sake and it produces knowledge to serve further purposes. In the former case, acquiring understanding of another culture or society can satisfy personal growth goals; in the latter case, it can form the basis for effectively living, working, and functioning in another society and culture.

What is clear, though, from the composite de Wit and Knight categories is that internationalization is not an end in itself. A very forthright expression of internationalization as a means comes from Madeleine Green in talking about fostering global citizenship: Global citizenship "puts the spotlight on the why internationalization is central to quality education and emphasizes that internationalization is a means, not an end. Serious consideration of the goals of internationalization makes student learning the key concern rather than counting inputs" (Green 2012a).

Perhaps internationalization is better viewed as part of a cause-and-effect chain (perhaps even a matrix) of motivations, means, and purposes. For example, international learning and engagement can help to connect localities and societies to a global market place of opportunity, thereby potentially improving economic well-being both locally and globally, and in turn creating conditions through inter-locked economies and trade to make peace a more attractive option than war.

Even though categorizing (compartmentalizing) motivations suggests a certain degree of separateness and individuality among them, it doesn't take much imagination to consider how the four categories are interconnected and cross-feeding. So, in a global environment, while motivations for internationalization proliferate, so do their interconnections, and so as a result do the pressures to widen the scope (breadth and depth) of internationalization.

Rationales and drivers for CI in a twenty-first century context

Beginning in 2011 and following publication of *Comprehensive Internationalization: From Concept to Action* (Hudzik 2011), the author began elaborating in greater detail at regional conferences in the United States, Europe, Asia, and Latin American what he saw as the four primary rationales driving higher education institutions toward more comprehensive commitments to internationalization (also see Hudzik and Stohl 2012). As displayed in Figure 3.1, these included:

- *The core mission driver.* The "business" or core of higher education is ideas and innovation. The core business manifests itself through missions which include the creation of knowledge through research, the transmission of knowledge to learners, and the translation of knowledge into action for society's benefits. With globalization, the business of higher education is increasingly conducted across borders in the flow of students, scholars, and ideas and in the formation of cross-border partnerships and other forms of collaboration. Higher education is functioning in a global marketplace of supply, demand, competition, and collaboration across *all* of its missions.
- *The customer service driver.* Higher education has customers. Among others we include students/graduates and perhaps parents, communities,

businesses, and employers. Life and work in or at least part of a *global* environment is increasingly an expectation for everyone. Our "customers" at home are global customers too. An OECD (2008) report noted that we are moving toward a more integrated world labor market, and that "work force ready" students has a global meaning and so must educational systems preparing them.

- *The social responsibility driver.* The social responsibilities of higher education have expanding global dimensions. It is not local vs. global but local *and* global because increasingly local prosperity is tied to global co-prosperities (Hudzik and Simon 2012). As part of these global social responsibilities, higher education institutions have a role to play in fostering global relationships, peace, and justice; enhancing peoples' position in the global economy; and improving cross-cultural understanding. Brooks and Normore (2010) use the terms "glocal" and "glocalization" to argue that education leaders must develop an integration of local and global across a number of key knowledge domains if higher education is to act responsibly in a twenty-first century context.

- *The globalization driver.* With globalization there is the emergence of a global higher education system based on a global spread of educational and research capacity; growth in mobility of students and scholars; emergence of multi-directional talent flows, collaborations, and networks; and global quality assessment and management systems. The impact of global higher education trends includes increased cross-border higher education trade and competition, collaboration, and stratification, which drives higher education institutions to be more strategically engaged abroad than before.

Together, these rationales and accompanying motivations drive higher education toward a more strategic and comprehensive engagement of internationalization. They imply a wide range of actions that must involve all institutional missions.

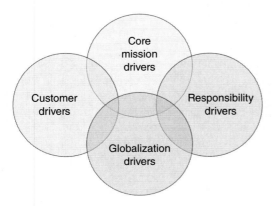

Figure 3.1 Rationales and drivers encouraging institutional CI.

They relate to the common overarching aspirations of CI presented in Chapter 1: mainstreaming access, integration into core missions, expanding who contributes and participates, and integrating across missions to produce synergies.

In sum and moving forward

If the various motivations and rationales noted throughout this chapter are indeed inexorably driving higher education toward more strategic and comprehensive forms of internationalization, the key issue turns on how one moves CI from concept to action to results. The remaining chapters focus on just that.

Chapter 4

Comprehensive internationalization

From rhetoric and concept to reality

There are few university presidents, vice-chancellors, or rectors who don't espouse the importance of internationalization. Yet, many fail to exert effective leadership for action to bring internationalization from a concept to reality and to engage the organizational change required to make it happen. Common omissions include: insufficient use of the persuasiveness of their office to engage an institution-wide dialog to build a culture of understanding and support for internationalization; inadequate attention given to development of an engaging campus vision for internationalization that includes goals for accountability and expectations for who must fulfill roles in the process of internationalization; failure to identify barriers to internationalization and attempt to ameliorate them; inability to engage bureaucratic and organizational change in a way that makes implementation a successful reality.

Of course there are many leaders who follow through, produce results, and demonstrate the art of the possible when it comes to the internationalization of higher education. If the general growth in cross-border higher education mobility, formation of cross-border institutional collaborations and partnership, and internationalization of on-campus curricula are an indicator, the climate within higher education for action appears to be improving. In reality, though, there remains a substantial gap which has been long-standing in the number of institutions and institutional leaders espousing the rhetoric and those taking action (Van de Water 1997; Green *et al.* 2008; Rodenberg 2010; ACE 2012).

Elspeth Jones (2011) decries another dimension of rhetoric vs. action in which of late the focus has been a debate over the meanings of internationalization and the best way to title it. Jones' solution is to call for an end to the debate and to get on with the institutional actions that will produce intended results and outcomes. Hudzik (2012), also tiring of definitional debates, noted in his *Chronicle of Higher Education* blog that while ideas and debates help guide action, he was hoping for "More Action, Not Just Talk, on Internationalization."

Organization change

The organizational change needed to bring comprehensive internationalization from idea to reality is not simply a matter of leadership but a willingness on the part of people and entities throughout the institution to become involved, to make contributions to internationalization in their own ways, and to confront the status quo where needed.

Inaction has many causes. Talk is cheaper than action. There is often a gap between wanting to accomplish an objective and knowing how to do it, or even where to start. The desire to preserve the status quo and the comfort of the familiar is a powerful narcotic turning attention away from change and the new. Assumptions about internationalization being costly, coupled to the inability to identify and marshal resources sufficient to completely fund or support internationalization, can amount to a death sentence for action—"We like the idea and want to do it, but we need much more money than we have to make it happen."

These and other rationalizations for inaction, while containing elements of reality, are at best half-truths and contrary to the experience and advice of many leaders, including one highly experienced US university president who in writing about internationalizing her institution has said,

> waiting for everything and everybody to be neatly in place before taking action guarantees inaction. Our orientation has begun with, "Why and how can we do this?" rather than, "How much will it cost?" Wide-ranging dialogue draws people into an understanding of internationalization, its connection to core institutional missions and values, and the rationales for it. From this evolves a framework for buy-in, concrete action, and resource allocations .... Getting on a road to internationalization is the important first step.
>
> (Simon 2013: 50)

Orientation of this chapter

This chapter focuses on overcoming the half-truths and moving the CI agenda forward. It is based in part on personal experience, but perhaps more importantly, on that of others who are also experienced in higher education internationalization and have come to understand what the key ingredients to action are, including elements of good practice.

This chapter models the need for action at two levels: (1) at the institutional, macro, or strategic level and (2) at the operational, tactical, or project level. In order for a strategic and comprehensive approach to be taken, both of these elements are needed, but only the second if the vision is more limited (e.g., learning for a few students as opposed to the many, involving only a few of the largely already "converted" academic and service units instead of most or all, or developing only one or two program dimensions of internationalization as opposed to a more strategic and comprehensive institutional approach).

Comprehensive internationalization cannot occur without a foundation being laid at the macro level and integrated into a broad institutional strategy. "Strategic inclusion" lays the foundation for CI by linking it to key decision-making and priority-setting processes in the institution.

This chapter does not seek to offer a single or "best" model of practice because there is none. There are practices that have been found to work, but which require a fit to particular institutional circumstances (see NAFSA 2014 for many examples). Recalling the point made in Chapter 1, higher education institutions are idiosyncratic, so the specific aspirations and practices that work for them will be, too. However, within this diversity of "good" practices some underlying principles of action are applicable. This chapter discusses them as well.

Taking action

By definition, CI impacts the entire higher education institution and enterprise; actions to bring it from rhetoric and concept to action and reality are similarly broad based. The action needed has a number of defining qualities including: long-term commitment; systematic and interconnected rather than piecemeal orientation, integrated into institutional missions, and built on a broad-based institutional culture of support.

Action needs to be guided by a vision that is both clearly directional and synthesizing. One version of such directionality and synthesis was presented in Chapter 1 where common aspirations associated with CI included mainstreaming, expanding involvement, mission integration, and achieving synergies. Each of these are likely to prompt organizational change.

Two levels of action

The breadth and depth of CI require activity at two institutional levels:

- The macro and strategic level concerns the institution as a whole and the extent of collective understanding of CI and support for it. It is building a broadly supportive institutional culture that views CI as an institutional priority and sees it as an imperative.
- The operational and programmatic level brings life and reality to CI through concrete programs, activities, and projects (e.g., expanding the number and integration of international students on campus, extending study abroad opportunities to all programs and courses of study, developing cross-border research partnerships and collaborations, internationalizing the on-campus environment and curriculum).

The macro/strategic and the operational/programmatic are mutually supporting. The former builds the environment and the foundation to support a wide range of activities and programs in support of CI and provides justification for giving priority and resources to CI. The operational and programmatic is what makes CI concrete in any institution.

While constructing a support culture is essential to achieving the breadth and depth of the common aspirations of CI, strategic culture building faces two challenges. The first challenge is that culture-building focuses on words rather than concrete actions with measurable results. The second is that culture-building takes time. The two difficulties taken together can give the appearance of perpetuating talk rather than action. A Japanese *haiku* may be relevant: "Much noise coming down stairs, no one appears." Talk and no action is a death sentence for getting an institution broadly involved in internationalization. People will lose interest and move on to other issues.

While action at the macro and strategic level ideally should precede that at the operational and programmatic level, both proceed apace as a matter of practical necessity in successful higher education internationalization efforts. There are numerous examples of institutions with long histories of international engagement which periodically undertake strategic institutional planning with respect to a more comprehensive approach to internationalization. Existing international programs and activities continue, but undergo strategic modification (see NAFSA 2014 for examples). Strategic planning exercises for CI will likely recalibrate priorities as well as the breadth and depth of international activity; but it also can be a dialog that refreshes an institutional understanding of and commitment to internationalization.

There are numerous examples described in the NAFSA Simon Award for Comprehensive Internationalization at large US institutions such as Michigan State and the University of Buffalo, and smaller institutions as well. Examples are also discussed in the institutional case-story chapters of this book.

Stephen Toope, President of the University of British Columbia, described an 18-month process of building UBC's strategic plan for internationalization. Toope described the process as neither top-down nor bottom-up but rather one involving broad interactive exchanges up, down, and throughout the institution. Although ostensibly a strategic planning process, the 18-month dialog could also be seen as building aspects of an institutional culture for a more strategic and comprehensive approach to internationalization (Loveland 2011a). Similarly, the Community College of Philadelphia employed wide-spread campus dialog to build the case and culture for internationalization. The College rewrote its mission statement to embrace the goal of giving students increased awareness and appreciation of a diverse world and interdependence. But it was campus dialogs, fora, town-hall meetings, and publications that built a culture of understanding and support (NAFSA 2014).

The elements of dialog to build a strategic support culture

Successfully building a support culture emanates from dialog that has an educational function as well as the objective of building buy-in through a conversational and an intellectual process of involvement. A strong agenda for a campus dialog on CI has a number of key elements:

- What is CI? Expand understanding of its key elements and build on earlier notions of internationalization.
- Why do it? Rationales/motivations driving CI.
- Connect to institutional missions. Particularly, how will CI enhance existing missions?
- What are the anticipated outcomes, impacts, and benefits from CI?
- What would constitute an energizing but realistic vision for CI?
- Who and which parts of the institution have roles to play in bringing CI about?

A mission-connected strategic dialog would add discussion and answers for:

- What are our missions (and responsibilities) in an increasingly global environment?
- How do we prepare our graduates for a global environment?
- What is the value of connecting teaching/learning and research/scholarship to global pathways of talent, ideas, and capacities, and the benefits and pitfalls? (See Jones 2013b.)
- Given the intertwining of local and global, how do we simultaneously serve the local community, national interests, and the broader global community?
- How will CI impact internal organizational structures and procedures?

A successful dialog around these kinds of issues refines understanding of what CI is, its importance, and expectations for actions, outcomes, and involvement.

A dialog should aim to achieve a level of understanding and justification for CI that widens and deepens support in general terms, but provides space for seeing value, action, and justification from a number of vantage points. A successful dialog is less a matter of building consensus over specific programs for comprehensive internationalization than it is to build a sustainable view of it as an institutional imperative. And it lays the groundwork for the strategic inclusion of internationalization into the institution's key planning and decision-making processes.

Strategic inclusion

Strategic inclusion provides the means by which a campus culture for internationalization exerts its influence through many means including planning, policy-making, budgets, and decision making (see Figure 4.1). Unless culture activates desirable behaviors it is of limited value. The elements of strategic inclusion tie the culture to certain key leadership and management behaviors. Six main areas for strategic inclusion are important to shaping peoples' commitment and institutional behaviors for CI. In concert, they help to determine whether an institution will treat CI as a priority in the allocation of time, effort, and resource investment.

On-going inclusion in:

- Leadership messaging
- Institutional missions and visions
- Institutional strategic and budget planning
- Institutional fund-raising
- Reviews of institutional policies and procedures
- Institutional moments of change

Figure 4.1 Elements of CI strategic inclusion.

1 *Leadership messaging.* Is there consistent and frequent senior leadership messaging to both internal and external stakeholders on the importance of CI for the institution and its future? Frequent and consistent messaging sustains attention.

2 *Institutional mission and vision.* Is internationalization clearly articulated in the mission and vision statements of the institution? It is hard to be included in strategic planning and resource allocation if CI doesn't have an entry point that links internationalization to the core of institutional values and ethos.

3 *Strategic and budget planning.* Is there integration into institutional strategic planning? Is there integration into annual budget planning? There are many ways this can be done as discussed in Chapter 7, but the key point is that unless internationalization is connected to these core priority-setting and investment activities, international activity is likely to be substantially marginalized and largely rhetorical. Additionally, there is benefit from inclusion not only in institutional planning and budgeting, but in sub-levels as well (colleges, departments, units).

4 *Fund-raising.* As fund-raising and expansion of contracts and grants income grow in importance for purposes of institutional revenue diversification, is internationalization included as a fund-raising goal? While fund-raising has been largely a US phenomenon, it is becoming a topic of interest in other systems faced with budget shortfalls.

5 *Reviews of institutional policies and procedures.* Is internationalization included in the periodic reviews of institutional policies, rules, and bureaucratic procedures for helping and hindering impacts? Rules and regulations developed with a local or domestic context in mind may easily complicate institutional functioning abroad, in a globalized regulatory environment, and in other cultures (e.g., relating to health insurance, safety, financial and personnel policies, and values such as academic freedom or intellectual property rights).

The key issue is whether an adaptive bureaucracy exists and can it be adjusted to international engagement. As no system of rules anticipates perfectly in all circumstances, especially when working across legal and cultural systems, are there timely ways to deal with bureaucratic barriers to CI when they arise? How resistant is institutional bureaucracy to changes in procedures and practices? Relatedly, is CI a part of regular discussions about updates and simplification of rules, policies, and procedures? At one institution a decision to change its health insurance carrier for employees was about to be made on cost criteria when it was discovered that the preferred low-cost carrier would have no provision for health and accident coverage when employees were in another country, even when there on institutional business.

6   *Institutional moments of change.* Is CI a part of discussions during defining moments and critical events in an institution's life? Defining moments are sometimes called "unfreezing" events because they open opportunities to question practices that have seemingly been operative since the Stone Age. Some of the more frequently occurring unfreezing moments include periodic accreditation and re-accreditation events, change in senior leadership, periodic curricular reviews, quality and ranking assessments, and institutional strategic planning exercises. Getting CI into the conversation of change by implicitly or explicitly incorporating it into these unfreezing events is critical.

Integration of "international" into *all* of these elements of strategic inclusion is not necessarily essential for success, but common sense would suggest that the wider and deeper the inclusion, the more explicit the attention will be to international activity because of the overlapping reinforcement given it through these several points of entry.

Institutions will vary in the degree to which there is strategic inclusion of internationalization in these processes. Taking an inventory of whether and how notions of internationalization are included and expressed in these key areas is a way to concretely assess the breadth, depth and stability of the basic foundation for CI. While strategic inclusion doesn't guarantee strategic follow through at the level of concrete actions and decisions, it does set the stage for such action and signal intent. And, most importantly when think about resource allocation for internationalization, prospects brighten considerably the more a culture of support is given meaning through inclusion of CI in these key institutional elements and processes.

Key enabling strategies and tactics

Additional strategies and tactics will further define and strengthen inclusion strategically and operationally. These can also be viewed as a set of enabling conditions that bridge between rhetoric and action, establishing the environment within which action and programs will produce intended results. The most important of these enabling conditions are outlined below and in Figure 4.2, although some of them will be dealt with again in subsequent chapters in greater detail.

I Define the meaning of success

Action is rarely taken without some expectation of results. Accountability requires prior thought about what will constitute success, or achievement of desired ends.

> 1 Articulate and define a vision of success
> 2 Reward success: What is counted is what counts
> 3 Integrate CI as value-added into core missions
> 4 Extend the leadership team for CI
> 5 Challenge the status quo
> 6 Recruit and develop human resources for CI
> 7 Articulate a bold vision and goals
> 8 Allocate money and resources

Figure 4.2 Key institutional enabling strategies for CI.

Motivation to act is at least partly stirred by the promise of success defined by criteria or measures that signal intended benefits. When all is said and done will there be an agreed basis for answering the question whether success was achieved in intended ways? Having some sense about the definition, criteria, or meaning of success is, therefore, partly motivational, partly the basis for accountability, and partly a directional guide for the kind of actions that need to be taken.

The issue of defining success is treated in greater detail in Chapter 6 in the context of the differing lenses through which various stakeholders will define successful impacts and outcomes from internationalization. Stakeholders share some criteria for measuring success but each will also use individual criteria and view success through different filtering lenses. Many times criteria can be in conflict with one another and not fully resolvable (e.g., cost vs. quality).

Consider, for example, efforts to mount a more fulsome student mobility program, whether outbound or inbound. What will constitute the measures of success: number of students or participants; standards of quality; faculty assessments of intellectual value and student satisfaction with the experience; finance (e.g., viability, break even, surplus models, and revenue diversification); academic outcomes (e.g., student completion rates and academic performance, knowledge gain, personal attributes and life skills, intercultural competence development, enhancement of global perspectives and multi-cultural skills)? The companion question is which of these (or other criteria) are necessary and which are sufficient as means to measure and establish success?

Do the criteria for defining the success of CI relate to the core missions of higher education: teaching and learning outcomes, research and scholarship, and community service and outreach outcomes? If so, the focus of defining success will be on strengthening institutional curricular and research capabilities and on sustainable institutional capacity building. Is the definition of success focused on enhancing the qualities of graduates, or on research and scholarship that is at the cutting edge, or on expanding institutional rank and reputation, or on projects that feed the entrepreneurial needs of the institution to diversify revenue streams, or all of these?

In Nokkala's (2007: 11) terminology, is the definition of success weighted toward "the science and knowledge discourse," "the civilisation and well-being discourse," or "the competition and competiveness discourse"? The answer will vary across institutions. Having some basic understanding of how success will be defined in a particular institution helps to define its CI priorities and starting points as well as selecting actions and routes for internationalization that will connect to criteria of success.

2 Reward success

What is counted and rewarded is what counts. Students understand what is important through curriculum requirements, electives, and opportunities to engage internationally. As internationalization is the product of peoples' efforts, what is there to indicate that their efforts to engage internationally will be rewarded? The incorporation of international activity, whether in teaching, research, and/or service, into institutional promotion and other personnel decision practices sends a powerful message on its importance (further discussed in Chapter 5). The allocation of resources is not only an enabling condition but also a measure of institutional commitment and what it counts as important; the role and means of resource allocation is discussed in Chapter 7. In sum, making it clear at the beginning that CI counts in the institution's system of accountability metrics is essential for turning rhetoric into action.

3 Build support through integration

Many will see CI as in competition for scarce resources and other institutional purposes. "We have too much to do already; we can't afford a 'fourth' mission; we can't serve local and domestic students and clientele as well as ones abroad." There is some truth to these utterances because there aren't enough *new* funds available to virtually any institution to fully or even substantially undertake an ambitious CI effort. The main alternative is through reallocations and "dual purposing" existing resources. For example, adding new courses does not have to be the principal means of internationalizing the curriculum. One can integrate global, comparative, and international content to existing courses and curricula. Internationalization does not require starting new research thrusts from scratch but can build on existing institutional research priorities and strengths, and on existing faculty research interests.

The basis for "integration" is inculcating an understanding and appreciation during the process of building a support culture for internationalization that existing institutional resources can be "dual purposed" for mutual benefit (see Chapter 7). If successfully building a case for dual purposing, people and units see that sharing their resources for purposes of internationalization will directly benefit them and their programs. They need to be able to conclude that their capacities can be strengthened through integration of an international dimension.

4 Extend the leadership team for CI

Comprehensive internationalization is not possible if it is the responsibility of the international office alone. Success requires multiple points of leadership and influence (see Figure 4.3). Comprehensive internationalization requires the influence of

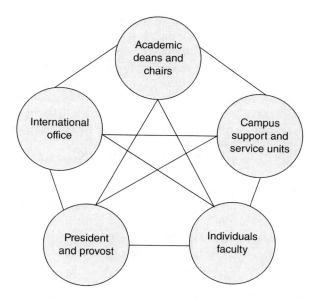

Figure 4.3 Multiple sources of leadership for CI.

influential people in multiple locations. Smithee (2012) views leadership for internationalization as having both individual and organizational dimensions. Included are people in leadership positions (e.g., presidents, provosts, deans), people and units in position to deliver key services (e.g., admissions, academic advising), and people with reputational influence (e.g., those with highly regarded specialty knowledge or who are themselves highly respected).

Smithee, referencing Barker (2002), notes that leadership is not necessarily hierarchical, and further referencing Chemers (1997), sees leadership as a process of social influence. Soft leadership is often the most effective in building coalitions, and soft leadership comes less from power and authority than it does from reputation and influence. That said, it remains that leadership for internationalization comes from many sources and among the most critical players and sources are:

- Presidents, vice-chancellors, rectors, provosts, and deputy or pro-vice-chancellors are the most visible elements of leadership to encourage internationalization. Academic deans and program leaders are also; they are not only highly visible leadership, but at many, perhaps most, institutions they sit astride the levers of action for the academic enterprise.
- Without active involvement of academic departments and their faculty and the substance of ideas embedded therein, internationalization risks becoming an intellectually vacuous process. In many systems faculty control the curriculum as well as promotion and job security criteria, and they drive the research

agenda and discovery, or at minimum have significant voice in shaping them. Those who advise students on academic courses of study and career paths are key links to students and their learning aspirations. It is difficult to imagine a single academic department, professional program or discipline today that isn't advantaged through CI or doesn't have a contribution to make globally.

- Highly regarded individual faculty exert leadership and influence simply by being involved internationally or being interested in global perspectives on their discipline and even more so if speaking strongly in its favor. The intellectual leadership of the institution will likely have as much or more influence than the administrative leadership.

- Often ignored, institutional service and support units have crucial roles to play in comprehensive and strategic internationalization efforts. What can be done in the classroom can be undone in the residence hall; efforts to recruit international students can be stymied by a registrar or admissions office inexperienced and unable to deal efficiently with materials and applications from different systems, cultures and in different languages; an institutional objective to expand research abroad or access funding from abroad can be marginalized if research support units or offices of contracts and grants are inexperienced outside domestic circles and sources.

- While the international office cannot do it alone, that office and its leadership (e.g., dean, vice-provost, PVCI, director, head)—generically referred to as senior international officers (SIO), are critical to the process. The absence of campus-wide senior leadership and coordination are serious impediments to successful comprehensive and strategic internationalization. The notion of comprehensive internationalization with no point leadership (and SIO) or at a senior person to assist in coordination seems absurd. Support offices for study abroad, international students and scholars, and others (often under the administrative leadership of the senior international officer) provide other essential aspects of leadership, as well as support. However, if offices of international programs are seen by others as responsible for internationalization, the concept of collective engagement and collective responsibility for internationalization is weakened. Academic, support, and service units need to be broadly engaged in the process of internationalization.

5 Challenge the status quo and encourage adaptive bureaucracy

A comprehensive or strategic approach to internationalization is almost certain to produce organizational change as well as highlight the need for organizational change. A key enabler of change is an institutional openness to: (a) examining policies, procedures and rules that were designed for a different age and primarily for domestic stakeholders; (b) assessing curricula that may now be parochial to prepare students for global citizenship; (c) considering new learning systems or methods of research collaboration congruent with contemporary learning preferences and technology; and (d) responding to outside calls for greater accountability and efficiency.

6 Recruit and develop human resources for internationalization

Higher education institutions come to be defined in important ways and their successes determined by whom they attract. CI is driven and delivered by administrators, faculty, staff, and students who, as a minimum, need to have an interest in and see the importance of international engagement. An important enabling condition therefore is whether the institution has and seeks to attract such individuals. If few individuals are interested in or capable of delivering on the idea of internationalization, it will remain mainly an idea.

Does the institution advertise its commitment to international engagement in its institutional branding and in messaging to prospective students through its promotional materials? When advertising faculty vacancies, does it express interest in hiring those who have demonstrated expertise, professional networks, and experience across borders? Relatedly, what commitment is the institution willing to make to further educate and develop its existing faculty and staff for international activity through professional development opportunities? After all, existing faculty and staff will provide the core of personnel resources for some time to come.

7 Articulate a bold vision and goals

A bold vision for internationalization that is rooted in the institution's "soul" can galvanize an institution and attract support. Audacious visions can drive goals and actions further than timid "vision" statements which merely tweak the status quo.

The success of Apple Inc. was driven by visions that initially seemed audacious, now seem commonplace, and the question is whether audacity will continue to drive its future. Several years ago a relatively new president at a very large institution in the United States set a goal of 40 percent of graduates having studied abroad; it was at that time about 8 percent and would mean growing the number of annual study abroad students to about 2,800 per year. Everyone saw the goal as audacious and bold, many saw it as crazy and unachievable. The reality is that the boldness of the goal attracted and sustained such a level of campus attention that it became a primary driving force exploding participation to nearly 30 percent.

8 Allocate money and resources

An institution unwilling to allocate resources to internationalization is not serious about it. A strategy to blend new money and tap into existing resources through dual purposing tied to an institutional strategic planning process is essential. A public commitment to such an integrated resource strategy is the first stage in acquiring needed resources. This is the subject of Chapter 7.

Establishing a mindset for shared responsibility and collaboration

Comprehensive internationalization has a difficult and perhaps impossible road to travel if it is seen as adding a fourth mission to the existing higher education missions of teaching/learning, scholarship/research, and service/outreach. Unless a strategy of integration is followed, moving from concept to action will be marginalized. The notion of integration coupled with the practice of strategic inclusion sets the stage for a way of thinking (a mindset) that values collaboration and shared responsibility as a means to advance internationalization. In effect, it is not simply expanding the leadership team for internationalization that is important, but also collaboration across offices and individuals. It is at the level of individual offices and programs where such collaboration builds meaningful shared responsibility. Following are some examples drawn from an earlier publication by the author (Hudzik 2011: 37–38):

An Education Abroad Office

- Actively identifying institutional barriers to expanded study abroad participation and collaborating with academic units, academic advisors, student service and support units, and campus leadership to reduce barriers.
- Partnering with curricular committees and academic units to connect study abroad program design and learning objectives to broader curriculum and institutional learning outcomes.
- Teaming with academic units, advisors and student campus-based support units to prepare students for successful study abroad and maximizing desired outcomes.
- Designing study abroad programs which do not delay graduation.
- Helping students re-enter campus life after study abroad and apply their experiences to continuing internationalization of campus living and learning.

An Office of International Students and Scholars

- Partnering with campus and academic leadership to develop a strategic international student recruitment plan based on institutional needs as well as the diverse needs of academic units.
- Defining the specialized academic and other support services needed by international students and scholars and building collaborative support networks with academic departments and staff, institutional support units, and within the community to meet these needs.
- Working with a variety of institutional and community-based groups to welcome international guests, provide means to expand contacts and build friendships.
- Partnering across campus to facilitate international students and scholars as valuable assets for overall CI efforts by developing outlets for their knowledge and skills, e.g., helping prepare students for study abroad

in their native countries, using native language skills in teaching and research, and systematically providing cross-cultural contributions to classroom settings.

An English Language (English as a Second Language) Program

- Developing programs to meet the needs of various ESL constituencies, for example: (a) institutional recruitment and "feeder" systems; (b) provisionally accepted international students; (c) accepted students who could benefit from additional intensive or on-going English learning, (d) undergraduate and graduate students needs; (e) the needs of students in programs with substantial community or general public contact; (f) English proficiency related to being instructors or teaching assistants.
- Matching development of pedagogies to specific clientele needs and capabilities.
- Collaborating with academic units and student support units on campus to reinforce language skills and proficiencies of ESL students.

Academic Departments

- Recognizing that the pivotal role they play in curriculum and research to actualize institutional goals and objectives make them the key sources of intellectual drive and content for the CI agenda.
- Actively defining, implementing and setting their goals for internationalization and actively engaging with international program components to achieving them.

Language Departments and Programs

- Working with campus and community groups to identify and define language proficiency needs of differing learner groups (e.g., liberal arts undergraduates, undergraduates in professional programs, study abroad students, graduate students, community constituencies, those engaged in research settings abroad or in development activity abroad).
- Developing outcome based measures and goals for oral and written language proficiencies that meet the differing needs of various learners.
- Developing cost-effective learner-centered pedagogies that are responsive and linked to differing learner life situations and language outcome goals.
- Partnering with departmental faculty and academic leadership to spread "language across the curriculum" programming.

Leaders of Student Service and Support Units

- Working to sensitize offices and staff to the kinds of problems experienced by international students and scholars (particularly recent arrivals) and developing culturally informed approaches to problem solving (e.g., counseling services and programs, residence hall and food service, libraries, and academic and faculty advisors).

- Registrar and offices of admissions and international students and scholars working to keep various service units on campus informed of present or arriving international populations on campus and their housing, living, and dietary restrictions, and religious practices, needs and accommodations—accommodating their needs in ways that also contribute to further CI of the on-campus environment.

Institutional Outreach and Engagement Offices

- Building community/campus partnerships and collaborations for CI both on-campus and in the community.
- Identifying the needs of community and other clientele groups for knowledge and skills for a global environment and facilitating campus resources to meet needs.
- Facilitating community access to information and education programs relating to globalization and cross cultural learning.
- Facilitating use of community-based international members and community-based cross-cultural assets to enhance campus CI efforts, e.g., to assist in teaching less commonly taught languages and for building a supportive internationalization climate.

Offices of International Programs and VPs for Research

- Collaborating to align institutional research thrusts and priorities to opportunities to enhance institutional research stature and outcomes through international partnerships and collaborations.
- Identifying not only opportunities and funding for such opportunities, but identifying and ameliorating bureaucratic barriers to cross-border collaborations.

It is also the case that "integration" needs to be thought of as a cohesive set of actions that produce a desired programmatic end. Elspeth Jones (2013a) identifies ten key elements of integrated internationalization for the purpose of producing globally competent graduates. The list of actions to be integrated is fairly long but reasonably obvious to produce globally competent graduates: (1) rationale and strategy for internationalization; (2) governance, leadership, and management; (3) internationalization of the formal curriculum for all students; (4) international campus culture and informal curriculum; (5) student diversity; (6) guidance and support for students outside the classroom; (7) staff development, recognition, and reward; (8) broad and deep international partnerships; (9) resources follow strategy; (10) monitoring, reflection, evaluation, and review.

Points of leadership for organization change and coordination

The more "comprehensive" the internationalization vision and the more expansive the range of actions associated with it, the greater the need for some kind of "point leadership" for coordination, overall monitoring, identifying incompatibilities, and looking for new opportunities to advance the CI vision. Also, the more complex its support infrastructure is likely to be. Who will give organizational leadership and drive to visioning, building, and nurturing CI, and what must the support infrastructure be?

The answers to these questions require reference to an institution's existing preferences and practices for organization, leadership, and authority. For example, is there precedent for central offices to provide campus-wide leadership in key areas (e.g., for graduate programs, information technology) and do these provide sufficient precedent for establishing a central leadership model for internationalization? What is the tradition of productive collaboration between such offices and academic units? Is there a culture for organizational crosswalks and partnerships between service and academic departments? Among academic departments, is the culture one of "silos" or cross-disciplinary collaboration?

Given traditions for organizing leadership and affecting coordination, whether centralized or decentralized, and whether heavily coordinated or more laissez faire, established institutional models and practice should not simply be ignored. A decision to try something new will need to take into account potential costs and resistance.

Support infrastructure for internationalization doesn't need to mirror tradition but shouldn't ignore it. There is also the reality of competing models for organizing leadership and coordination which has been previously summarized:

> At the center of most discussions about organization and structure on campuses is whether there should be a centralized office to lead and coordinate internationalization, or whether decentralized models are best. Centralization is touted by some as delivering more effective coordination, greater efficiencies, and focused drive toward strategic objectives. Others see centralization as exploding red tape, stifling creativity and initiative on the "shop floor," enforcing "cookie cutter" rules and regulations onto an extremely heterogeneous set of departments and motivations, and, ultimately, destroying "ownership" of internationalization at the departmental and college levels.
>
> (Hudzik 2011: 22)

To centralize or not is a false dichotomy, there being other options. One is the matrix-style organization structure which in various forms has elements of hierarchy, decentralization, and significant direct collaborative (horizontal) crosswalks among contributors, as well as cross-functional project management team building (see, for example, Bartlett and Ghoshal 1990; Galbraith 2008). There are aspects of Henry Mintzberg's "adhocracy" in such organizational designs (Mintzberg 1979).

Versions of a matrix organizational structure characterize how some of the largest and most complex higher education institutions are organized to support CI. Various individuals and units contributing to aspects of international activity are located under separate reporting lines but with communication and coordination crosswalks, as well as dual reporting lines in several instances.

As an example, one can find area (world, regional) study centers and language departments reporting to a dean of liberal arts and social sciences (or to the SIO, but with dotted-line relationships to an academic dean); individual thematic centers in, for example, global public health, international business, or global food sustainability and safety reporting to deans of medicine, business, and agriculture respectively (perhaps with a dotted line to the SIO); student mobility support offices (both inbound and outbound) might report to an SIO because the services provided are institution wide, or because legal and other vulnerabilities in these offices require rationalization of the services.

There will be some ambiguities regarding lines of authority in these kinds of models and not everyone will be comfortable with the ambiguity, but complex and flexible organizational arrangements may be necessary to support something as multi-faceted as CI at larger institutions.

Several institutions have found the matrix-style model not only workable but potentially more flexible in dealing with the complexity that is inherent in CI, *but* there is still the need for some form of overarching leadership and coordination. A complete absence of coordination (e.g., through an SIO) increases fragmentation in the internationalization effort.

Anecdotal evidence is strong for a preference and a trend in higher education globally to create a central staff leadership position near the top of the organizational hierarchy with several functions: (a) to help orchestrate an institutional strategy for CI; (b) to be an advocate for it throughout the institution; (c) to expand participation and roles of both academic and service/support units; (d) to advise senior institutional leadership; and (e) to encourage collaborations across institutional silos. Such positions and their roles have become important; a good US-based guide exists for those in these positions (Heyl *et al.* 2007).

It varies greatly across institutions whether such a position exercises authority through reporting-line relationships or mainly influence because the organizational chart is matrix, dotted line, and full of crosswalks. There is also the reality of the diversity of higher education institutions and their organizational cultures with the result that models of organization for internationalization vary substantially, as does the position and responsibility of an SIO. In consequence, the best model for any institution is the one that best fits it: "Ultimately, the plan put in place must reflect the university's particular history and culture; failure to respect the institutional context puts the initiative at risk" (Biddle 2002: 10).

Leading from the top, bottom, and middle

Given earlier comments regarding the importance of multiple points of leadership to help drive CI, it seems likely that a combination of leading from the top, leading from the bottom, and leading from the middle will have practical value in moving from rhetoric to action. There is the additional reality that top-down command

and control models do not fit well with higher education institutions. Partly this is a matter of traditional governance models which vest significant decision-making authorities with the faculty via academic governance models. The models (which are under some revision—discussed in Chapter 5) balance academic governance and administrative leadership through either delegated authorities to the faculty or through shared governance models. In areas critical to internationalization such as curricula and academic personnel decision-making, academic units, and academic governance structures typically have extraordinary powers.

Some institutions have a history of and prefer loosely coupled and shifting matrices of organization. In these cases an SIO not too powerful in a command and control sense will be complementary to this loose and shifting environment. Other institutions have history and preference for centralized offices providing leadership and coordination with varying degrees of authority assigned to the central office. An appropriately empowered SIO will be complementary in this kind of tradition.

Building a coherent institutional strategy for internationalization across the work of either a few or numerous internationally engaged offices and programs requires leadership that is (a) senior and influential enough to promote development of an institutional consensus and strategy for CI as a whole; (b) leadership that can help facilitate development of synergies across the programming components of internationalization; and (c) leadership that can exercise influence across a wide array of actors and interests.

Summary

This chapter has focused on core strategies, tactics, and structures necessary to moving CI from concept to action. As presented in Chapter 5, doing all suggested in this chapter may not be enough to move from action to results. Despite best organizational intentions to put in place the means for action, barriers may still exist to move from actions to results. Chapter 5 is about dealing with the barriers.

Chapter 5

Barriers and barrier reduction for comprehensive internationalization

Chapter 4 focused on the gap between "rhetoric and action." It emphasized: (1) putting in place an institutional culture for internationalization; (2) strategic inclusion; (3) recognizing and engaging organizational change; and (4) setting in place a number of enabling strategies and tactics. To move beyond rhetoric to action, and then to results, it is important to identify and reduce barriers to internationalization. CI, because of its multiple dimensions, organizational scale and scope, and the range of individuals involved and affected, can massively expand the sources and the strength of barriers to its implementation.

Chapter 4 highlighted some barriers to CI of a structural nature, for example: bureaucratic rules and regulations out of synch with cross-border, cross-cultural, and non-domestic activity; the absence of leadership; insufficient resources; institutional silos impeding collaboration; disconnection from key processes such as budget planning, and so forth.

There are also important behavioral, motivational, and attitudinal barriers at the levels of individuals, departments, and the institution as a whole that can become either powerful barriers or effective enablers of a more comprehensive approach to internationalization. Structural and behavioral barriers interact and while both are considered in this chapter, emphasis is given to the behavioral, motivational, and attitudinal side of the equation.

The IAU Fourth Global Survey of International of Higher Education referenced earlier in Chapter 3 (Egron-Polak and Hudson 2014) queried a global sample of institutions regarding internal and external obstacles to internationalization. Twelve internal obstacles and eight external obstacles were identified. In both lists, the obstacles could be seen as mainly structural rather than behavioral per se, but one could infer some behavioral dimensions to some of them.

For internal obstacles, 49 percent of respondents listed insufficient financial resources as their number-one-ranked obstacle (69 percent listed it among their top three obstacles). Similarly, for external obstacles, 34 percent rated limited public funding as number one (73 percent rated it among the top three obstacles). The focus on inadequate resources is not surprising and is discussed further as a general issue for internationalization in Chapter 7.

The rankings of other internal obstacles based on percentages of respondents rating the item among their top three barriers included: limited experience/

expertise of faculty, 30 percent; inflexible curricula, 26 percent; bureaucratic impediments, 25 percent. Percentages of respondents rating other external obstacles among their top three included: language barriers, 53 percent; difficulties in recognizing qualifications (from other countries), 48 percent; visa restrictions on incoming students/staff, 36 percent; internationalization not a national priority, 29 percent; and visa restrictions on outbound student/staff, 20 percent.

While these results are useful, and in many ways confirm aspects of structural barriers raised in Chapter 4, there is still the issue of barriers relating to behaviors and attitudes.

Is rhetoric to action enough?

If actions identified in Chapter 4 are reasonably addressed, an institution may seem to be on the way to internationalization because: institutional rhetoric champions a more comprehensive and strategic implementation of internationalization; there is talk *and* action reaching into academic and service units to reinforce its importance; there is a broad-based campus culture that understands CI's importance; and there are expressions of commitment and examples of program initiatives widely spread to bring it into reality.

Looks good: the plan is in place, foundations and enablers have been activated, but is this enough? What if the level of implementation and success in results doesn't reach expectations or doesn't seem to address the motivations for undertaking internationalization in the first place? If so, a revision of the Chapter 4 *haiku* is in order: "Much noise coming down stairs, something appears, not clear what." Without tangible results, it will still look like a lot of talk, a lot of work, but little valued because there are few, if any, desirable and measurable results.

Overcoming barriers to span action to results

Failure to achieve results when change is complex usually has several causes. All innovations requiring organizational change benefit from on-going detection and amelioration of barriers that easily arise at both the organizational and individual levels. As Childress' (2009) research about the fruitful development of faculty engagement in internationalization suggests, successful implementation only just begins with the strategic plan and getting action underway; the real work is in the on-going confrontation of expected and unexpected barriers to achieving results.

Barriers arising from scale, organizational resistance, and human nature

Strong rhetoric supporting internationalization, followed by good planning and programs in place will still encounter barriers—some are typical of any organizational change, some particularly germane to internationalization. Implementation of comprehensive internationalization is not like buying a new ready-to-go music system, "No assembly required, just plug it in." Declaring that we have a plan for CI does not guarantee intended outcomes, nor does having structural enablers in place.

Barriers to behavioral change or simple resistance to adopting desired behaviors, whether in individuals or in organizational units, are often the most confounding of impediments, including for implementing CI. While barriers to change are present in all organizations, their saliency is not equal across all organizations and individuals. Some people and organizations are naturally inclined toward or prepared for change; others appear to be the opposite, particularly if the organizational culture and leadership champion the status quo. CI has a reasonable chance in the former environment, much less in the latter.

Two actions are important for catalyzing effective action to reduce barriers, whether structural or behavioral. One is sensitivity to detecting them and understanding their causes. The second is on-going leadership attention to monitoring and ameliorating barriers. The good news is that proactive identification and assessment for potential barriers also often uncovers natural pockets of support for internationalization that can be built on. Identifying pockets of support is as important as knowing the opposition.

Many of the barriers to internationalization are not simply a matter of inadequate understanding and the "logic of the plan" but also acceptance of its utility in personal and organizational terms. Geoff Scott (2003: 26) in "Effective Change Management in Higher Education," quotes George Bernard Shaw that "Reformers have the misplaced notion that change is achieved by brute logic." Relatedly, Carl Jung notes that "We cannot change anything until we accept it" (Jung 1969: 519).

A starting point for thinking about barriers to CI

The sources of barriers to internationalization are many; one categorization includes:

1   *Common individual and organizational barriers.* Chapter 4 identified several of these which, depending on how one views them, can be seen as structural (but also as influencing behaviors). Included were an absence of clarifying and mobilizing aspirations; not knowing what to do, which priorities to set, or even where to start; preference for the status quo and comfort with the familiar; ineffectual leadership, and perceived unaffordability, to name a few.

2   *Structural barriers arising from higher education organizations.* The higher education institution is a distinctive organizational form (Winston 1998). Kezar (2001) identified twelve institutional features of higher education (largely structural) based on research findings. Five are particularly relevant as potential barriers to affecting the kind of change needed for CI: (a) inter-institutional and disciplinary interdependencies reducing autonomy; (b) institutional status tied to traditional missions; (c) loosely coupled internal structure; (d) organized anarchies driving decision making; and (e) shared governance.

One conclusion to be drawn from this list is that conditions of leadership and authority tend to be murky in higher education organizations. Such an organizational reality can present significant barriers to innovation including adoption of CI which requires coalition building and some degree of coordination for clarity of purpose and direction.

3   *Barriers arising from internationalization.* To the "converted" internationalization sells itself as a twenty-first century imperative; but many people and departments are unconverted. For the latter, internationalization is not a natural sell because of beliefs relating to costs and competition for scarce resources and time, or attitudes and personal discomfort with the notion of cultural and social differences, coupled to high value placed on uncertainty avoidance and concerns how internationalization will impact the job (Sporn 1999: 69).

In Australia a step in credentialing for more senior positions has included appointments abroad to externally validate stature. As Sporn notes (69), this practice is now spreading in Europe. Having to work abroad to be credentialed is problematic, unattractive or an insurmountable challenge for some. Internationalization also carries with it more diverse student and colleague populations; the value of diversity is not recognized or accepted with comfort by all.

Cross-reinforcement of personal, job-related and structural barriers

In the case of change and resistance to it in organizations, the sources of resistance can be cross-cutting and reinforcing: resistance to change can be personal (general discomfort or fear of the new and unknown); job related (I have mastered my job routine and don't want that upset); organizational (this is the way we've always done things and it works fine). Cross-cutting and reinforcing barriers are the most salient.

Dealing with resistance to organizational change has produced a large consulting industry. In Australia, for example, there are now National Competency Standards in Organizational and Community Change Management, and there is an Australian Diploma of Organizational Change Management accredited through the Australian Qualifications Framework. A casual internet search of the topic will display a myriad of learning and consultation services. Change management modules or courses now find their place in numerous business and executive training programs.

Other barriers to comprehensive internationalization

I Uncertainty without proof and fear of results

Kumari Beck (2012) suggests that resistance to internationalization in higher education relates in part to the absence of hard data about its actual results and also because of simplistic (documented and undocumented) assumptions about the evils of globalization generally as well as for higher education. A contributing factor in Beck's view is conceptual confusion over the meanings of and expectations from internationalization. In the absence of hard data substantiating the actual impacts and outcomes from internationalization (comprehensive or otherwise), people are asked to accept largely at face value that internationalization produces benefit.

Without answers to questions such as "How do we know what study abroad actually accomplishes?" or "What is the evidence that forming cross-border research partnerships are cost effective and capacity increasing?" significant effort and resources are nonetheless being reallocated, peoples' jobs changed, and institutional priorities altered. Uncertainty leads to neutrality among some and hostility in others because of the fear of the unknown as well as previous experiences with other "grand experiments" from magical cures for illness, to get-rich-quick schemes, to failed models of international development efforts.

Beck's solution is to open discourse on these issues rather than continuing to ignore their relevance. The airing of issues through critical discourse contributes in his view to a conceptual strengthening of internationalization (ibid.: 143). Yet, while "airing out" issues is a reasonable start, the question remains, "What is the evidence of benefits?" Chapter 6 explores modes and mechanisms for documenting the impact, outcomes, and results of CI. While hard empirical and systematic data are somewhere between hard-to-find and non-existent, Beck's solution, while far from perfect, enables sharing of data about results that are available even if these data are largely anecdotal and case based.

2 Low tolerance for change and ambiguity

This category is related to but not quite the same as the one above. There are both organization and individual levels to it. People and organizations can be risk-averse and they often gravitate toward and reinforce one another. Madeleine Green points out, based on research conducted by the American Council on Education, that resistance to internationalization can easily be a product of "connection between individual and institutional obstacles" (Green 2005: 11, 2007). Where both the dominant organizational culture and individual preferences are uncomfortable with internationalization, they reinforce one another. Socialization to the job by peers in the workplace can further reinforce: "This is the way we do things here and what we think is important, and always have; you need to follow the rules; if you aren't comfortable with that, find a job someplace else." The not too subtle message is "get in line with our established priorities and modes of operation."

Of course there can be individual and organizational cultures that relish change, are often entrepreneurial, and see risk taking as the road to the future. "Your job is to find new markets, new ways of doing things, and your job success depends on it." These cultures, though, are not typical of higher education organizations, at least in the past. However, financial and other system stress may strengthen change cultures out of necessity.

Uncertainty avoidance and power distance barriers

Delgado-Marquez *et al.* (2012), examining characteristics of the top-200-ranked higher education institutions in the world, conclude that two variables, "uncertainty avoidance" and "power distance," play important roles in shaping institutional internationalization. An institution that places high value on uncertainty avoidance relies heavily on regulations and structures to minimize departures from the status quo (Mueller and Thomas 2001). The allied characteristic of high "power distance" is reflected in strong organizational hierarchies, low communication through organizational levels, and deference to higher authority (Delgado-Marquez *et al.* 2012: 6, noting Shane 1993).

Delgado-Marquez *et al.* (2012: 11) conclude from their research that low power distance improves the organization's creative atmosphere and the free flow of ideas. This implies that comprehensive internationalization is more likely to occur in institutions which are not strictly top-down in structure and authority patterns, but rather are more flexible, perhaps more matrix in design. If true, this fits well with higher education institutions being loosely coupled organizations. Delgado-Marquez *et al.* also conclude that low levels of uncertainty avoidance "will foster the comprehension and consciousness about ongoing trends and demands in the education market to help universities to be more active in their strategies of internationalization."

There can be little doubt that individuals and organizations with low tolerance for ambiguity will have a hard time swallowing CI without some help to re-orient knowledge and thinking. The fixes are partly organizational and partly educational. On the organizational front, there won't be innovation and change unless the institution signals receptivity to it and unless it rewards those who attempt it. There also won't be much experimentation if those whose reasonable efforts are unsuccessful have their heads handed them.

Change and experimentation is inherently risk-taking. An institution that negatively values risk-taking is not a friendly environment for CI. The signal needs to be sent that change toward internationalization is not only desirable, but that it will be rewarded, as will to some extent those who at least reasonably try. Intentional risk-taking needs to be encouraged, and failures looked upon as "opportunities to learn and not as reasons to blame or abort" (Hudzik and Simon 2012: 179).

On the education front, exposure of individuals and the institution to information on trends, what other institutions are doing and success stories can help reduce concerns about being trailblazers. Given that barriers constantly arise from lack of information and understanding, "education" as part of a strategy to ameliorate barriers is especially important for those who have a low tolerance for ambiguity.

3 Not being first

Some individuals and organizations thrive on being at the cutting edge, viewing it as both an advantage in the market place, and also providing notoriety. Others, probably the majority, think otherwise, being particularly risk-averse if without company. Robert Tucker (2010), a higher education consultant who facilitates institutional discussions and actions to engage innovation, has written: "the first question college presidents ask me in the context of discussing a specific innovation is, 'who else is doing that?' If the answer is, 'no one, you can be the first,' the discussion is over." In its October 25, 2009 edition, in the midst of fears about the "great recession" and global meltdown, *The Chronicle of Higher Education* reported "College leaders may be thinking strategic change but few are engaging it" and concluded that at least part of the reason was fear of being first (Blumenstyk 2009).

In reality, higher education internationalization has been underway for decades and expanding rapidly in the last decade and a half. There is little if any risk of being first. The problem is that if nothing is known about who has done what, anything will appear as a first. This reinforces Delgado-Marquez *et al.*'s preferences for broadly educating leaders and staff about trends outside the institution. It also suggests the importance of identifying success stories. The NAFSA Simon Award winners are a place to start; identifying germane sessions at NAFSA, AIEA, APAIE, IEAA, EAIE, and the like for cutting-edge examples of successful programming in higher education internationalization will provide help.

4 Top-down is at odds with loosely coupled structures

Higher education is not known for its speed and few, if any, have accused higher education institutions as relishing change. Weick (1991) sees higher education institutions as loosely coupled structures. Kezar (2001: 70) describes loosely coupled organizations as "uncoordinated, ... differentiation among components, ... specialization among workers, and low predictability of future action, including change." Tightly coupled organizations are "highly centralized, non-differentiated, and highly coordinated, with strict divisions of labor."

If one accepts Weick's and Kezar's characterization of higher education organization as "loosely coupled," it doesn't take much imagination to recognize that heavily "top-down" approaches to the implementation of internationalization will not find much purchase in the bowels of most higher education institutions. Kezar references Hearn (1996) who notes the high degree of intra-organizational independence characterizing higher education institutions with the consequence that change is experimental in pockets and incremental, as well as improvisational and reactive to signals for change, rather than being strategic and proactive.

An important implication of this is that on-going attention needs to be paid to cultivating pockets of internationalization in strategic locations within the institution. Strategic pockets include those where there is receptivity to internationalization and where visible results can become a beacon to others. Not everyone and everything needs to change at once. Nurturing and growing strategic pockets is sensible in terms of manageable start-up but it is also essential in loosely coupled organizations because it underscores the value of both top-down *and* bottom-up strategies.

5 The drag of mature enterprise

Another organizational barrier is drag of mature enterprise coupled to a belief about success in the existing ways of doing things. For example, James Duderstadt (2009) has characterized US higher education as "risk averse, at times self-satisfied and unduly expensive." In consequence, high costs limit and stratify access, and self-satisfaction lulls institutions and people into complacency and championing the virtues of the status quo, including failure in his view to respond adequately to the globalization of higher education markets. Self-satisfaction is a powerful narcotic and inoculation against change. While Duderstadt may not have intended to paint all higher education institutions with the same brush, there are certainly plenty of institutions to which the criticism applies. Duderstadt's appraisal shouldn't be surprising given Kezar's description of higher education that paints it as "relatively independent of environment ... loosely coupled, ... [having] organized anarchical decision making, ... goal ambiguity, ... and [concerned with] image" (2001: 61).

The drag of mature enterprise would not seem to be an assessment unique to US institutions. Sporn's and Nokkala's assessments of the situation in Europe offer parallels. Pressures for change in higher education institutions are strong throughout the world, especially with mature and long-established systems that do not measure up to global standards (see Rumbley *et al.* 2012: 19; Green *et al.* 2012; Deardoff *et al.* 2012b). If one examines the data demonstrating the global flattening of higher education capacity and increased global competition, the days of mature-systems lethargy may be challenged, with or without their conscious understanding or consent.

George Mehaffy (2012: 42) concludes that "higher education institutions have a confusion of purposes, distorted reward structures, limited success, high costs, massive inefficiencies, and profound resistance to change." Yet, Clayton Christensen and Henry Eyring (2011) assess higher education organizations as particularly vulnerable to disruption and ready for disruptive innovation. The title of their book, *The Innovative University: Changing the DNA of Higher Education from the Inside Out*, is intriguing for what the title suggests—that the source of change will be from the inside. There are cracks and pressure points for a commitment to internationalization; it is the job of leadership at all levels to widen the cracks and find the opportunities.

6 Internationalization is "their" job, not mine

For many institutions and leaders, it is a happy moment when they can answer "yes" to the question, "Does your institution have an international office." "Yes" is an indicator of institutional commitment to internationalization, but it may also have a less positive connotation—"Yes, we have an international office, they handle things" (with the implication being, so others don't have to become involved). Given the impossibility of comprehensive or strategic internationalization being the sole responsibility of an international office, this kind of responsibility displacement is a fundamental barrier.

Responsibility displacement, a time-honored coping mechanism in bureaucracies, has a couple of faces to it: one face is the institutional, "They handle that." Another face constitutes more selective finger pointing in the sense of designating certain anointed disciplines or professions as appropriately supporting internationalization (e.g., humanities and the social sciences for cross-cultural learning and effectiveness, or business for negotiating the global economy), but not others like the natural sciences "which are already highly internationalized because they read science journals from around the world." This last quotation was made by a Dean of Natural Sciences from a tier one research institution; however, his science graduates had precious little education and knowledge for living or working outside the domestic environment.

Josef Mestenhauser (1998: 272), an early highly respected leader in international education, foresaw "an advanced level of internationalization ... involv[ing] not only internationalizing key courses but also identifying the international dimensions of every single discipline." Overcoming the barrier of responsibility displacement is partly dialog and education and partly demonstrating the value added of internationalization for everyone. Building a sense of "we instead of they" is essential to counteract responsibility displacement.

7 Ranking schemes

Global institutional ranking schemes are a two-edged sword: they provide succor to institutions ranked highly, and concerns for those not. Most schemes are heavily driven by measures of research quality and capacity rather than necessarily teaching and service missions. They also drive institutional behaviors in that those seeking to raise image and competitive position within the higher education community learn to play to the limited ranking criteria. This is not the place for a wide-ranging critique of ranking schemes, particularly their methodological shortcomings, but it is worth mentioning some of their consequences. As Deardoff *et al.* submit, the ranking process "encourages institutions to link with more prestigious ones to elevate their visibility and brand ... and exacerbates the tensions around competition and collaboration" (2012b: 462). A thorough assessment and critique of rankings is provided by Ellen Hazelkorn (2011).

While rankings seem innocent enough at face value, there is a potentially pernicious side impacting institutional internationalization behaviors. Rankings assess the institution; yet, mobility has dimensions not only for selecting an institution, but academic departments and intellectual foci. Institutional rankings perpetuate a kind of aggregate fallacy, saying very little about within-institutional departmental program rank and quality. Among the "best" institutionally does not guarantee among the "best" in terms of particular courses of study. The same is true with respect to specific areas of research. As a result, ranking schemes tend to ignore niche institutional strengths and diversity (Hudzik and Simon 2012). A barrier to effective internationalization at the academic program level is driven by the fact that overall institutional rank (matching institutional pedigrees) doesn't guarantee and may impede forming productive partnerships at the departmental level where the work is done. Many very strong academic programs reside in middle-ranked institutions.

Unfortunately, there is a tendency for the most prestigious institutions to collaborate across borders by forming exclusive international "clubs" of institutions, or consortia. An alternative strategy put forth by Hudzik (2011) is that instead of a two-tier system of global engagement emerging with the top tier forming cross-border partnerships and the rest not, the more useful analog might be a continuum of engaged institutions by which each seeks the best partners substantively and intellectually defined, and by mission fit, rather than determined by general institutional rank and pedigree.

8 Faculty, academic units, and quality

While it is damaging enough if the faculty aren't allies of internationalization, it is "game over" if they are opposed or hostile to it. Several of the suggestions for strategic and operation actions made in Chapter 4 were aimed at academic staff but the companion issue is whether faculty in their departmental academic cultures will actively engage or will be passive observers, or worse, hostile toward international work and assignments.

Hostility can arise from a number of circumstances: (a) fear that internationalization will force a reprioritization or retooling of the faculty member's teaching and research; (b) concern on the part of both faculty and disciplinary units that international activity will not be given sufficient recognition by national disciplinary bodies who rate departmental reputations (and also less directly, faculty reputations; (c) concern by faculty as well as by academic units that they do not have the experience and skills necessary to engage internationally in a quality manner or in international subject matter; (d) fear that engagement of internationalization will divert limited departmental funding and positions away from traditional high-priority departmental strengths (e.g., in political science for example, away from domestic legislative or executive studies into positions of comparative politics or international relations); and (e) lack of clarity as to whether faculty who engage internationally will be appropriately rewarded not only by the institution, but by their home academic units. (Also, see Leask (2014) for a questionnaire on blockers and enablers for curriculum internationalization.)

These issues play out at both institutional and academic unit levels. Providing space in the promotion and job security (e.g., tenure) documents to include evidence of faculty international engagement isn't sufficient. The real issue turns on how such information is used, for what purposes, and by whom. Space in the personnel assessment process to indicate that international activity is permissible is one thing. It is another matter if inclusion implies that international activity carries weight in assessment of faculty. And, it is very much another step if the implication is that international activity is expected or required.

Implications and expectations defined at the institutional level are important, but so are (and perhaps more so) what criteria academic departments actually apply to their faculty promotion and reward decision recommendations. If the culture of the academic unit is hostile toward international activity, faculty will unlikely engage. If the academic culture is neutral, individual faculty might engage, while still realizing that it may not count for much.

It is well understood, however, that academic departments are not free agents to decide the appropriateness of criteria—institutional level criteria set parameters. They are subject to implicit or explicit standards promulgated by disciplinary professional associations (national or international) and sub-discipline priorities that emerge as a result. Discipline-based departmental structures may discourage giving priority to international activity, as well as discourage inter-disciplinary work which is a critical dimension of international teaching, research, and service (see Mestenhauser and Ellingboe 1998: 27).

The wider aspect of the challenge as put by Green (2007: 21) is that for faculty,

> developing an internationalized mind-set can be particularly challenging, since it requires examining assumptions underlying the discipline and developing or refining a set of intellectual skills different for those emphasized in their original graduate training and by their professional disciplinary association.

Effective barrier mitigation occurs if the academic or departmental culture is actively supportive of the international engagement of its faculty and also sees international engagement as advantaging and strengthening the position of the academic department. There is an obvious reciprocal relationship between faculty and their discipline in building a culture of support and international practice. As a result, the elements of building support among individual faculty are similar to building departmental support. Both are discussed in the next section.

Persistence as a strategy for barrier reduction

Although the preceding discussion may appear to suggest a somewhat bleak higher education environment for comprehensive internationalization and the changes it would prompt, it was neither the intention to suggest, nor is it true that all higher education institutions encounter strong resistance to internationalization. Indeed, a review of the institutional stories of the NAFSA Simon Award winners as well as many of the institutional case stories in Part II demonstrate otherwise.

The long view becomes important and so is persistence. Change is unlikely to be quick or widely embraced where deeply rooted resistance arises from lack of knowledge and understanding, or from personal distaste for it, or in organizational cultures that approach change in a very incremental manner, or in loosely coupled organizational settings where decision-making and follow-through on change typically begin in pockets and develop incrementally.

John Kotter (2012), an organizational change expert and a Harvard faculty member, presents an eight-step process for overcoming barriers to change. He begins with the need to establish a sense of urgency and building a "guiding coalition." These two steps are similar to those in Chapter 4 about building a support culture and establishing an understanding of the importance of CI. Another of Kotter's key steps is "planning for and creating short-term wins," to which should be added long-run persistence in committing to change and overcoming barriers.

Combining quick successes and persistence

One key to change in such environments is taking it on in manageable pieces. Starting with natural allies and manageable projects producing observable results relatively quickly will attract additional allies and more results and further change. Another key is persistence in understanding and dealing with barriers. Persistence, patience, and deliberateness advances organizational change of most situations, including those moving institutional ethos and practice toward more comprehensive and strategic internationalization.

The soft side of "forcing" change

Command and control models do not fit well with higher education institutions because of the balancing of academic governance and administrative leadership as well as the locus of curricular and academic personnel decision-making in faculties, departments, and colleges and schools. In many higher education organizations, decentralization is strengthened by the power and influence of the academic deans, which has led many to describe higher education institutions as akin to feudal systems.

With changing governance structures (e.g., a move toward corporate models of governance), and the appearance of stronger executives and managerialism, control from the top may be strengthening in higher education, but even under tight top-down corporate management models, the power of the dominant organization culture is not easily or effectively over-ridden. It can be argued that it took bankruptcy protection filing for the General Motors Corporation to finally affect change in the dominant organizational culture, even though prior successive leadership signaled change as the prime objective.

Dominant culture and resistance to change are not effectively manipulated by top-down command and control so much as by education, influence, and connection to individual and personal benefit. In their book *Blue Ocean Strategy*, Kim and Mauborgne (2005) emphasize that the toughest part of organizational change is dealing with entrenched culture, and doing so depends far less on power and authority and much more on persuasion. What they are discussing might be called the "soft side" of causing change which begins with an understanding of "the what and the why" of change, followed by close attention to motivating people to *want* to change.

Geoff Scott (2003), writing about change management in higher education, views that "a clear understanding of what motivates staff to engage in learning (change) is essential if they are to be adequately supported through the process (73). He adds that "change is not an event but a complex and subjective learning/unlearning process for all concerned"—individuals and organizations. And he notes that "managers are not the only important change leaders. In fact everyone can be a leader of change in his or her own area of expertise" (73–74). This last point connects to the leadership-enabling strategy discussed in Chapter 4. First, the leadership team for internationalization has to be expanded, particularly if the objective is comprehensive and strategic internationalization. Second, given the multiple dimensions of CI, leadership expertise needs to be assembled from many sectors and institutional levels, including from opinion leaders among the faculty.

Barnard and Stoll (2010) in their review of literature of organizational change management note that Balogun and Hope-Hailey (2004) report that generally 70 percent of change efforts do not reach their intended outcomes. While this finding is subject to interpretation as to the meaning of "reach" (partial, complete, or revised), Balogun (2001) notes pointedly that "change is about changing people, not organizations" and therein may reside the biggest challenge.

Edgar H. Schein (2009), concerned that there is not a clear or consistent understanding and meaning for "dominant corporate culture," offers the idea that the essence of an institution is the learned and shared assumptions about the organization that drive individual daily behaviors. Those shared organization/individual understandings constitute the dominant culture, reinforcing one another. Change must impact these shared assumptions. So while individuals need to understand and be motivated, organizations need to be sending and reinforcing the right message. Partly this is the role of dialog to produce a supporting culture for CI and partly it is establishing goals and expectations and rewarding the behaviors that lead to desired outcomes.

Identifying and ameliorating barriers to CI

Chapter 6 focuses on dealing with barriers related to finding evidence of outcomes and benefits. Chapter 7 deals with resource barriers. The focus of the remainder of this chapter is on various people barriers and on managing the scale of change.

In dealing with people barriers, the important institutional actions are education and motivation aimed at all those who are needed to bring reality to the vision through their collaboration and work. The foundation is provided by understanding the people involved, particularly in terms of what motivates them in their jobs (and by implication in their home departments) and how internationalization can

be tied to these motivations for mutual benefit. It also depends on carefully identifying with whom to begin. There is evidence to suggest that adding an international dimension to jobs increases job satisfaction and motivation (Jones 2012).

Expanding the circle of the motivated and engaged

There are three types of institutional stakeholders vis-à-vis their default views
toward expanded internationalization. At the ends of a continuum are "allies"
and "opponents." Allies are typically knowledgeable about aspects of international engagement and purposes and are committed or even passionate about
advancing it. They are usually also internationally experienced. It is understood
that a strong correlation exists between being an ally or an opponent of internationalization depending on experiences internationally and whether good or bad
(Green 2007).

In the middle of the continuum is the contested area comprising a group of
people and departments which are marginally aware of the concept of internationalization, but not engaged. This middle ground is composed of individuals
who will voice their support for internationalization but are themselves inactive,
and others who are neither vocal nor active because of stronger doubts or lack of
understanding.

While an obvious solution in dealing with the middle ground (and perhaps
opponents) is "getting them abroad or involved," there are barriers to staff
mobility that have to be dealt with. Simon Sweeney identifies these to include
"institutional inertia, lack of support from within departments, and the disruption
of one's own and colleagues' work patterns and responsibilities" (2012: 26). To
Sweeney's list could be added family and other private-life obligations and dis-
ruptions. Sweeney offers some solutions in the form of short, but more frequent
visits abroad, to which might be added taking advantage of the internet and
related electronic mechanisms, and modest institutional matching travel funds, or
support for international volunteering through extended vacation time.

Expanding the circle of allies from the bottom up

Knowing who is where on the continuum of supporters/opponents takes some
investigation; initial assumptions don't always prove out, in either direction.
Pushing out the circle of allies and particularly those who are committed allies is
a key ingredient in ameliorating barriers. The more allies, the wider the institutional culture of support, the greater the number of individuals and units engaged
internationally, and the larger the pool of individuals and units with a vested
interest in internationalization.

The bottom line is that as the circle of the engaged allies expands, the louder is
the voice for dealing with a myriad of barriers to internationalization. While leadership is important, expanding the circle of engaged allies is essentially building
support from the "bottom up." Allies need to be nurtured and kept as allies and

they often are the most fertile ground for further investment in start-up. Inactive supporters need cultivation through dialog and education, helping them to see how internationalization can advantage them, and having them see concrete roles for themselves. Monitoring opponents is important, but accept that opposition to some degree and in some quarters is inevitable; don't waste time converting them unless they occupy a strategic position in the institution which can effectively block key aspects of internationalization (e.g., an institutional recruitment and admissions office ignorant of how to recruit international students and opposed to the idea; language departments unwilling to experiment and expand innovative pedagogies for language learning for multiple purposes). Isolated opposition is less the problem. Opposition that gets in the way needs to be managed and this is when an expanded circle of active allies will be helpful.

Managing barriers by scaling implementation and staging development

CI is an ambitious undertaking, so much so that it requires manageable steps in building its scale and scope. Simultaneous attention to all aspects of CI dilutes organizational attention, leadership, and resources. It also ignores the fact that various potential areas of international activity may be at different stages of readiness (e.g., the institution may already be engaged in study abroad and inclined to expand opportunities in it; alternatively, basic discussions may not have taken place over the meaning and implications of internationalizing curricula at home). A strategic plan for staged implementation gives a sense of destination, steps and milestones along the way, and how individual actions fit within the larger and longer-range whole. It also means that the circle of necessary allies can be enlarged in manageable steps.

Institutions will differ by what they choose to start with or take on first. Some of the more important drivers for priority-setting are a matter of common sense and have been listed as (adapted from Hudzik and McCarthy 2012: 16):

- Build on strengths. What are your institution's strengths and expertise? Which of these are naturally inclined toward international engagement (e.g., languages, business, environmental programs, or perhaps public health)? Which of these will find interested and potential partners across borders for mutual benefit?
- Build on pockets of good will. Where can you find ally departments and faculty who are already experienced and or converted to undertaking international activity? Start building with friendly allies; don't spend start-up time trying to convince the hostile.
- Look for opportunities that can provide relatively quick and visible desirable results and offer the potential for scalability. It helps if projects have an intuitive appeal because of the likelihood of benefits that can readily be seen. Nothing sells like success or its promise.

- Look at manageability and feasibility. Projects need a fairly good understanding on how to move forward and what is required. If there needs to be a long planning and analysis period, before action, the advantage of quick start-up is lost.
- Have a strategic implementation plan that is ready with the next steps in scaling-up and broadening programming.

Expanding institutional allies and partnerships through mutual benefit

Most people and units will not allocate precious time and resources to projects unless they see benefit from doing so. The basic idea behind building allies and partnerships is simple: Productive partnerships between internationalization and existing programs leverage each partner's resources into something more than each could do on their own (discussed fully in Chapter 7). When thinking about becoming an ally or a partner, people want to know whether sharing some of *their* time and effort for *your* purposes will benefit *them*. Most will ask and will want to know in relatively concrete terms "how does internationalization help me do what I am already supposed to be doing?" Before looking for partners, be clear about what internationalization will offer, and focus on manageable projects that others can relatively easily understand and in which they see potential value.

To sell a plan, there needs to be one. What are the initial projects and priorities; what are the goals and objectives; what is the end game or long-range goal? Which allies and partners are necessary for initial and subsequent successes? What contributions are needed from them or what do they need to do?

Summary

This chapter has focused mainly on behavior and attitude barriers to organizational change for CI. These are powerful in their own right, but particularly so if combining with organizational and structural barriers. Recognizing and dealing with barriers to organizational change are essential to moving from concept to action to results with respect to CI.

The next two chapters focus on topics that if ignored will also offer powerful barriers. One is the need to document outcomes and value from CI. The other is to obtain the resources necessary to fund CI.

Chapter 6

Measuring outcomes from institutional comprehensive internationalization

This chapter connects comprehensive internationalization of institutions to measuring outcomes from doing so. Outcomes assessment measures the achievement of goals and results. As CI is a means to other ends and not simply valuable in and of itself, assessment begins by identifying what the ends or goals are, then measuring results. Because there are multiple stakeholders of internationalization with diverse motivations, there will be a multitude of goals and many aspects to outcomes assessment.

There are contextual dimensions for the meaning and practice around outcome assessment. The first dimension is the "level of analysis" and the second is how impact and outcome measurement fits within the larger picture of research about higher education internationalization.

Level of analysis

There are four levels of analysis when thinking about impacts and outcomes from higher education internationalization:

- *Level 4.* At the highest and most aggregated level are *global and supranational* goals of internationalization for, e.g., world peace and justice, the global economy, the global environment, and global prosperity. Assumptions are that the more widespread international knowledge and cross-cultural sensitivity, the more people are able to participate in the opportunities of a global market place and the more aware they become of a shared sense of common problems and solutions for, e.g., global warming, communicable disease, poverty, and causes of local and global instabilities).

- *Level 3.* Analysis is typically at the level of the *national* entity which overlaps with distinctive societies and cultures, and also with a *national higher education system.* At this level, outcomes assessment of internationalization might focus on building an educated and knowledgeable citizenry, enhancing national capacities, and providing the basis for a citizenry and workforce to compete and collaborate successfully across borders. Or how successful is the higher education system in developing higher level literacy, numeracy, and analytical skills as measured by the OECD (2013d) Programme for the International Assessment of Adult Competencies (PIAAC)? Higher national skill levels are associated with the higher levels of national economic development, GDP per capita, and cutting-edge position among the world's knowledge economies (Van Damme 2014).

- *Level 2.* Assessment focuses on the *individual higher education institution.* What are the institutional outcomes from its comprehensive internationalization: for example, institutional reputation or rank; enhanced institutional instructional and research capacities; increased or diversified revenue streams; or access to global pathways of opportunity? **micro**
- *Level 1.* The focus is on outcomes relating to *institutional students and other clientele* it serves. The term "clientele" references a broad array of potential institutional external stakeholders and customers including, but not limited to governments, communities, businesses and employers, contractors, professional groups, and so forth; students too are clientele but may be seen as first in line for most institutions.

What have students learned or what can they do as a result of completing an internationalized curriculum? Or, what are the community problem solving applications and consequences of institutional cross-border research partnerships? How does CI help meet the work force needs of employers?

Chapter focus

This chapter and book have an ostensible focus at Level 2—the institution. However, it would be an unacceptably narrow discussion if not connected to the institution's goals for outcomes related to Level 1. In an ideal world, all four levels of outcomes and their interconnections would be assessed. However, while ideal, such a spread for this chapter would be unmanageable and deflect from the theme of this book. So, with acknowledgment of these other levels and their connections, the focus is on Levels 2 and 1.

The wider research context for CI outcome assessment

Assessment research has an application in mind. The application can be retrospective (what was done; what was achieved; what worked and what didn't). For example, we internationalized the core undergraduate curriculum, but what were the outcomes for student learning? Assessment can also be prospective (what are the lessons for the future; what can be improved and how). To focus only on the past is suboptimal; the real payoff from assessment is thinking about lessons learned and options for strengthening. Can we change content and pedagogy in the interest of improving student learning further? Or can we change the features of cross-border research collaborations to improve research outcomes or institutional research capacity?

There are other types of research that fall broadly under a label of international research on higher education. But there is often confusion between the purposes of these other kinds of international research and the purposes of assessing outcomes. Hans Weiler (2008), writing about "international research on higher education," parses research topics into those about (a) student and scholar mobility; (b) cross-border research and related collaborations; and (c) the international properties of higher education systems. He further elaborates some of this research in terms of: policy, goals, and prescriptions for higher education; overviews of national higher education systems; and databases and statistics about higher education systems (e.g., provided by UNESCO, OECD, and the World Bank). These data allow describing and comparing national post-secondary structures in terms such as funding, student participation and completion rates, etc. However, Weiler's classification doesn't give explicit attention to the emerging need for research on the outcomes of internationalization.

Teichler's (2009) portrayal of higher education internationalization in Europe is noteworthy because a portion of the discussion is on systematic and strategic internationalization including that of higher education institutions but, as he notes, without a coherent view of internationalizing the higher education institution.

Kehm and Teichler (2007: 261, 264) reported substantial growth in the literature of higher education internationalization from the mid-1990s and further elaborated prevalent research themes in this literature to include:

(1) Mobility of students and academic staff; (2) mutual influences of higher education systems on each other; (3) internationalization of the substance of teaching, learning and research; (4) institutional strategies of internationalization; (5) knowledge transfer; (6) cooperation and competition; and (7) national and supranational policies as regarding the international dimension of higher education.

The fourth category in this list, "institutional strategies of internationalization," comes closest to having an institutional focus, while the other categories can be seen to begin identifying a set of elements or dimensions for looking more comprehensively at institutional internationalization. These also begin to lay the foundation to engage outcomes assessment in broad terms.

Kehm and Teichler (2007: 262–263, and later Kehm 2011) note a number of other research developments, three of which suggest linkage of other research topics to the internationalization of institutions and assessing outcomes:

• One is the linkage of internationalization to institutional management, policy, funding, etc. This linkage naturally flows from integrating internationalization into core institutional missions, governance and administration and growth in scale, scope, and diversity of motivations and stakeholders of internationalization. It is a small step for research to include assessing impacts of internationalization on higher education institutions themselves as well as on outcomes desired by institutional leadership, students and other clientele.

- A second set of linkages is the "systematic analyses of international dimensions of higher education." This means looking systemically and strategically at the interconnection of a broad array of activities (e.g. study abroad, internationalization of curriculum at home, research engagement abroad) and is consistent with the notion of comprehensive internationalization.

- The third linkage arises from the emergence of increasingly "theoretically and methodologically ambitious" research about internationalization. Theoretical underpinnings are important for moving research beyond being exploratory and descriptive toward establishing causality ("what causes what") which is useful for policy analysis and decision-making—if you want Y outcomes, research shows that you should do X. For example, what does research show about the nature and degree of student learning outcomes (Y) from study abroad if including pre-departure preparation (X_1), immersion in the host culture (X_2), curricular integration (X_3), and so forth? What theories or models of learning or development provide a basis for understanding such causal relationships?

  While establishing causality is usually very involved and difficult, it remains important because it provides answers for decision makers who want to know whether spending time and money on doing X causes or is responsible for desirable outcomes Y.

These three areas of linkage reflect the growing complexity of higher education internationalization, as well as emergence of more sophisticated understandings of the motivations, models, and outcomes of internationalization. This expanding level of complexity and sophistication has yet to produce a "dominant disciplinary, conceptual, or methodological home" for the study of internationalization. In part this reflects the relative newness of research on higher education internationalization, but also its inherently inter- or trans-disciplinary nature.

Research on areas of international activity

There are rapidly growing bodies of research and literature in specific areas of internationalization activity, for example, on mobility and on internationalizing the curriculum and on the substance and pedagogy of teaching and learning related to them. Mobility has become one of the most widely researched topics within higher education internationalization, and perhaps an exponentially growing one. The Forum on Education Abroad (2012) assembled a bibliography of outcomes assessment studies in education abroad. It listed 100 such studies appearing between 2006 and 2012, 50 studies between 2000 and 2005, and 18 studies between 1976 and 1999. The Twombly *et al.* (2013) review of research on the impacts of study abroad is an excellent overview, although not particularly laudatory about the current state of the art. The internationalization of curriculum, teaching, and learning also has a growing and important literature (e.g., Jones 2013a; Leask 2013). Beyond mobility and curriculum, there is growing discourse on matters of cross-border higher education collaboration, knowledge transfer, and collaborative knowledge development (Brandenburg *et al.* 2009).

Descriptions of country and regional higher education systems that come from the World Bank, OECD, or UNESCO, although useful and can be seen as "international" because they allow cross-border comparisons, are really quite different than the kinds of research issues that focus on connections between institutional behaviors and subsequent outcomes and impacts from internationalization.

Methodological issues

The methodologies employed in many research studies about internationalization activities and programs have limitations: limited sample size and reliance on case studies and, thus, questionable representativeness challenging generalizability; weak theoretical underpinnings making it difficult to establish the basis for cause and effect; lack of rigorous statistical standards (e.g., use of parametric statistics with non-parametric data); reliance on self-reported and often subjective assessments; and sometimes questionable objectivity in designing the research and reporting findings. On matters related to cost/benefit analysis of institutional internationalization, the analytical models typically avoid the measurement of outcomes, focusing instead on inputs and outputs. For further wide-ranging discussion about methodologies and limitations see Beerkens *et al.* 2010; Cuthbert *et al.* 2008; Deardoff and van Gaalen 2012; Green 2012b; Hudzik and Stohl 2009; Leeuw and Vaessen 2009; and Musil 2006).

Quality assurance projects

Quality assurance projects and models related to internationalization typically include considerations of goals, strategies, processes, policies, leadership, programming, staffing, and budgets; but measuring results or outcomes tends to be weak. Examples include the IQRP supported by the Institutional Management in Higher Education Program (de Wit and Knight 1999), the IMPI Project of the European Union (Beerkens *et al.* 2010), the Nuffic MINT project (Nuffic 2013), the Netherlands Flemish Accrediting Association (NVAO) assessment framework (NVAO 2011) and the International Association of Universities and the American Council on Education qualitative review instruments. As Green rightly implies, such efforts at quality assurance come up short if not measuring actual outcomes (e.g., "paying close attention to what students are learning") (Green 2012b: 8). The NVAO project is interesting and with potential for aspects of outcomes assessment in that several of the features of its framework for assessing the internationalization of degree programs include identification, measurement, and provisioning for student learning outcomes (Aerden *et al.* 2013).

The importance of assessing outcomes

In a climate of resource stress, CI needs to demonstrate its value-added in outcome terms. There are many assumptions without hard data concerning the outcomes of internationalization, relying instead on anecdotal evidence and "beliefs" about what we hope to be true. An example comes from suppositions in the OECD 2012 report on higher education internationalization (Hénard *et al.* 2012) where higher education internationalization is purported to:

- Increase national and international visibility.
- Leverage institutional strengths through strategic partnerships.
- Enlarge the academic community within which to benchmark their activities.
- Mobilize internal intellectual resources.
- Add important, contemporary learning outcomes to the student experience.
- Develop stronger research groups.

Although one can see these as desirable goals apt to produce intended outcomes to some degree, the absence of systematic data to verify outcomes and the absence of analysis about which approaches to internationalization produce the strongest results are shortcomings.

Scale and scope of outcome assessment

CI substantially broadens the scale and scope of research interests and questions about outcomes from internationalization. By expanding internationalization to encompass all institutional missions, research interests widen beyond assessment of teaching and learning to include impacts and outcomes relating to research and service missions. It brings to the fore questions about impacts relating to institutional ethos, image, reputation, networks, capacities, organization, and impacts, and outcomes for various students and other clientele. It widens the circle of stakeholders wanting to know what the returns are from investing in institutional internationalization.

Who wants to know what: stakeholder lenses prioritize criteria for impact/outcome assessment

Various stakeholders of CI wear different lenses when peering into the cauldron of research topics suggested by a comprehensive approach to internationalization (see Figure 6.1). Each lens tends to highlight certain issues based on a viewer's institutional position, interests, and biases. Although the lenses differentially prioritize research interests, comprehensive internationalization encourages a wide and *systemic* research agenda which over time will build a broad-based body of knowledge across the lenses regarding institutional behaviors and outcomes from internationalization.

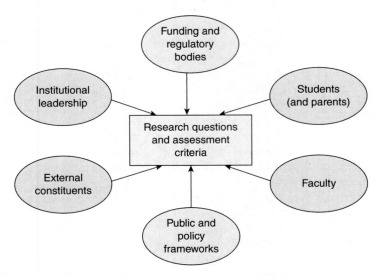

Figure 6.1 Stakeholder lenses filtering outcome assessment issues.

- *Administrator/leadership lens.* Presidents, vice-chancellors, provosts, deputy vice-chancellors, deans, and chairs are interested in impacts on: institutional reputation, niche position, stature, branding and identity; funding; governance structures; changing roles, structures, and functions of both academic and service units; institutional strategic management; inter-institutional collaboration and competition; academic quality and outcomes in the eyes of institutional constituents; and documenting both sides of the internationalization cost/benefit equation.
- *Faculty lens.* Interests are about: scholarship (e.g., opportunities for research, funding, and publication, or access to post docs); careers (e.g., tenure, job security, promotion, and career opportunities); and intellectual legitimacy and quality. What benefits (and costs) does internationalization bring to faculty teaching, research, and service roles? Does internationalization facilitate or reshape the research and teaching perspectives of faculty?
- *External constituents lens.* Are graduates attractive to employers: do they come with the right knowledge and skills sets, including those relating to internationalization? Does institutional internationalization have payoffs for external clientele (e.g., communities and business in problem-solving, gaining knowledge and access to global markets)? The many clientele of higher education will want to know what the payoffs are for them *in their terms* from institutional internationalization.
- *Students and parents lens.* This lens encompasses a panorama of issues: (a) logistical ones such as added requirements from internationalization or difficulties in matching credits across systems, thereby causing possible delays to degrees;

(b) documentable value added in learning, skills, and abilities; (c) cost; and (d) down-the-road impacts such as in careers.

- *Governance and funders lenses.* How do governance (both institutional boards of trustees and academic governance), funders (e.g., governments for public institutions and donors for both public and private), and policy-makers view the costs and benefits of internationalization? What are their expectations for and assessments of payoffs from internationalization?
- *Public policy lens.* Nations and other political entities will set policy preferences and priorities for their higher education systems. Policy-makers will want to know what the documentable impacts are of internationalization on key policy priorities such as workforce preparedness, competitive position in the global market place, and access to global cutting-edge knowledge. What are their expectations for outcomes and impacts from investments in internationalizing higher education?

The foregoing lenses are examples of how different stakeholders may prioritize questions and issues. Another way to differentiate interests is related to key higher education functions and missions.

- *Teaching and learning lens.* Those focused on pedagogy and curricular content will want to examine the meaning, models, and impacts of internationalization in shaping teaching and learning and who has access. What does it mean operationally to internationalize curriculum and learning, what are the options in pedagogy and content for doing so, and with what outcomes? For example: (1) adding content, concepts, themes, and perspectives to the curriculum without changing its structure or its pedagogy; (2) infusing the curriculum with content that reflects diverse perspectives and a framework for understanding differences and similarities; (3) transforming—transitioning from exploring cultural diversity to critical thinking e.g., learning through different perspectives, new methodologies, and different epistemological questions. The first two options are clearly suboptimal.
- *Research and scholarship lens.* What are the impacts of internationalization on: institutional research capacity, priorities, quality, and reputation; access to funding; connections to global pathways of innovation and talent; and knowledge transfer? Are there shifts in the balance between top-down and bottom-up research agenda setting? Examples of outcome measures for research and scholarship include:
  - o   refereed publications in international journals and citations;
  - o   invited speakers at international conferences;
  - o   institutional position in global rankings;
  - o   faculty and staff international awards, prizes, and recognition;
  - o   research discoveries of intellectual consequence and/or problem solving;
  - o   commercial applications income;
  - o   strategic cross-border collaborations that contribute to institutional mission objectives and strengthen institutional capacities.

- *The service lens.* How does an institution's internationalization impact the various communities it serves? For example: assessing methods of cross-border technology transfer; community engagement and empowerment; economic and social development; the saliency of models of co-production aimed at least in part at solving problems where people live and work. In the end, what are the outcomes and impacts on peoples' conditions at home and abroad, for example:

  o   economic
  o   health
  o   education
  o   nutrition
  o   safety/security
  o   access.

Models and approaches to evaluation and assessment

There are a number of potential models to assess impacts and outcomes of CI. Four models have relevance: (1) the program evaluation model; (2) the program learning and results model; (3) the systems model (input–output–outcome); and (4) a variant of the third option labeled "the logic model" which differentiates outcomes and impacts (Rogers 2008); the logic model also distinguishes between activities and outputs. All of the models have a progression of assessment criteria from simple to more complex and difficult, and from less costly to expensive. All include criteria of results, outcomes, or impacts as essential to meaningful evaluation and assessment.

The program evaluation model

This model has its origins nearly 50 years ago and its major initial popularity in the United States was associated with the emergence of the Johnson Administration's "Great Society Programs" and the resulting need to assess the consequences of hundreds of billions of dollars being spent on a wide array of social programs (Suchman 1967; Hatry *et al.* 1973; Bennett and Lumsdaine 1975). Typical evaluation and assessment components of this model include:

- *Effort.* The description and analysis of funds spent and work or activity undertaken (e.g., amount of money allocated to study abroad programming, number of programs offered, number of students participating).
- *Efficiency.* Analyzing the cost of programs, often summarized in unit cost terms. For example, $50,000 was spent internationalizing ten courses in the core undergraduate curriculum for an average cost of $5,000 per course. If the criteria of program success emphasizes efficiency, then the objective of policy-makers can easily become lower unit cost (cost-cutting).

- *Effectiveness.* Measuring the degree to which program objectives or goals have been met. For example, student learning outcomes, successful community problem-solving from research applications (e.g., clean water in remote villages, controlling the spread of tropical and communicable diseases). Efficiency and effectiveness criteria need to be balanced against one another.
- *Process.* Determining whether the program (money spent and activity undertaken) was responsible for achieving goals (effectiveness). This component of the model attempts to establish cause and effect. For example, were student gains in intercultural skills the result of the study abroad program, or simply from their being abroad, or is study abroad even necessary or sufficient for improved intercultural skills?

It is probably a matter of common sense that evaluation and research become more difficult as one moves down the list. Most organizations have legal requirements to keep data on resource expenditures and work activity so effort and efficiency can be relatively easily calculated. Effectiveness is more difficult because defining outcome measures and collecting data on them are much more involved. Process or cause/effect assessment is the most difficult principally because research designs and data are complex and expensive for gathering strong evidence, let alone proof of the impacts of a particular program intervention. Measuring long-term effects is particularly costly. Consider measuring effectives of study abroad on careers; this requires data collection over many years from students and employers.

The program learning and results model

This model owes its origins to Donald L. Kirkpatrick (1977) and was initially developed to assess organizational training programs (also see Hudzik and Wakeley 1981), but has obvious applications to aspects of higher education internationalization. The Kirkpatrick model measures four dimensions:

- *Reactions.* Did participants or students "like" a particular program? Surveys or interviews of their satisfaction with various aspects of, for example, a study abroad program, or their assessment of a particular course in the international curriculum can be multi-dimensional (relevance and attractions of the course content, logistics, pedagogy, instructors, etc.). Reactions assessment, while producing valuable "customer" feedback, is inherently subjective.
- *Learning.* What principles, facts, techniques, or skills were learned by participants? Measures can be subjectively assessed, e.g., "Do you think you learned much on the program or in the course?" Or they can be more objectively determined by utilizing objective pre–post tests of knowledge, attitudes, and so forth.
- *Behavior change.* To what degree can one observe changes in participants following a program or course? For example, is there a difference in their behaviors, reactions to events and situations, opinions or attitudes, abilities

to cope with or analyze situations, interpersonal skills, and applying learning to behaviors on the job or in life, etc.

- *Results.* To what degree did the learning and behavior changes bring about desirable organizational or societal results or impacts? Examples could include assessing how returning study-abroad students reshape the classroom dialog and learning environments, or the ways in which internationalizing the curriculum reshapes faculty as well as student orientations and perhaps institutional ethos.

The "reactions" component of the Kirkpatrick model is regularly applied to study abroad and also to assessment of courses in the on-campus curriculum through course and instructor evaluation forms. Most institutions require these at a minimum. Courses and programs typical have tests, papers, or other means for somewhat more objective appraisals of learning, the second component of Kirkpatrick's model.

Some programs or courses, but typically not many, will pre–post test knowledge in order to assess knowledge gains. Even so, there are deep suspicions about how much students actually learn in college generally (Arum and Roska 2011), let alone through study abroad (Vande Berg *et al.* 2012). Very few programs or courses follow up on subsequent behavior change or other results such as impacts on career paths, global orientations, or retention of new ways of thinking or behaving. A few may use standardized inventories to measure changes in attitudes, changes in orientations or ability to manage in other cultures or unfamiliar situations, and so forth, as a result of international engagement. (See for example BEVI (Shealy 2004) and the IDI Intercultural Development Inventory (Hammer 2012)).

The systems model (input–output–outcome)

The origins of this model are in systems engineering and analysis. Its popularity in policy terms grew with the advent of program budgeting where budget and resource allocation decision-making switched from an emphasis on trying to control resource expenditures (inputs) and achieving greater efficiencies from work and activity (outputs) to assessing whether desirable results and goals were being achieved. This model has three main categories:

- *Inputs:* Resources (money, people, policies, etc.) applied to internationalization efforts.
- *Outputs:* The amount and types of work or activity undertaken in support of internationalization efforts. Some have differentiated between outputs as in establishing capacity (e.g., number of study abroad programs) and use of such capacity (program enrollments) (Deardoff *et al.* 2009), but this seems an unnecessary refinement of the core model for purposes of this chapter.

- *Outcomes:* Results, impacts, and end results. It is these that are usually most closely associated with measuring goal achievement, advancing institutional missions, and achieving ends. Longer-range outcomes are expressed by some as impacts.

In this input–output–outcome model, if more money is provided to departments to internationalize their courses and more courses are internationalized (inputs), and students complete these courses (outputs), assessment ultimately turns toward outcomes (e.g., what do they learn or what skills do they develop?) (see Table 6.1). Limiting assessment to expenditure analysis, numbers of courses, and numbers of students participating is suboptimal because it falls short in assessing results. Indeed, if assessing only input and outputs, it is almost as if the goal of internationalization is spending a lot of money and doing a lot of work—ends in themselves?

It is at times a matter of choice whether a particular item might be listed as an input or an output (e.g., is the number of study-abroad programs an input or an output?). There is also the challenge that in almost any measurement progression from inputs, through outputs, to outcomes there will be strong desire to establish cause and effect. Doing so is rarely straightforward. There can also be multiple and confounding outcomes. For example, we may want to assume that greater diversity in study abroad options provide better fit to diverse student needs, thereby leading to more students studying abroad and better fit with their learning needs. But more options may reduce program economies of scale, raising student costs and thereby limit access.

So, too, many assume that increased research funding increases research output and valuable outcomes. But it is not always true that more money spent per faculty member on research yields an equivalent or greater return in valued research outcomes. It might just yield more low-impact publications.

Is there a real difference among the terms "outcomes, impacts, and results?"

The answer is a matter of opinion and how one chooses to use the terms. In line with the systems model, outcomes are a measure of goal achievement, or ends realized. Goals are seen to have a value in themselves. Spending money and doing work (effort) to internationalize is a means to ends as argued in earlier chapters. The "results" of internationalization include desired outcomes, but some results may be unanticipated, and some of these undesirable. For some the term "impact" serves as a label for both long-term (Rogers 2008) and cascading results as well as multiple cause-and-effect relationships—for example the long-term and eventual effects of an internationalized curriculum on jobs, careers, and then on economic development (Earl and Smutylo 2001; Vickers and Bekhradnia 2007).

Table 6.1 Dimensions for assessing CI

Core institutional mission	Sample input indicators	Sample output indicators	Sample outcome indicators
Discovery	Institutional research expenditures per faculty member in support of international, global, or comparative research. Or, external research dollars for ... etc.	Publications, patents, incidence of citation, grants, and contracts from external sources from international activity	Enhanced institutional reputation, awards, commercial applications income, economic development of communities or regions, community problem-solving, etc.
Learning	Number and diversity of study abroad options; extent of on-campus curriculum that incorporates global, comparative, or international content; institutional financial support for such courses or study; number of faculty with relevant expertise	Number and diversity of students studying abroad, enrollments in courses with global, comparative or international content, curricular integration of international content; number of faculty delivering this content	Impacts on student learning, knowledge gain, attitudes, beliefs, life skills, careers, etc.
Engagement	Money, people, and other resources applied to community or international development problem-solving and engagement	Numbers of projects, locations, and people abroad involved. Problem-solving domestically that incorporates methods and learning from other societies and cultures	Impacts on people's well-being and condition—economic, health, income, nutrition, safety and security, access, etc.

Measuring learning outcomes

A detailed consideration of approaches to defining and assessing learning outcomes is beyond the scope of this chapter. However, as the teaching and learning missions of higher education have been and remain core components of internationalization, a few additional points are in order. First, the categories of learning are diverse. Some can be seen as more immediate such as assessing knowledge immediately after a learning experience, and some are long term. Among the latter are the "staying power" of knowledge gain or changes in attitudes and beliefs. Other longer-term issues concern the consequences (or impacts) of knowledge and skill gains and attitude changes for jobs and careers. Even further out is the impact of these on increasing national position and competitiveness in a global economy, or in the nature of global relations. Included among a fairly diverse set of learning outcomes and impacts are matters such as, but not limited to:

- identifiable knowledge competencies or learning objectives met;
- standardized levels of language competency achieved;
- impacts on attitudes, beliefs, skills, and abilities;
- impact on careers and workforce development;
- increased capacity to learn from and with others from different cultures;
- meeting requirements of internationally defined credentials.

Madeleine Green (2012b: 9–18) provides an excellent summary of the main issues in assessing learning outcomes as well as several examples of learning assessment. Also see: Olson *et al.* (2007) for a taxonomy of learning outcomes when considering both international and multi-cultural education; Jones (2013a) on internationalization and student learning outcomes; and Sternberger *et al.* (2009) on designing a model for international learning assessment. (For further general reading on levels and dimensions of learning see Banks 2004; Green and Mertova 2009, 2011; Leask 2004, 2012a; Hanson 2008; Mestenhauser 1998; Rea 2003; Rhoads and Szelényi 2011).

There is also the issue of uncovering and applying theoretical models which explain how and why particular learning has taken place. Theoretical models abound, for example: social learning theory (Bandurra 1977, 1986); a multitude of cognitive and related learning theories (Leonard 2002); attribute theory (Jones *et al.* 1972). Also see Bloom's (1956) classic taxonomy of educational objectives. An informative annotated bibliography on learning theory has been compiled by Infed, a UK-based non-profit (see Smith 2003). (Also see Deardorff *et al.* 2009.)

These and other applicable theories and ways of conceptualizing learning help provide a theoretical foundation for understanding consequences from international learning opportunities. There are interesting twists on data collection that show promise for uncovering depth and nuance in learning. For example, the American Council on Education in partnership with the Fund for the Improvement of Post-Secondary Education developed a student e/portfolio approach to gathering information about a wide range of learning dimensions (ACE 2014). Kalamazoo College in the United States has been using portfolio assessment methodologies for a long time.

Evidence vs. proof of outcomes

In evaluation and assessment research it is one thing to describe apparent outcomes on key dependent variables (global knowledge and understanding, cross-cultural awareness, research collaborations and partnerships abroad, access to sources and levels of funding, institutional reputation, and so forth). It is quite another matter to establish that institutional internationalization programs actually cause any of these and to what degree. What does study abroad or internationalizing the curriculum cause in terms of outcomes, what do institutions and its various stakeholders get out of an institutional commitment to comprehensive internationalization?

The answer to such questions moves beyond the realm of descriptive research to explanatory research and invokes questions about what is necessary to produce evidence of cause and effect, let alone proof of it. Thousands of research methodology books and scholarly articles explore research requirements for evidence and proof of cause and effect. The range of issues cannot adequately be dealt with in a chapter, let alone in a book, but there are a few points that seem particularly germane to the discussion in this chapter. One has to do with research design and the gathering of evidence about cause and effect. The second concerns data and data sources. A few brief points will raise the important issues.

Research design

Without being able to establish some level of evidence about cause and effect *there is no objective way to establish the outcomes, results, or impacts of international programming*. This point cannot be emphasized enough. Evidence requires not only establishing a conceptual basis for why X would lead to Y, but also requires reducing error in data collection and minimizing rival explanations.

Two classic scholarly publications relating to experimental and quasi-experimental research design maintain their relevance today (Campbell *et al.* 1963; Cook and Campbell 1979). Both outline conditions needed to gain evidence (from strong to weak) or proof that X caused Y. They form the basis of this brief note regarding research design (see Figure 6.2).

A simple example used earlier is worth repeating: X (study abroad) causes Y (knowledge gain and attitude change). There is a rudimentary conceptual basis established if the subject matter and pedagogy of study abroad was related to intended outcomes (what was taught is what was tested). But it is possible that other factors intervened outside the study-abroad experience to produce certain outcomes (e.g., what happened during independent travel before or after the program, or perhaps students who study abroad are already well informed and have

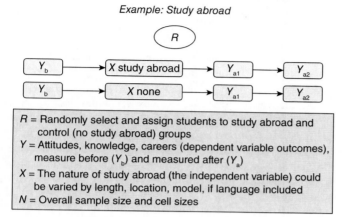

Example: Study abroad

R = Randomly select and assign students to study abroad and
   control (no study abroad) groups
Y = Attitudes, knowledge, careers (dependent variable outcomes),
   measure before (Y_b) and measured after (Y_a)
X = The nature of study abroad (the independent variable) could
   be varied by length, location, model, if language included
N = Overall sample size and cell sizes

Figure 6.2 Research design for assembling evidence and proof of impact/outcomes.

"conducive" attitudes). Or, if we simply measure Y after the program, what can be said about the level of Y before the program? Maybe there was no change in Y.

The classic experimental design (see Figure 6.2) attempts to control for these issues in the following ways. First, there is a control group (no study abroad) and an experimental group (study abroad). Second, there are expectations and measures of outcomes for Y. Subjects are measured on Y_b before the program and then after Y_a. To measure permanence or staying power of results or outcomes, Y may be remeasured at one or more additional points in the future $Y_{a1,2,3}$.

To control for extraneous variables (for example that those electing study abroad are already "with it" while those who don't aren't), it is important to establish that there are no systematic differences between those in the control group and the experimental group. Random selection and assignment to the control and experimental groups is supposed to "even out" the systematic differences between the two groups. Measuring on Y before is an additional check. There is much more to it than this, but these are the basics.

Practical limitations and options for assessing internationalization cause and effects

The reality is that most actual situations involving assessment of outcomes from internationalization can rarely approach the ideals of the experimental model. Random assignment would mean that some students are mandated to study abroad, while others are prohibited from such experiences. Realistically this is a political and ethical nightmare.

Measuring Y_b and Y_a for students studying abroad is reasonably possible. Measuring the same for students not studying abroad is not quite as easy but is possible if a group of non-study-abroad students are willing to be tested before and after (even with randomization not being possible). Long-term, time series data collection on $\Upsilon_{b1,2,3}$ is necessary for assessing staying power of changes, but getting access to subjects becomes more difficult with time.

There are projects in study-abroad impact assessment that are designed to collect data across control and experimental groups, mostly focused on assessing retention and graduation rates (e.g., Center for Global Education 2014). These studies, while not meeting many requirements of the experimental design, are a step in the right direction.

The minimum that should be done to begin collecting evidence on impacts and outcomes (whether assessing study abroad, internationalization of curricula at home, assessing internationalization's outcomes or impacts on institutional research or service missions, or other internationalization activities) are the following in research design terms:

1   Accurately describe the elements of the international activity or program (X).
2   Define intended outcomes (Υ).
3   Establish a "logical" connection between doing X and achieving Υ.
4   Develop objective criteria and verifiable measures for X and Υ.
5   Measure Υ before and after.

Doing more in terms of meeting classic design requirements is better, but these five elements are a good and realistic start. While these five elements will not provide proof of outcomes attributable to a particular internationalization activity, they can begin to provide evidence. The key is that the criteria for outcomes (Υ) relate to goals and objectives and outcomes rather than to measuring input and outputs, and that data being collected is as objectively based as possible.

Data for assessment

Again, the issues and options are many and complex. The two key issues are data validity and reliability. Data validity concerns how we measure or operationalize an abstract concept. The important issue is whether what actually is counted or measured is what we intend to stand for the concept. For example, it is a matter of common sense and established practice that learning objectives for internationalized curricula should be operationalized by valid measures of the intended elements of learning (facts, figures, analytical or reasoning capabilities, etc.).

Self-reported data is inherently subjective in that it is based on what an individual believes or feels, unless one is asking about verifiable data (such as age). Objectivity in data means that different people will look at the same data or information and draw roughly similar conclusions (reliability). If I ask, for example, "How is the temperature in this classroom?" I am likely to get "hot, cold, OK" as responses from a group of people. Who is right? Everyone. If, though, I ask "What is the temperature in this room?" and have everyone look at a thermometer, I will get very similar answers.

The problem in assessing impacts and outcomes of internationalization is that much current data collection is subjective, based on self-report, or asking people to assess a situation without reference to objective and stable measures and standards. This, frankly, is one of the difficulties with many of the current institutional ranking schemes because a large component of rank is dependent on quite subjective peer assessments where criteria may not be standardized or uniformly applied across the rankers. The same is true with assessing study abroad, curricular impacts, and growth in research capacity from internationalization, and so forth. The need is to find measures based on data that are objective and verifiable.

Pre-post tests using objective data can be a step in the right direction. Pre-post knowledge tests and use of standardized attitude inventories can help. If increasing cross-border joint publications is an objective, incidence and rates before and after can be counted, as well as citation incidence. If access to more money from sources abroad is the objective, this too can be objectively measured before and after. If the assumption is that international engagement will improve institutional rank, one can look at before and after ranks, but in this case changes may be in the long run, and it is difficult to separate rival explanations for improvements in ranks.

Qualitative and quantitative research asessment

There is the reality that objective and numerical data are often not available, maybe because outcomes and goals themselves are stated in a way that do not permit quantitative measurement—we can't quantitatively and objectively measure for the question being asked. Recall the "temperature" example. Qualitative data collection methods include observation, interviews, opinion surveys, and document analysis as examples. Many disciplines use qualitative analysis, such as the social sciences, marketing, leadership, and management. Use of the method is particularly valuable for exploratory purposes—laying the groundwork for understanding what key variables may be involved and later to generate research questions capable of quantitative analysis. However, arriving at objective conclusions using qualitative methods that are generalizable is difficult and impossible in some cases; they don't provide a firm basis to establish cause and effect (but they can establish a reasonable cause-and-effect hypothesis); and they rely heavily on self-reporting and interpretative conclusions of the researcher.

Qualitative research provides information different than research based on quantitative and objective data using experimental research designs. The hardened skeptic is rarely satisfied by qualitative data. But good qualitative research can expand the boundaries of understanding among those willing to concede its value.

Bottom-line reality

The world of outcome assessment research requires a balancing of the ideal and the possible. Qualitative research plays a strong role and valuable role in assessing the impacts and outcomes of internationalization. In many cases it is the only realistic approach available. Some assessments will remain in the realm of relying on anecdotal data, subjective and opinion-based measures, and beliefs and hope. In this imperfect world, the minimum objectives of assessing impact and outcomes from internationalization are to:

1   Know what the goals are.
2   Devise impact and outcome measures that relate to these goals.
3   Improve the objectivity of data measures and research design as much as possible.
4   Continuously focus on valued intended outcomes.

More research on issues identified under the stakeholders "lens" would be useful for building a body of knowledge on the outcomes of internationalizing higher education institutions. Research findings would inform institutional decision making and policy, and provide a basis for assessing value. Research questions will need to be prioritized for manageability. Eventually fitting the pieces into the larger context of comprehensive or strategic internationalization and its holistic impact on institutions would be a very beneficial result.

Chapter 7

Sustainable resources for comprehensive internationalization[1]

Comprehensive internationalization widens challenges to finding sufficient resources to support and sustain its many dimensions. The hunt for resources is a core responsibility of leadership in any organization—perhaps more challenging for leadership of CI because it requires building resource collaborations throughout the institution. There is no easy or one-time solution, but there are strategies and tactics which can measurably improve the odds of getting necessary resources. Several such strategies are discussed in this chapter:

- Treat money and resources as allied concepts but not as synonyms; they are related but not the same, as explained later.
- Build on an institutional culture for internationalization and tie resources through strategic inclusion.
- Tap into existing institutional resources, which include faculty, staff, programs, and activities. This strategy requires the integration of internationalization into core institutional missions, building partnerships of mutual benefit throughout the institution and dual-purposing the use of resources.
- Link manageable steps forward within a long-range strategy to acquire needed resources.
- Diversify the revenue stream for internationalization which requires creativity in accessing and blending resources from several sources.

All five strategies will be shaped by institutional budget practices and bound by institutional and environmental fiscal realities and constraints. Each, though, is an important element in the long-term assembly of resources needed for comprehensive internationalization.

Compatibility and integration with institutional budgeting policies and realities

Institutions differ widely in the details of their budget planning and resource allocation practices. Established rules and procedures need to be known and understood in advance because they define the legal parameters as well as the pathways to money and other resources.

Rules and pathways fall into two broad categories: (a) fiduciary and financial accounting responsibilities and (b) policy and procedures for setting resource allocation priorities. A detailed description of the first category is not within the confines of this book, because they are intricate and idiosyncratic for any institutional setting and shaped differently across political and policy jurisdictions. Suffice to say that audits monitor compliance with budgeting and accounting regulations. Regulations define acceptable sources of resources, allocations of resources, how their use is governed and authorized, and expectations for record keeping. Internationalization cannot play by a different set of rules except where convincing argument can be made and accepted in advance that modifications are warranted. So we will concentrate on the acquisition of resources for internationalization as a part of the institutional resource planning and priority-setting process.

Budget planning models and comprehensive internationalization

Higher education institutions vary widely in how they approach their budget planning and allocation priority setting. At one end of a continuum, change-resistant institutions approach budgeting as a preservation of the status quo. They emphasize what is commonly referred to as "baseline" budgeting; the current year's budget allocations are adjusted for inflation and take into account other typically minor changes at the margins and then rolled forward as next year's budget—year after year. Little of past or present practice is challenged, and change is rare.

At the other end of the continuum are a growing number of institutions which are either choosing, or are being forced, to review allocation priorities in the interest of managerialism, accountability, and greater efficiency and effectiveness. These kinds of pressures, coupled to increasing resource stress in higher education, argue strongly for strategic planning and strategic change.

It is difficult to imagine the successful adoption of comprehensive internationalization in an institution oriented toward preserving the status quo. If Sporn (2003) and others are right to signal strategic change in leadership and management orientations and greater accountability expectations, strategic resource allocation and reallocation will grow and provide an important base for the reallocation of institutional resources to comprehensive internationalization.

Strategic budget planning and resource allocation for CI: a force for change

Figure 7.1 graphically shows the principal elements of a generic strategic planning process for institutions. It depicts that the large-level drivers of organizational strategy consist of missions, values, vision, the external environment, and an assessment of institutional strengths, weaknesses, opportunities, and threats (SWOT). These in turn shape program and operational priorities.

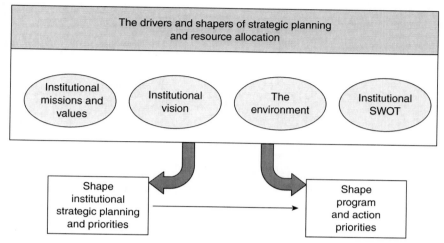

Figure 7.1 Types of issues that shape strategic planning and resource allocation.

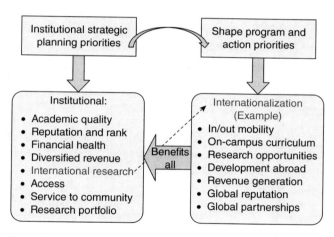

Figure 7.2 Inclusion and integration of CI into strategic planning.

Figure 7.2 elaborates on Figure 7.1 and places internationalization ("international reach") into a list of priority institutional strategies. Incorporating internationalization as one of the institution's priorities is at the heart of strategic inclusion. A second aspect of strategic inclusion is the flow from the bottom-right to the bottom-left where internationalization is expected to strengthen other institution priorities. In this way, strategic inclusion is a reciprocal relationship: on the one hand, the institution defines internationalization as a strategic priority; on the other, the benefits of internationalization are intended to be defined in a way that enhances all

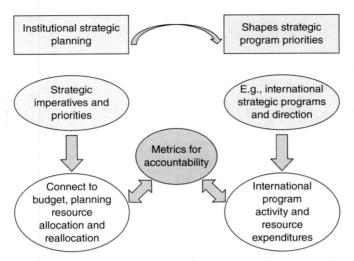

Figure 7.3 Strategic inclusion of CI into planning, budgets, and accountability.

other institutional priorities. Benefits are seen as all-around and essential to gaining broad-based institutional support for CI.

Figure 7.3 takes the process two additional steps forward: first, connecting internationalization to resource allocations, and second, addressing expectations of mutual benefit and measurable outcomes for accountability. It is the expectation that institutional and CI accountability metrics will be compatible and reinforcing, certainly not working at cross-purposes.

Table 7.1 is an example of a list of possible institutional metrics (a mix of input, output, and outcome)—an amalgam of sorts from recent activities of US institutions to define institutional metrics for accountability. These can be related to the kinds of assessment measures listed for internationalization in Chapter 6 and as way to measure change.

Money and resources

It is limiting and counter-productive to think of resources only as money. While money is one form of resource, there are others in the form of existing institutional academic staff, programs, service and support units, and their collective time and effort. Tapping into these existing resources is a productive strategy for supporting internationalization, so much so that although it may be counter intuitive, getting new money for internationalization is usually the smaller part of the equation for sustaining internationalization. The meaning and means of tapping into existing resources is covered later in this chapter.

There are several reasons why getting new money is problematic. First, as discussed in Chapter 2, in many countries higher education is under financial stress

Table 7.1 Sample of input, output, and outcome metrics

Students, learning, and curricula

1 Number and diversity of students in activities abroad (study, research, internships, etc.)—graduate and undergraduate
2 Range and availability of courses and curricula having international comparative or global content
3 Numbers or proportion of students' enrollment in courses with international content
4 Numbers of students achieving level 1, 2, 3, or 4 competency in a second or third language
5 Evidence of outcomes relative to learning objectives
6 Evidence of impact on students: e.g., knowledge, attitudes, beliefs, skills, careers
7 Number of international undergraduates and graduate students and their diversity of "country of origin" and "major preferences"
8 Incidence and quality of integrative living/learning experiences between domestic and international students

Faculty, research/scholarship

1 Faculty with credentials from abroad and/or native of other countries
2 Dollar value growth above inflation of contracts and grants awarded to support international activity
3 Diversification of the sources of international contracts/grants
4 Levels of internal and external support for faculty projects and activity abroad
5 Levels of internal and external support for students engaged in study, research, and internships abroad
6 Incidence of faculty and staff publication in international journals, invited speakers at international conferences

Institutional capacities, quality, and impacts on stakeholders

1 Institutional positions in global rankings of higher education institutions
2 Institutional and faculty/staff awards, prizes, recognition, for international activity (instruction, research/scholarship, service)
3 External funding for international-development activity abroad
4 Number of faculty engaged in international teaching or research or projects abroad
5 Strategic joint ventures/alliances with peer institutions abroad that meet or exceed alliance objectives
6 Global strategic alliances linked to institutional strengths and priorities for program enhancements
7 Measurable outcomes from institutional international research and scholarship: e.g., enhanced global/national reputation and awards; commercial applications income; contributions to economic development of locations/regions; solving problems of various communities
8 Outcomes from outreach and engagement: e.g., impact on people's condition: economic, health, education, nutrition, safety/security, access
9 Outcomes for students and other stakeholders from international/global/comparative curricular and learning: knowledge gain, change or strengthening of attitudes, change in or widened basis for beliefs, intellectual skills, life skills, personal capabilities, career options and directions

owing in part to reduced public support—a shift in part from seeing it as public good and more as a private gain. Stress arises also from the inability of public coffers to support burgeoning demand for higher education particularly in rapidly developing systems and the growing needs for life-long education.

Second, regardless of the centrality one may assign to the importance of CI, it must compete with other core institutional functions and missions for scarce resources; probably the best to be hoped for is competition on a somewhat level playing field. Third, because of the rising costs of higher education, typically above general inflation, institutions are under increasing pressure to control or reduce costs; among the key strategies for doing so is achieving multiple payoffs or benefits from existing allocations of resources.

Within a somewhat pessimistic fiscal environment, there is good news for CI in the results of the IAU Fourth Global Survey of the Internationalization of Higher Education (Egron-Polak and Hudson 2014: 82) fifty to seventy-five percent, or more, of respondents report funding has increased or remained stable for internationalizing curricula, research collaboration, outgoing mobility, faculty and staff mobility, international student exchange, off-shore programming and distance learning, and international development and capacity-building projects. All of these are significant elements of a comprehensive approach to internationalization. The largest percentages of respondents reporting increases were related to research collaborations, student mobility and exchanges, and mobility for faculty and staff. These results are particularly encouraging given that the period following 2007 included the deepest global recession in decades.

Yet, about half of IAU survey respondents reported that insufficient internal funding levels were the number-one internal barrier to advancement of internationalization, while about a third rated insufficient public funding as the number-one external barrier. Neither result is surprising, as the IAU authors point out, given significant costs of internationalization. But it is also not surprising given that the lack of funding is a widespread complaint in higher education, almost no matter what the issue.

Tapping into existing staff, programs, and their associated resources to support internationalization decreases the pressure to rely on getting new money, integrates internationalization into existing institutional priorities and programs, and improves institutional efficiency by achieving multiple benefits from a given set of resources.

The advantage of multiple sources

Acquiring new money and tapping into existing resources are linked and can be mutually reinforcing in a number of ways. No single source or kind of support will be sufficient for CI. Tapping into the existing resources of numerous campus units and programs widens access to support but also the circle of those involved in internationalization. The latter expands the "political" base for seeing internationalization as a widely embraced undertaking. While offering no guarantees, a wider political base for internationalization makes it easier for central leadership to allocate new money to it, especially if in partnership with tapping into existing resources.

Managing scale and scope of need

When engaging CI, trying to do everything at once is an unmanageable approach. Not everything can be done at once and not everything can be afforded at once. Affordability is possible if effort *and* cost are staged in manageable bites and follow a long-term strategic plan of build-up. Huge sums of new money to be spent in the short run are often mismanaged because of scale; examples include large new government grant programs where spending the money can easily degenerate from goals to spend it smartly to "moving the money out" before policy-makers think the money isn't actually needed. Smaller sums of money built up over time are not only more manageable but allow adjustments in how resources are used. It is a matter of strategy and the environment one inhabits, however, because in many situations, the first budget is the most important one with getting more money later a challenge as was the case in the United States with Title VI funding. The answer may be staged allocations for staged expenditure growth.

Comprehensive internationalization can easily seem impossible if discussion begins with "A huge amount of new money will be needed to make this possible." Responses are likely to vary between "Are you insane, where will we find that much money?" to "Hmmm, guess we better think this over for a while." Either way, CI will have likely lost its day in court. Affordability looks very different and more realistic if viewed as a multi-year strategy. Loans for home purchase are an example; so is a multi-year plan of technology upgrade; so is CI.

Staged growth according to a plan

The key is to know what the long-term plan is so that the manageable staging of effort and cost can be synchronized with a longer-range goal in mind. What are the more likely action components of a comprehensive approach to internationalization: inbound and outbound mobility; internationalizing the curriculum at home; language study; building institutional partnerships abroad; internationalizing support for faculty and staff; branch operations abroad; internationalizing faculty research; enhancing institutional instructional, research and service capacities; and so forth?

A long-range vision gives some sense of intended scale and phase-in over the long run, including: (a) what to begin with and what follows (sequencing); (b) what is the intended growth in these and over what time; and (c) what are the probable resource needs over time. At one institution a ten-year plan was developed to increase study abroad participation four-fold through the staged building of program options. At another institution the plan was to increase international student enrollments to 20 percent from about 10 percent of total institutional enrollments. Both institutions met their goals. With no need to go into the detail here, there are management tools to help manage this staging (Klastorin 2004; Project Management Institute 2013).

Implications

The implications of managed action and resource needs are twofold. First the journey to CI is a long-term commitment; second, success is the product of a cumulative set of steps heading someplace as opposed to appearing to be wandering in a desert. At another institution emphasizing engineering disciplines, enrollments in language courses had significantly declined. Starting small, engineering collaborated with the German language department to link language learning with the engineering course. Over time the program grew to include other languages, eventually having 25 percent of engineering students graduate with dual degrees in engineering and a language.

A three-part strategy for securing resources for CI

A strategy for sufficient and sustainable resources has three major foundation blocks (see Figure 7.4). The first is building the institutional culture of support and its strategic inclusion into key institutional decision-making and priority-setting processes. The second is tapping into existing institutional resources. The third is recognizing and meeting the need for new money.

The three are like a three-leg stool, take one leg away and the stool is unstable. Long-term sustainability is heavily dependent on culture and strategic inclusion. Successive sections of this chapter deal with that first and then move on to strategies for tapping existing resources and then acquiring new resources.

1 Building and reinforcing a support culture through strategic inclusion

Chapter 4 discussed at length the element of building a support culture for CI and its companion action "strategic inclusion." The core of the message there was

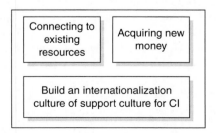

Figure 7.4 Three-element strategy to acquire resources for CI.

that a campus dialog was essential to building a broad base of understanding and support for CI. Dialog done well, while educational and building understanding to support internationalization, is rhetoric without practical follow-through. Strategic inclusion provides the essential architecture for follow-through. Chapter 4 listed six key elements of strategic inclusion with integration of CI into institutional strategic and budget planning processes being one of the most important. Rhetoric turns to action and supports strategic change when CI is built into key institutional decision-making processes, culminating in bringing resources to bear.

Centralized and decentralized strategic inclusion in budget planning

How CI fits into strategic budget planning depends on whether institutional budget processes are highly centralized (mainly top-down), decentralized (bottom-up), or a combination. It is infeasible at most institutions to have either a purely top-down or bottom-up process. Most have a combination of the two, varying in the degree to which input from departments is expected, the degree to which departments participate in setting resource allocation priorities, and who makes final decisions.

The place of CI in the budget process strengthens if the practice is for international issues to be addressed centrally in overall institutional budget planning documents *and* as part of budget planning documents at the department level. In such a combination, institutions include CI among their strategic budget planning priorities. College deans and departmental chairs are expected to focus a portion of their budget planning on their units' CI goals. Some institutions provide budgetary incentives for units which actively engage internationally.

2 Connecting CI to existing resources

In the Fourth IAU Global Survey of Internationalization of Higher Education, Egron-Polak and Hudson (2014: 82) report that, for the global sample of institutions, 53 percent of funding for internationalization comes from the institutional budget, 24 percent from public funds including grants and programs, 6 percent from international student fees, and well under 5 percent each from five other sources. These data likely focus on actual budget or money allocations. Yet, institutions have substantial resources not just in terms of money but also in people, time, programs, and effort deployed to support various missions and purposes.

Most resource allocations fund multiple purposes. For example, budgets provided to academic units support faculty teaching, research and service activities, as well as undergraduate and postgraduate education. There is a long history in higher education that the allocation of unit budgets is typically dual- and multipurposed in pursuit of outputs and outcomes. In this, there is an expectation of integration and synergies across various missions and responsibilities within units—research and teaching functions cross-advantage, products of research feed into community problem-solving and service functions, and so forth.

The key for CI is that people see the potential for internationalization to strengthen existing missions. This is one reason why internationalization shouldn't be viewed as an end in itself; rather, it is a means to other ends, particularly to strengthen existing missions of teaching, research, and service. There will be those locked into the view that CI is akin to adding a fourth mission. Yet, if the arguments in Chapter 3 carry weight, then CI strengthens core missions in a twenty-first century context and becomes a substantial benefit to academic and service units through integration.

Re-purposing and dual-purposing of existing resources

There is sometimes confusion over these terms because both relate to tapping existing resources, but they are substantially different in meaning and practice. Nonetheless, both can be very important to finding resources to support CI. Re-purposing is moving money from one purpose to another. Dual-purposing is combining an existing purpose with another, using the same money or resources for two or more purposes simultaneously. There might be a preference to consider re-purposing first—that is taking money from a program or activity no longer an institutional priority and reallocating it for purposes of internationalization. However, relying too heavily on the re-purposing strategy and being too successful at it can carry negative consequences in the form of advocates of internationalization being seen as predators gobbling up someone else's money at any chance. This is why dual-purposing can be a more politically palatable alternative for accessing existing resources. Dual purposing has more potential, but is more involved in selling it to others.

Dual-purposing is seen as less predatory if it produces win–wins for internationalization and for academic units. This depends substantially on whether academic and support units see an advantage to them from incorporating an international dimension into what they are already doing. Many institutions, small and large, employ dual-purposing for internationalization. One US liberal arts undergraduate institution estimates that a quarter of its faculty are engaged internationally through dual-purposing. Similar proportions exist for a large number of the big Midwest US research institutions. Although data from Europe and elsewhere are limited on this point, an inference can be drawn loosely from data reported in the IAU Fourth Global Survey where only 22 percent of respondents listed faculty inexperience or disinterest as a significant barrier to internationalization. No world region in the survey ranked faculty inexperience as a significant factor (Egron-Polak and Hudson 2014: 69). This suggests a resource pool available among existing academic staff for internationalization.

Partnerships and integration of effort

The essence of dual-purposing is building partnerships for mutual benefit and integration. It helps if CI initiatives bring some monetary incentives to the table in the form of, for example, grants to support internationalizing courses or sub-jects, faculty development, international travel support and the like. The equally important contribution is that those already experienced with aspects of interna-tionalization bring their knowledge to the table in helping to integrate interna-tional dimensions into existing activity.

Higher education already spends many billions globally developing and teach-ing courses and subjects. A modest retooling of the learning objectives and design of existing courses can expand internationalization of curricula in cost-effective ways. Hundreds of US institutions are using such a strategy to internationalize the general education component of the undergraduate curriculum. Accredita-tion and other self-monitoring quality control efforts in fields such as business and engineering have championed integration of internationalized components into degree programs.

Another example of integration and dual-purposing is building on existing faculty research interests and expertise. If faculty have expertise valued at home, it is likely to have value abroad. In turn, applying that expertise in other countries and cultures will further enrich the expertise. The issue is not so much chang-ing faculty research and teaching priorities as it is discovering ways in which an internationalization of faculty engagement will further increase their research and instructional capacities. Faculty want research, funding, and publication oppor-tunities; a well-designed effort to internationalize the research activity of existing faculty can produce desired benefits all around.

Through dual-purposing, internationalization brings an orientation and opportunity to enhance the quality and relevance of core higher education missions, thereby also providing support resource platforms.

Laying the groundwork for dual-purposing partnerships

Forcing partnerships top-down is not a productive tactic; it usually produces either unwilling participants or at best those who will only half-heartedly play along. Before looking for and spending time cultivating partnerships or collabo-rations, it is important to have decided:

- what areas for building CI will come first (inbound mobility, outbound mobility, internationalizing the curriculum at home, or cross-border research collaborations, etc.);
- for these, who/what are potential partners/allies for advancing program priorities.

It is useful to consider who the natural allies for the priority CI activity might be—i.e., those already converted through knowledge and experience to the importance of CI. Do any of these existing allies align with program development priorities? Setting initial priorities for collaborative action (partnership building for dual-purposing of resources) is helped by identifying such potential matches.

What cooperation can be expected from them, and what are the prospects that they will join in and be able to contribute? The most important first step in dealing with this question is coming to understand partners—their jobs and responsibilities and to think from their perspective or from within their shoes:

- What are their responsibilities and to whom and what are they accountable?
- Work and dialog with them about how CI could advance meeting their responsibilities.
- Make them full partners in the CI idea-development process.
- Most importantly, understand what will motivate them to become involved.

Resolving these questions begins the serious business of building partnerships for internationalization and dual purposing.

Integrated reciprocal resource strategy

Recall from Figure 7.4 that the basic three-part strategy blends establishing an institutional culture for internationalization and strategic inclusion, accessing existing resources, and acquiring new resources. Each portion of the strategy leans and builds on other portions of the strategy (i.e., organizational culture supports getting new resources as well as accessing existing resources; existing resources help leverage new resources; and, reciprocally, new resources leverage existing resources.

3 Acquiring and using new money for internationalization

The focus initially was on accessing existing resources, recognizing that higher education budget constraints make getting new money a challenge. However, no matter how successful connecting to existing resources is, some new money is always needed. As one president put it to his SIO, "you need some 'walking around' money to attract interest and to leverage other resources."

An institution unwilling to allocate or attract new money to build CI over time is sending the signal that internationalization is not a priority. Many forms of leveraging are made possible when cash can be brought to the table, particularly as match or as incentive.

The productive strategy is one that seeks to cross-leverage new money and existing resources. Sources of new money for internationalization come from inside (re-purposing) or from outside sources (e.g., grants). Both inside and outside sources need to be combined for maximum effect.

The guiding principle for getting either is connecting an idea for funding to a source of funding having similar interests. This is the same as the principle noted in the previous section of finding matches between program priorities and potential allies in connecting to existing resources.

Laying groundwork

The general principles mentioned at the start of this chapter govern not only the overall quest for sufficient and sustainable resources, but also the search and acquisition of new money for internationalization. Similar groundwork is needed:

- Building a case for new money is strengthened if: (a) an institutional culture via strategic inclusion establishes CI as an institutional priority, and not simply a whim; (b) priorities are set—not everything can be done at once; this gives potential funders a sense that thought has been given to a manageable and staged action plan; and (c) such a case is made in terms attractive to those who have the money.
- "Attractive" has a particular context when looking for new money. It involves matching institutional program priorities with funder's priorities in a way that meets *their* objectives. A good case in point involves seeking grants, whether from government agencies or from private foundations. Each will have circumscribed their priority interests for giving; proposals to fund a particular aspect of CI will need to match their preferences and this requires investigation in advance as to what those are.
- Another important aspect of groundwork and prior analysis is determining where the most important resource gaps existing to support CI priorities. In other words, where is the absence of resources most acute?

Finding a match between filling the most acute needs and sources of funding begins with "inventorying" existing resources. There are at least three kinds of resources to be inventoried: (1) people, units, and programs already actively engaged; (2) those who could become engaged with encouragement; and (3) cash or money resources already in hand. In institutions both large and small, but particularly in larger ones, surprises abound when systematically surveying what is already available, who or what is already internationally engaged, or who might want to be.

Figure 7.5 shows one way to organize an inventory; there are others. In this particular example, the focus is on outbound mobility and sources of support (money, people, units, and programs already involved) arranged across two dimensions. One dimension is source of funds (e.g., general fund support vs. other sources, and combinations. The second dimension attempts to place the locus of support along a centralized vs. decentralized continuum—meaning mainly are these sources at the institution level or at a department level, or both? For example, endowment funds to support study-abroad scholarships might be found in institutional-level accounts or in departmental accounts, or a mix of both.

Focusing this kind of analysis on a particular area of activity (e.g., outbound mobility) maps support for it and after such a grid is laid out, it can be used in conjunction with an analysis of support gaps, eventually identifying priorities for new funds. For example, consider scholarships for mobility. If insufficient, questions

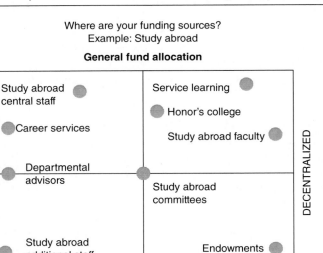

Figure 7.5 Taking inventory of various existing resources for CI components.

might be: Where on the inventory grid is scholarship support presently provided? What sources already on the grid might be a source of more (e.g., general fund sources or fund-raising, the institutional scholarship office, or individual academic units)? What new sources might be cultivated (e.g., a private foundation)? The bottom line is that to inventory existing resources not only documents what you have but identifies the gaps so that when requests are made they can be justified.

New money from the inside

RE-PURPOSING

New money from inside the institution can take several forms. One form is "re-purposing," discussed earlier. Its potential is relative to the on-going churn of resources in an institution through reallocation of resources prompted by discontinuing, reducing, or reconfiguring existing programs, thereby freeing money for reallocation. Regardless of amounts, the essential strategy for internationalization advocates is to have established a front-row seat for internationalization at the reallocation part of budget planning.

STRATEGIC INVESTMENT AND INCENTIVE FUNDS

Other sources of new money involve accessing institutional strategic initiative and incentive funds. These funds are different from emergency reserves which exist to cover unexpected contingencies. Strategic investment or seed funds typically exist centrally on an on-going basis to support start-up projects of all kinds, including for CI (e.g., getting a new partnership with an institution abroad off the ground).

Incentive funds act as an inducement for departments or staff to undertake certain actions such as developing materials to internationalize an existing course or to present research and papers at international conferences. In both cases, but especially for accessing incentive funds, match is required from other sources such as the staff member's home department. And in most cases allocations are temporary (non-recurring) mainly to jump-start something new.

The existence of strategic initiative pots is extraordinarily important for growing support for CI. Allocations from these funds should not only synchronize with long-term CI strategic goals but also with near-term priorities for manageable steps forward.

Allocations from incentive funds support particular kinds of activities on a regular basis but typically in one-time allocations for the activity. Examples include:

- a travel grant for a conference presentation;
- a grant to internationalize an existing course or subject;
- expanding research capacities fund (e.g., support travel or other costs to meet with a colleague to develop a collaborative cross-institutional research grant);
- a study-abroad scholarship;
- an international professional development training/education grant.

Few presidents, provosts, or deans will establish such funds unless the groundwork has been laid for internationalization being an institutional priority and unless there is a clear plan guiding priorities and what the money will be used for, usually attached in clear ways to institutional and internationalization strategic priorities. Applications for funding need to highlight these strategic connections.

RECURRING AND NON-RECURRING ALLOCATIONS

Additional issues concern the nature and conditions of disbursements from investment and seed funds. A critical issue is whether the disbursement is recurring or non-recurring; in the former, money is allocated permanently, year after year—it comes to "rest" in some activity permanently as a part of the base budget. Non-recurring allocations are sometimes referred to as a "one time" allocation of funds (e.g., for one year, or perhaps for two or three, but it is not permanent). In the case of recurring allocations, constant attention needs to be given to replenishing money for the funds—a difficult task and risky. On the other hand, once a fund is established on a recurring basis and if only non-recurring allocations are made from it, the fund remains a stable source of money.

MATCH AND LEVERAGING

Fund managers also need to figure out how to have their money go further through leveraging. Requiring match becomes an important leveraging strategy—"We will provide half the start-up cost if you will commit the remainder from departmental funds." Requiring match is also a way of assuring that those receiving the allocation have their interests in the project clearly demonstrated by having to allocate their own funds and/or finding additional outside support. A "free lunch" can be abused and without the requirement of match, it is difficult to judge the depth of sincerity and commitment to the project being funded. It is human nature to be more seriously committed if one's own money is also involved.

Allocations from funds can also act like bait on the hook to get others to buy in. It often doesn't take much to motivate others to join in. A few hundred dollars or euros (or equivalent) from one of these pots can attract matching resources to support travel abroad to present at a conference, conduct research, or gather materials to internationalize a course. A study-abroad scholarship meeting a portion of a student's costs can be a powerful motivation for students and families to find the rest elsewhere. Of course, allocations can be bigger for bigger projects, but so will be the expected match in those circumstances.

New money from the outside

CI will have numerous programs and many dimensions; each will naturally connect to different sources of money and support. No single source of funding can make it all happen (whether from the inside or the outside). As very few outside funding sources are open ended, getting new money from the outside must be a diversified strategy that links particular projects with particular sources of money.

Almost all foundations, grant agencies, and private donors will have priorities. Access foundation websites (e.g., Gates, Ford, Rockefeller, Mellon, the World Bank, Soros Foundation, Wellcome Trust, and hundreds of others which may be locally, nationally, or globally based) to view their priorities (which by the way will change over time, so keep current).

PURSUING MULTIPLE SOURCES OF FUNDING

Gaining critical mass to sustain internationalization almost always means feeding the resource needs from several sources and directions at once. Figure 7.6 combines internal and external sources of money consistent with the opening points of this chapter that blending resources and money from multiple sources, and from internal and external sources, is required to support comprehensive internationalization.

There are numerous sources of outside funding that seemingly are only limited by ability to find and tap them. Many institutions have specialists whose job is to constantly survey the external environment for sources of funding for institutional strategic priorities. An important question is whether they have been given a charge to support internationalization as a priority in their investigations.

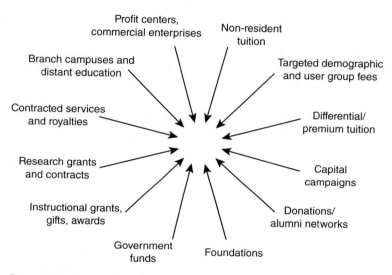

Revenue diversification

- Profit centers, commercial enterprises
- Non-resident tuition
- Branch campuses and distant education
- Targeted demographic and user group fees
- Contracted services and royalties
- Differential/ premium tuition
- Research grants and contracts
- Capital campaigns
- Instructional grants, gifts, awards
- Donations/ alumni networks
- Government funds
- Foundations

Figure 7.6 Internal and external sources of resources for CI.

Fees beyond tuition

A contemporary reality that most internationalization leaders will face, sooner or later, is institutional interest in fees as a source of meeting costs and balancing the budget. Competing interests and positions around fees need to be thought through. This includes what place fees might have in addressing the overall internationalization balance sheet, and perhaps above all, if fees are imposed on customers, will they still see value from services they receive, or more as a disincentive to participate? And finally, there is the market place of supply and demand and with competition and price sensitivity.

DEVELOPMENT FUND-RAISING

Development and donation fund-raising is not evenly developed as a strategy across country and regional higher education systems, nor even within given systems. With growing pressure on higher education generally to diversify revenue streams, interest is growing globally in this source of revenue. The potential is huge. In the United States, for example, higher education endowments worth billions and in some cases tens of billions of dollars are a reality. While gift-giving to higher education is not a strong tradition in many societies, it is spreading not just because of the need for revenue diversification, but also because of the sizeable growth in the global middle class and global number of millionaires and billionaires able to give serious consideration to philanthropy.

GOVERNMENT GRANTS

Governments fund higher education generally and as well as for specific purposes such as internationalization. The Title VI program of the US Department of Education is one example. Several exist in Europe, such as the Marie Curie program, Erasmus, STINT in Sweden, and many more. There are equivalents in Asia such as the Chinese-funded Confucius Center programs, and others in Japan, Singapore, Latin America and Africa as examples. There are also significant international development funding programs in the United States, the Netherlands, and Japan, to name a few. (For a convenient and fairly expansive list of country-based and regional sources see http//en.wikipedia.orgn/wiki/list_of development_ aid_agencies. Also, see Hudzik and Pynes 2014).

FUNDING TO SUPPORT RESEARCH

The great majority of institutions with a research mission have pots of money to support research and research start-up. The key is to tap into existing institutional pots or grant funds to support internationally connected research. It is important to break down artificial barriers that may suggest there is a difference whether research is conducted domestically or internationally. Only where national security interests and regulations invade do such barriers exist in practical terms. Breaking down such barriers also aids in tapping transnational sources of money to support research such as from the World Bank, the Asian Development Bank, corporate partnerships, off-shore foundations and donors, or to build funding partnerships with higher education institutions abroad, etc.

CONTRACT INCOME

Contract income is revenue for specific services performed. While research for the sake of research and discovery is rarely the emphasis of contract work, work that solves problems and achieves practical results produces useful findings that are opportunities for publication and other forms of scholarly output.

Finding contract linkages is similar to the other forms of linking discussed earlier in this chapter but also requires some preparatory work. What are you good at doing? Is there a need abroad for what you are good at doing? Does applying institutional talent abroad in a contractual arrangement fit institutional priorities and values and those of a granter? One catch in both development and contract grant work is that, increasingly, funding sources like USAID, the Millennium Challenge Corporation, the World Bank, and other development agencies expect at least in-kind contributions in the form of match, recognizing that institutions themselves benefit from engagement abroad.

Institutional due diligence before accepting outside money

Not all outside sources of money are necessarily a good thing. Obtaining money for the sake of money can create substantial disconnects between institutional values and priorities and those of funding sources. Institutional due diligence is needed in considering implications of the following issues:

1   compatibility in priorities, values, and objectives;
2   most grant, foundation, and contract funds have an end date and are non-recurring;
3   impact on institutional core values.

The first issue is really asking "Are you only after the money? Or, are you after money that will advance institutional priority objectives for internationalization?" The second question raises a thorny issue. Often, an outside funding source will invest in an idea for a start-up period with an expectation that the institution will find a way to sustain it when their money ends. Is there a realistic plan for sustaining the activity if it is to continue post grant funding?

The third question is potentially the most serious challenge. Will accepting the terms of the money challenge or violate core institutional values, raise legal issues, and generate unacceptable campus strife? There are innumerable examples:

- Funding to start a branch campus abroad will result in discriminatory admission requirements, or seriously limit open or balanced inquiry in the classroom. Will these violate core institutional values? Should you do this? Can you do it? What are the costs of violating core values?
- Engaging in research and drug trials abroad that do not meet institutional standards for protections of human subjects is another example.

Thinking through such potential conflicts is essential.

Emerging sources of outside funding

There are two emerging sources of outside money worth a special mention: (a) public–private partnerships; (b) funding from abroad or from supra-national organizations such as the British Council or the EU.

Partly as a result of globalization, the private sector is increasingly engaged and connected abroad for business as well as other reasons. We mentioned earlier trends in the privatization of higher education (both growth in private institutions and enrollments in them) as well as the emergence of private-like forces in public higher education (see Chapter 2).

In many countries there are also public–private partnerships to build certain institutional capacities on a contractual basis or on a fee-basis (for profit or not-for profit basis). Private vendors of many kinds are offering contractual services from recruitment, to operating "bridge" programs, to offering certain kinds of academic programming (for example language learning) in both public and private institutions. The vendors invest up front to build institutional capacity and will achieve payback from revenues, usually on a shared basis. In effect they become a source of investment for certain internationalization activities.

The second trend is looking outside the home country for money. As economies strengthen globally, the proportionate growth in international sources of funds from previously less developed countries and regions may exceed funding growth in developed countries and regions. This global economic growth translates into a myriad of funding opportunities abroad. Three contemporary examples come to mind:

- Many institutions when thinking about opening branch campuses or other forms of presence abroad have found that governments and corporations in host countries are willing to invest and partner. This is similarly an option when thinking about development work in a host country, or in providing technical assistance for a variety of purposes.
- International alumni are becoming prime prospects for development fund-raising. Keeping in touch with international alumni in positive ways can cultivate their later generosity. There have been numerous examples of international alumni contributing millions and tens of millions to their alma maters.
- Another cross-border opportunity for funding arises from the fact that cutting-edge teaching, research, and service capacity is rapidly developing elsewhere in the world along with the money to support it. Partnering with those capacities can strengthen home capacities.

Cross-border programming will increasingly be funded from cross-border partnerships and the cross-border blending of resources. Examples include: cross-border dual and joint degree programs and other forms of cross-border collaborative curriculum; pooling research expertise in cutting-edge areas; engaging problem-solving or development abroad that connects to grants from global bodies (e.g., the World Bank), host-country sources and matching funds from your institution.

Summary

This chapter has emphasized several strategies and tactics for accessing the funding needed to support internationalization. The most important is to think about an integrated strategy that combines building a campus culture to support internationalization coupled to accessing existing campus resources as well as new money.

The importance of having a long-range vision and strategic view, but biting off projects and resource needs in "manageable pieces" has also been emphasized. A diversified and multi-sourced revenue strategy is essential. CI will need multiple sources of support (revenue diversification) for success. And, different kinds of internationalization projects will naturally attract different kinds of funding.

Building an institutional support structure for internationalization can take time, but getting started early is important as is building a level of understanding among potential partners within the institution that internationalization will advantage their core responsibilities. Success breeds replication. When people see concrete and hopefully valued results from one set of actions and expenditures, they are more inclined to think that more will get more.

Note

1 Portions of materials in this chapter are based on previous work and Power Point presentations made at various conferences by the author, also in Hudzik and McCarthy (2012), and as also in Hudzik and Pynes (2014).

Part II

Institutional case stories

Introduction

Eleven institutions were identified for case stories of how they have approached more strategic and comprehensive forms of internationalization. The eleven institutions vary in terms of region, size, and missions. Some have long institutional histories and others were formed more recently. They vary in their starting points and traditions with respect to institutional internationalization. And most importantly, their case stories reflect the diversity of how institutions come to define and implement more comprehensive and strategic forms of internationalization consistent with individual institutional missions, core values, priorities, and modes of institutional operation. A reading of the case stories will reinforce the view expressed frequently in Part I that there is great diversity in how institutions individually approach more comprehensive and strategic internationalization, but that also there are several common aspirations that can be detected across diversity of means.

Case authors were given a broad-based outline to guide the writing of their respective chapters, but they were also given much latitude to tell individual institutional stories in ways most germane in their judgments. Each was asked to provide a brief overview of the following issues: institutional and environmental context about their institution's internationalization; the institutional vision for internationalization and whether this represents a change and new directions; what key actions have been undertaken in moving forward, and with what results; and prospects and lessons for the future.

Organization of Part II

In the pages that follow, each case story is presented in a separate chapter. The last chapter of Part II and the book, Chapter 18, blends and summarizes key themes from Part I with a sample of findings from Part II.

Chapter 8

Beloit College

Internationalization in the American Midwest

Elizabeth Brewer

On a March Saturday morning, students, faculty, and staff gather on the Beloit College campus to read and analyze essays by returned study-abroad students. Intended to facilitate reflection and meaning-making, the essays also become the basis for assessing learning outcomes. This morning's task is to look for evidence that study abroad is furthering two of Beloit's goals: the development of life-long learning skills, and the ability to contribute positively to a diverse society. Findings from the workshop will inform a range of activities aimed at strengthening study-abroad learning outcomes: advising, messaging about study abroad, outreach to academic departments, and curriculum and faculty development.

The workshop will also encourage ownership of study abroad, for while an Office of international Education is charged with facilitating internationalization, Beloit's internationalization is a shared enterprise. In fact, on the strength of this shared ownership, Beloit received NAFSA's Simon Award for Comprehensive Internationalization in 2011.

How did a modestly resourced, liberal arts college[1] of 1,250 students in a small city in the American Midwest come to lay claim to an international identity? The story begins shortly after the College's founding.

First impulses: 1846–1959

By charter, "religious tenets or opinions" and attendance at religious services could not be a requirement for teaching and studying at Beloit College (Council and House of Representatives of the Territory of Wisconsin 1846). Nonetheless, the early College was shaped by its members' Christianity. Indeed, its founding by New England pioneers was motivated by a Christian missionary drive to spread civilization through education.

Unsurprisingly then, the College's nascent internationalization began when alumni became missionaries in countries "in need of American instruction and assistance" (Hoffa 2007). In this, the College followed trends in American higher education of the time: a desire to bring American undergraduate education to non-European countries, while looking to Europe to fill in gaps in American higher education at the graduate level. Edward Dwight Eaton, Beloit College's second president, observing Beloit missionary alumni serving in China, proudly noted in 1898 that

> A very few days in P'ang Chuang [. . .] could not fail to give anyone a new impression of the wide zones of influence of Beloit College, and [. . .] the splendid way in which Beloit ideals are worked out into practical expression all around the world.
>
> (Siegel 1992, p. 11)[2]

Conversely, as early as 1867, Beloit graduates traveled to Europe for further education; some returned to join Beloit's faculty ranks (Siegel 1992, p. 12).

Initial reciprocity

Even as Beloit's alumni, faculty, and students felt superior to much of the world, the world began to penetrate the College. Missionary alumni returned to lecture about countries and peoples encountered, wrote about these in books and letters read on campus, and arranged for local youth to attend Beloit. The campus newspaper featured country-specific articles, students debated questions of race and nationality, and gifts of objects helped establish anthropology and art museums. The curriculum internationalized slowly, however: French and German were added in 1858, but otherwise modern and non-Western worlds remained largely absent.

Then, in 1924, Beloit College Dean George Collie ignited debate across the United States by proposing to solve the world's "racial" problems. If 60 percent of the College's students came from abroad, the resulting clash of viewpoints would "shake each one out of his preconceived opinions and his more or less provincial views."[3] The college curriculum would be modified to include a focus on "problems associated with race and race relationships" so that "the representatives of the varied nationalities [. . .] could give expression to their national hopes and desires" (Collie 1924). No longer would American voices be held superior.

Opinion beyond Beloit doubted the plan could work, although some thought it should be tried. At Beloit College, the president proposed moving slowly. A brochure for international students was published, and in 1930, trustees ruled that college funds could support study abroad for one junior per year. The depression, World War II, and other challenges prevented the College from taking further steps until the late 1950s, and neither the composition of the student body nor the curriculum significantly changed in the intervening years. Now, however, broad-based discussions would result in a multi-pronged internationalization plan.

Commitment

What next? Several years of discussion led to a 1960 call to bring "the world to Beloit College" so students would understand the "interrelationships and interdependence of the aims and aspirations of the nations of the world" (Beloit College 1960a). Echoing Collie's earlier vision, now a Beloit education would be "specifically designed to produce enlightened citizens [. . .] more fully *aware* of man's common store of knowledge and thought, the interrelationships and interdependence of the aims and aspirations of the nations of the world" (Murray 1960).[4]

Already in 1942, Midwestern faculty and students had met at Beloit to discuss international affairs, and by 1958, programs in Russian Studies and International Relations were on the way. The curriculum would continue to internationalize, the number of international faculty and students increase, and study abroad grow. A new World Affairs Center coordinated activities and a grant helped create a language laboratory. Faculty-led seminars traveled to Belgium, France, Spain, and Taiwan.

More radically, the 1964 Beloit Plan called for all students to spend one or more terms off-campus. By 1970, 100 students were studying abroad. When the Plan was abandoned,[5] numbers dropped; in 1983, fewer than 40 students studied abroad. To continue keep its internationalization commitment, Beloit offered 10 days of language instruction during new student orientation. Today, a center offers an intensive summer language program.

In 1989, the first full-time director of the World Affairs Center arrived. Faculty-led seminars began to give way to exchange programs, and study-abroad numbers grew once more. Exchanges brought benefits: institutional partnerships, increased international-student enrollments, lower study-abroad costs, and a diversification of study-abroad opportunities. However, as faculty involvement decreased, international education came to be equated with student mobility: study-abroad and international-student enrollments. Ironically, the appointment of a full-time director had led to a waning of campus-wide ownership of internationalization, and the College's early foray into international education threatened to become "a handicap resulting in a lack of innovation" (Jones & de Wit 2014, p. 28).

Internationalization at home

In 2001, Beloit College adopted a new strategic plan. International education was to remain a core component of the college mission. New targets were set for international-student enrollments (12 percent) and study abroad (60 percent),[6] and an additional hire in international relations was anticipated. Although the plan discussed international education in terms of numbers, questions about "why," "how," and "so what" demanded to be addressed, and to find answers, the College joined the Internationalization Collaborative of the American Council on Education (ACE). The new collaborative hoped to move institutions away from discrete international activities toward comprehensive internationalization, a "process of infusing an international, intercultural or global dimension into the purpose, functions, or delivery of postsecondary education" (Knight 2003) that also "shapes institutional ethos and values" (Hudzik 2011, p. 1).

In this, the ACE and its collaborative were responding to a similar recognition in Europe that the international mobility of some students and faculty members was neither significantly impacting teaching and learning at home institutions, nor creating institutional structures to support international and multicultural engagement. The European response was a call for Internationalization at Home (IaH), an integrated approach involving the entire institution (Nilsson & Otten 2003).

At Beloit, there were concerns about changes to current practice. Faculty members in area studies and modern languages worried these would erode and study abroad would weaken, if international education became more inclusive. Faculty members in other disciplines wondered about their roles: what could they contribute when the principles they taught applied regardless of national borders and language? How was international education, and study abroad more particularly, relevant to their students?

Five strategies helped Beloit College move beyond fears toward shared ownership of internationalization.

Campus conversations

To help the campus avoid a potential impasse, Dean David Burrows took interdisciplinary teams to Internationalization Collaborative meetings to discuss the whys and hows of comprehensive internationalization. On campus, three annual, day-long faculty conferences were devoted to the topic. With international education at Beloit strongly associated with study-abroad and international-student enrollments, questions focused on their educational outcomes. Also addressed were the international education of non-mobile students, the role of faculty members in delivering international education, and structures supporting international education.

The mandate of the Office of International Education[7] broadened from supporting international students and study abroad to facilitating campus internationalization; the charge to its faculty oversight committee similarly changed. Next, an international education mission statement was adopted that did not privilege any discipline, instead calling for all Beloit graduates to

> understand their own identity and their relationship to others; be sensitive to commonalities and differences among and within cultures; have the ability to understand multiple perspectives; be knowledgeable about global forces, both human and physical; understand how their status and actions impact others; and contribute responsibly to humane and positive change.
>
> (Beloit College 2002)

Equip the faculty

Beloit College is a teaching institution. However, students can only receive an international education if faculty members are equipped to deliver it. Equipping the faculty, therefore, has been a central strategy, and its success has rested on "faculty ownership, choice, and support," its integration with "other internationalization strategies," and the inclusion of an ever-expanding "circle of engaged faculty" (Green & Olson 2003, p. 78).

International faculty development at Beloit College operates at three levels: (1) informational (receipt of information about international education facts, developments, and priorities in briefings and written materials); (2) activities that inform advising and may contribute perspectives to teaching (study-abroad site visits, participation in workshops, service on the international education committee); and (3) curriculum development (extended workshops and seminars). Level 1 activities reach most if not all faculty members. Over 50 percent of the faculty have participated in level 2 and 3 activities, with level 2 activities generally by invitation, and level 3 activities by application.

Activities at all three levels encourage a campus climate supportive of internationalization, but level 2 and 3 activities are most impactful. As one participant reported, they have "led me to develop courses, write essays, forge better relationships with colleagues, and continue to be the sort of learner that I want to model for my students." Further, 98 percent of respondents to a survey reported that faculty development activities significantly impacted their understanding of international education at Beloit College; 100 percent reported that the activities influenced their teaching and advising, and increased their understanding of study abroad (Brewer 2013).

Two examples can illustrate the scope of activities, their intersection with other internationalization efforts, and the implications for student learning.

Under the *Cities in Transition Project*,[8] initiated by faculty in 2008, students at selected exchange sites take courses taught via the internet and Skype by faculty members in Beloit. The project responded to a problem: students had a hard time leaving the veranda (see Ogden 2007). Learning goals and experiential learning methods were developed in workshops, and students studying in China, Ecuador, and Russia now take Cities courses. A Japanese Cities course comes on line in fall 2014.

As a result, students now leave the veranda to engage with their host sites, and an extended project of each student's choosing encourages connections between the students' interests and their host cities. Thus, a Moscow in Transition project enabled one student to combine his passions for soccer, Russian, and international relations. His language skills and his knowledge of Russia and its people grew steeply, and the project became the basis for his senior capstone paper.

Through the Cities Project, faculty members are once more directly involved with learning during study abroad. They are also more comfortable with experiential learning methods. Additionally, the project has led to other curricular innovations on campus, benefiting students who do not study abroad, and exchange partnerships are stronger.

The *Caribbean Initiative* emerged from faculty desire to teach about the Caribbean. A campus fund supported visits by experts on Jamaica and Cuba and a workshop on conceptions of the Caribbean. In a second stage, the College's

Weissberg Program in Human Rights supported a year-long, three-stage Cuba project: fall semester seminar, January visit to Cuba, and spring semester course development. A joint publication on teaching about Cuba is in the planning, and a new course on the history of Cuba–US relations will soon launch, along with modifications to other courses. The project is being disseminated to the campus, and opportunities for study abroad in Cuba are being explored.

Study abroad: intention and integration

In Beloit's first formal forays into study abroad, faculty members helped students prepare, accompanied them abroad, and taught a follow-up seminar upon return. Resource intensive and limited in disciplinary focus, this form of study abroad eventually gave way to unaccompanied study abroad. With faculty members no longer directly guiding study abroad, desired and actual learning outcomes became unclear. Reinstating faculty-led study abroad was not the solution given prohibitive costs, faculty time constraints, and the desire to make study abroad possible in every major.

Instead, in a series of steps, learning goals were adopted, an annual International Symposium established to share the study-abroad experience, the study-abroad application changed to emphasize planning and connections to on-going studies, reflective essays replaced a study-abroad satisfaction survey, and learning outcomes began to be assessed. The Cities and other projects connected faculty members to study abroad in new ways.

Today, study abroad is understood as integral to students' studies, and an experience that can help them grow and learn in ways not possible on the Beloit campus. Its potential is better understood. Thus, instead of "Let her go, hopefully she'll get something out of it," today a student's study-abroad application will be met with "What else can he do before and after to get the most out of it?"

Support for international students

George Collie not only wanted to bring more international students to Beloit, he wanted American students to pay attention to them; Beloit's international students were "lonely figures in college life, without influence" (Collie 1924). He presciently understood that the mere presence of international students would not guarantee cultural exchange, something others have belatedly concluded (Brewer & Leask 2012, p. 252).

Beloit invests to help ensure international-student success: financial aid is generous; international students can take full advantage of the College's offerings, including study abroad; ESL courses ease adjustment to US culture and academic life; a host family program provides a glimpse into American family life; and faculty members take both degree and non-degree international students seriously. Indeed, an exchange student was astonished to be appointed a teaching assistant in her second, final semester on campus. The Office of International Education works hard to make international students feel at home, but it takes the larger campus and area community to do so.

High-impact programming

Nearly daily, an international event—lecture, performance, exhibit, film—takes place on the Beloit College campus. However, it is high-impact programming that contributes most successfully to campus internationalization, and the Weissberg Program in Human Rights exemplifies this. Centered around the annual residency of a leading advocate for human rights, the Weissberg Program not only highlights a particular issue each year, but brings students into contact with practitioners, expands faculty members' knowledge and teaching capacities through reading groups and faculty development activities, and, through job-shadowing and grants for independent study projects, gives students hands-on experience. Synergies are found with other campus programming, alumni return to campus to share their insights, and public events engage community members. High-impact programming not only brings the world to Beloit, but helps prepare students to contribute to the world.

Final lessons

Institutional "transformation 1) alters the culture of the institution by changing underlying assumptions and overt institutional behaviors, processes and structures; 2) is deep and pervasive, affecting the whole institution; 3) is intentional, and 4) occurs over time" (Eckel *et al.* 2001, p. 5). Further, transformative change, spans the academic program, budget, and self-image (Heyl 2007). This case study discusses Beloit College's transformation, over many decades, from domestic and regional to international. Some final lessons:

- *Make international engagement visible.* At Beloit, study abroad became stronger when an annual International Symposium was created in 2002 to allow returned students to discuss and reflect on their experiences. Other students received inspiration to plan their own study abroad, while faculty members paid more attention to helping students prepare for and build on study-abroad experiences. The study-abroad application was modified to encourage more intention. Today, study abroad is an "integrated part of an educational sequence of student experiences" (Twombly *et al.* 2013, p. 113).
- *Deploy resources strategically, adopt wise policies.* At Beloit, international students receive the same kinds of scholarships as domestic students, and financial aid applies to study abroad. Exchanges, direct enrollment, and strategic use of provider programs keep study-abroad costs manageable for both students and the College. These policies and practices encourage international-student enrollments, and enable students, no matter their financial resources, to study abroad. Foundations and donors have been enlisted to support internationalization. Strategic use of resources and wise policies matter.

- *Provide evidence of results.* Comprehensive internationalization requires the contributions of many individuals, campus units, and external supporters. But good will is not enough—students, parents, faculty, trustees, and donors want to know that their investment will bear fruit. No matter the activity attached to internationalization, thinking ahead to not only the anticipated outputs (numbers), but the outcomes (capacity-building) will help focus the activity and tell the so-what story.
- *Find synergies and partnerships.* If you work at a college or university campus, you will know that at any one time, competing events and efforts are taking place. Internationalization will require new events and efforts, but should also find synergies with what already exists. Partnerships should be leveraged for collaborative opportunities that advance student learning.
- *Focus on learning, not numbers.* Numbers matter: internationalization requires a critical mass of invested students, staff, and faculty. However, student learning is what is at stake. By focusing on student learning, Beloit College's international program is stronger than it was in 2001, when targets were set to increase international-student and study-abroad enrollments. The targets have yet to be met, but students' international education is richer. "There are so many ways to be "internationalized"' at Beloit College, reported a senior survey respondent.
- *Persist and nurture.* Internationalization is a process, not a product. Think of it as a garden that if nurtured well, will bear rich harvests. Some ideas will fail, but organic methods will ensure long-lasting health and growth. Outside ideas will be helpful, but will need to be adapted to local conditions and aims. Cultivating a garden requires patience, steadfastness, creativity, faith, and regular tending. So does internationalization.

Notes

1 The liberal arts college arose in the early United States where, according to a Yale College report, a "republican form of government render[ed] it highly important, that great numbers should enjoy the advantage of a thorough education" (Committee of the Corporation and Academic Faculty 1828). To support democratization, education should prepare graduates not for specific professions, but for life-long learning, and residential campuses would foster close interactions among students as well as between students and faculty. Today, students study the humanities, natural sciences/mathematics, and social sciences, while a major allows for some specialization. A small segment of the US higher education, liberal arts colleges have had a disproportionate influence in terms of their graduates' contributions to society. Beloit College was modeled on Yale.
2 Beloit alumni were instrumental in establishing and leading Doshisha Academy (now Doshisha University) in Japan, Tarsus College (later Tarsus American College) in Turkey, and Robert College (now Bogazici University) in Turkey. Hoffa (2007) argues that this is where American missionaries had greatest impact.
3 At the time, 90 percent of Beloit students came from Wisconsin and Illinois, with the remaining 10 percent coming from elsewhere in the United States, China, Japan, and Persia (Burwell 2011). Beloit College admitted its first female students in 1895, although Collie's use of pronouns does not make this clear.

4 Students countered that awareness was not enough. They needed the intellectual skills to "approach social and political problems" (Beloit College 1960b), anticipating a current emphasis on applying the liberal arts.

5 Under the plan, the curriculum was offered over fall, winter, and summer terms, and faculty members taught in two out of three terms. Faculty governance became problematic with one third of the faculty absent in any given term, while staff members, who worked year round, had no time to catch up or plan.

6 At the time, these percentages were 11 percent and 45 percent.

7 Formerly the World Affairs Center.

8 The Cities in Transition Project was noted in NAFSA's Simon Award citation.

Chapter 9

Embedding internationalization at the University of Helsinki

Markus Laitinen

Internationalization for modern universities and other higher education institutions is considered extremely important, sometimes in a way making it a precondition for their existence. Unfortunately there is often a significant disconnect between the rhetoric and what actually takes place. The following case study looks at the experiences of the University of Helsinki in embedding internationalization in a very dynamic global operating environment. The question worth considering is whether internationalization is too important to be left for an international office.

Background

The University of Helsinki is one of the European pioneer institutions in what is referred to as embedded internationalization. Sometimes this approach is called comprehensive, deep or even mainstreamed internationalization but somehow the verb "to embed" seems to best capture the idea of making internationalization part of all the university's core activities and their support functions. But before describing any of the details of this approach, it will be important to offer some information about the university and its operating environment.

Finland is a relatively small and northern European country. The land area is fairly large but the population is currently at around 5.4 million. During the course of the country's history it was part of the Swedish kingdom and the Russian empire before gaining independence in 1917. Finland has never had colonies or any other significant presence beyond its national borders. Traditionally, and still partly today, Finland has a fairly low number of immigrants. Linguistically, Finnish belongs to the Finno-Ugric languages but the languages within this group are not mutually understandable. All of this poses some challenges to internationalization. For example, there are no significant pools for recruitment of international students or faculty internally or externally. On a more positive side, the level and appreciation of education and research are high compared to other countries and foreign languages, predominantly English, are taught to and spoken by a very large majority of the country.

The University of Helsinki was established in 1640 and for quite a long time it was the only university in the country. Throughout its history it has often been seen as a national flagship institution and still today it is the only provider of certain fields of study in Finland. Having this prestige certainly has positive consequences but when it comes to internationalization, it also presents some challenges because the university is often seen as having a leading role in the preservation of Finnish academic culture, including Finnish as a language of academia.

Since its establishment the University has had, as most likely all universities, internationalization somehow on its agenda. But in a more mass-scale, things started really changing in the late 1980s and early 1990s, culminating in 1995 when Finland became a member of the European Union. At that time, however, internationalization was rather one-dimensional and meant mostly student mobility. And in the very early phase the University was mostly concerned with outbound mobility only. However, with the introduction of courses taught in English the inbound mobility really started picking up in the late 1990s.

Since these times the agenda for internationalization has broadened significantly. First the University became a member of some European university networks and subsequently it started attaching importance to offering English-taught full degree programs at the Master's and Doctoral levels. More recently the University has been attracting more research funding from abroad, and engaging transnational education, Massive Open Online Courses (MOOCs), rankings, active recruitment of international academic staff, branch campuses outside Finland and other forms of presence abroad. These and many other topics have entered the scene. It is safe to say that university internationalization looks very different and much more diverse than 20 years ago.

It would be nice to be able to say that in 2003 the University of Helsinki realized that the world had changed and was changing still and that it needed to adopt a new approach to internationalization. But that statement would be false. Yes, the seeds of embedded internationalization were sown then but this was a result of a more generic change and reorganization of the central administration. The result was, among many other things, a decision to dissolve the central international office and place former office members in teams and offices throughout the organization. Again, this decision really did not come from a careful analysis of how internationalization would be best served. It was only later that the University started to realize that the reorganization really had opened the door for embedding internationalization as opposed to something that would be a responsibility of a single office or a select few.

Key developments in embedding internationalization

When the University of Helsinki first embarked upon the embedded route it operated like most universities still do. It had a central international office dealing with international exchange and mobility and related agreements. It also periodically published an international strategy or an action plan. There was a central committee for internationalization, which discussed various issues related to the

University's international activities and the University community held internationalization in fairly high regard, albeit not very actively. Almost all faculties offered courses in English, mostly aimed at the increasing number of incoming exchange students, although the University already had some 1,000 international degree-seeking students (Figure 9.1).

The first step on the road toward embedding internationalization was the dissolution of the central international office. The staff was placed in different parts of the central administration, mostly with Academic Affairs and Student Services. At around the same time two new people were recruited to reinforce internationalization within Academic Affairs, a unit responsible for the development of teaching and learning at the central level, especially concerning the development of fully English-taught degree programs. These new recruitments later became vital for internationalizing Academic Affairs from within, as they were able to generate interest toward internationalization in a unit which previously was very domestically oriented.

In 2003 the University also put together and confirmed an Action Plan for Internationalization for 2004–2006. This was to become the last such document and since then internationalization has been considered only as an integral part of the University's main strategic documents, such as the Strategy proper and various action plans for the enhancement of teaching and research. Initially this meant including a separate chapter for internationalization in each of these documents, but later on international considerations became more truly embedded strategically.

Today one really has to read the Strategy[1] of the University of Helsinki thoroughly, to fully grasp what role internationalization plays for research, teaching, and

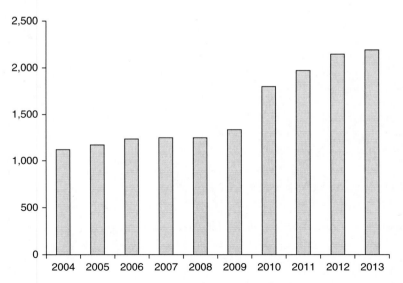

Figure 9.1 Number of international degree students at the University of Helsinki.

engagement. But realizing that the Strategy actually also covers internationalization does not require a magnifying glass or a code book. Among the measures to be taken to reach the University's strategic objectives the following are mentioned: participation in international research infrastructures; improving the recruitment and integration of international students and staff; promotion of bi- and multilingualism; enhancing participation in international exchange programs; these are just a few.

The preparation of the 2004–2006 Action Plan also marked the end of a central Internationalization Committee. The committee was considered somewhat ineffective and redundant in the sense that international issues began to permeate the central committees for the University's core activities and there seemed to be fairly little for the Internationalization Committee to discuss beyond what was covered by the committees for research and teaching respectively. For various reasons the Internationalization Committee also ended up being little more than a discussion group where members mainly represented their own interests, not those of the University as a whole.

One of the ways the University of Helsinki promoted interest in expanding internationalization was through the use of an internal result-based funding instrument. This was first established in the 1990s and faculties were initially rewarded with extra funding, first for their output of international student exchange and later also for the number of Master's and Doctoral degrees completed by international students. At first this instrument was very effective, much beyond the sum of money involved, as becomes clear from Figure 9.2.

In the end, most faculties earmarked this money and invested it back into their own support measures for internationalization. But as embedding gained ground,

Figure 9.2 Student exchange in selected programs.

it was realized that an instrument which, on the surface, seemed to support inter-nationalization mainly managed to marginalize it, as faculties were disinclined to take up international activities beyond those included in the instrument's indicators. Thus, by 2007 this internal funding instrument was discontinued.

Another milestone on the road toward embedding internationalization also took place in 2007. It is rather curious that even though research has always been considered international, the word "internationalization" and activities of "international office" seem to refer mostly to issues related to teaching and edu-cation. Similarly, the services that are considered normal for incoming exchange and degree-seeking students are often lacking for incoming academic staff. This was also the case for the University of Helsinki, until a decision was reached to establish a central service to facilitate the arrival and integration of members of academic staff from abroad. Before this, only one or two internationally active research units had dedicated personnel to advise and offer services for new inter-national research and teaching staff. Elsewhere, things were handled ad hoc and case-by-case, which lead to inefficiencies and unprofessionally provided services.

As the numbers of international academic staff gained strategic importance for the university, and as the numbers started to grow quite rapidly all over the University, the pressure mounted to improve the services. At this time, the Uni-versity no longer had an international office where the new service unit could be placed, so the only real alternative was to establish it as part of the Personnel Office. Similarly to Academic Affairs described above, the Personnel Department had previously had a very domestic outlook, but through the establishment of "International Staff Services"[2] things started to change both for the department itself and for the University as a whole. Currently the number of non-Finnish academics is more than 20 percent.

International university networks started to appear in Europe some 20–25 years ago and initially they were mostly a response to issues related to intra-European student mobility. Things have certainly changed since then, but the appearance of a new network established in 2002 really started changing the picture for the Uni-versity of Helsinki. The League of European Research Universities (LERU)[3] was initially a club of leading European universities' Rectors and Vice-Chancellors and mainly aimed to become influential as a lobbyist on the members behalf toward the European Commission and others involved with European research funding. This still remains central for LERU, but over the years benchmarking and other collaboration among the member universities has increased significantly.

Today there are various communities and other groupings within LERU, where the members exchange best practice for issues such as research careers, doctoral training, open access, university communications, donations and alumni-related issues, and research ethics, to name just a few. As a consequence, many people from the University of Helsinki not previously exposed to international cooperation have been required to represent the University in regular meetings. This would not have been possible if this kind of international cooperation would have been allowed to be seen as a responsibility of an "international office." Still today in many universities in Europe and elsewhere something that takes place beyond the national borders gets "dumped" to dedicated office or unit for internationalization.

Yet another important part of the process of embedding internationalization at the University of Helsinki is the so-called International Staff Exchange Week (ISEW).[4] Since the mobility of non-academic university staff became possible within the Erasmus program in 2007 many European universities started organizing special, dedicated weeks instead of just receiving individual visitors. Helsinki was no exception in doing so, but the approach chosen was different from most others. Whereas most of these weeks were organized by international offices and for international officers, the University of Helsinki chose to exclude people with clearly international job descriptions. The reason for this was realization that these people already had ample opportunities for international cooperation and networking.

The Helsinki edition of ISEW invites partner university staff members representing various administrative areas such as financial and personnel administration, university archives, information technology issues, libraries, PR and communications, and many others. There are two distinct advantages with this approach. First, the incoming staff members are often people who have had very few opportunities to travel abroad in a professional capacity. But in addition to this altruistic benefit, receiving visitors in the different sectors of administration requires the hosting units to be able to talk about their work in English, have related documentation also in English and to be overall receptive to internationalization. The experiences have been extremely positive both from the side of visitors but also from the hosts. It is safe to say that as a result of ISEW, the institutional capacity for internationalization has grown tremendously.

The final and latest example of how embedded internationalization has been adopted at the University of Helsinki is the Teachers' Academy,[5] which is intended to be the University's institutional boost for the promotion of teaching and learning. It consists of individual teachers from different disciplines from humanities to natural sciences interested in promoting teaching at the individual, departmental, and institutional levels. The Academy was first formed in 2012 and one of the first working groups thereunder deals with internationalization of teaching and learning. This group is working toward designing high-quality courses meeting the expectations of international students, with the aim to increase the interest level worldwide in the University's research-based education as well as establishing international teaching cooperation through joint courses and by offering courses at partner universities. It also seeks to explore various options in transnational education in order to promote the Finnish pedagogical methods.

It needs to be pointed out that none of the working groups was dictated from above, but they were all self-organized. The creation of the internationalization working group, therefore, is a testament of the chosen teachers', as well as the University's, dedication toward internationalization.

Through no longer having a dedicated office, strategy, or central committee for internationalization the University of Helsinki has, as demonstrated by the examples above, been able to demonstrate its continued commitment to internationalization on a broad front.

Success factors and benefits of embedded internationalization

In September 2013 the University of Helsinki was given an award by the European Association for International Education (EAIE).[6] The application for the award was the first written document to describe the University's approach to embedded internationalization. Until then the ten-year process had been mostly practically oriented. In addition to describing the various aspects of embedding, the application also listed four key words as the success factors, which were excellence, cooperation, communication, and embedding. These words encapsulate the essence of embedded internationalization for the University of Helsinki.

Excellence, for a university aiming to be one of the top-50 universities in the world, is in many ways a precondition for everything it does. This is also the case for international activities, and everything the University does internationally should contribute to its strategic goals. In the past, the focus was on expanding partnerships and increasing the numbers, but through embedding, all the necessary qualitative aspects will receive deserved attention. Even though international rankings and league tables have been of some interest to the University, the more important aspects of excellence are thought to include the quality of recruited academics and the conditions the university can offer for them in terms of services and infrastructure. Rising in the rankings is very much a secondary consideration.

Where no central international office exists, cooperation and constant attention to internal and external communication will be required. The risk with embedded internationalization is that different players start pulling in their own directions, rather than finding synergies and working together. This can be prevented by creating joint activities in which actors from different parts of the organization come together to create added value. Relatively simple things like joint meetings, e-mail lists, and creating common visibility in the internet are very important in keeping the actors on the same page. It is crucial that even though there is no single office for internationalization, experts and services are easily locatable without an intimate knowledge of the University's organizational chart. The University of Helsinki, for example, has a dedicated website,[7] which looks like a regular international office website but actually consists of contributions by actors in various parts of the organization.

Even if the University no longer has an international office, it has a small, two-person unit called International Affairs, and the author of this chapter is one of the those two. The main responsibility of International Affairs is to maintain overall coordination of the University's many international activities and to chair related meetings. An important aspect of this work is also facilitating cooperation regarding issues which are not the responsibility of any single unit. It would be too simplistic to say that working in International Affairs is just like heading an international office anywhere minus the direct supervisory responsibilities for finance and personnel.

So far, the University of Helsinki has seen many clear benefits from embedding internationalization. One of the main benefits may be called the "Contamination Factor," which refers to the idea that by placing international actors in formerly domestically oriented units, internationalization spreads more easily throughout the University. The consequence of this is that by involving people not previously engaged internationally, it is possible to add resources toward internationalization while not increasing staff numbers correspondingly.

Through embedding internationalization it is also possible to extract and make use of expertise from others, e.g. marketing and service development are more readily available for Internationalization and does not have to be regenerated or reinvented in an office. Institutionally the embedded approach results in internationalization receiving a broader recognition and a sense of participation and ownership throughout the University. In the experience of the University of Helsinki new developments in internationalization, such as HR issues, rankings, transnational education, MOOCs, etc. become more easily adopted and receive appropriate attention in the embedded model.

It is worth repeating that for the University of Helsinki the road toward embedding did not start immediately or in a uniform way. Different parts of the University, especially within the central administration, have had significant differences in the pace with which they have committed themselves to internationalization, and in many respects this is still work in progress. It may be possible to take a different route and to start embedding overnight. A more cautious approach is perhaps less prone to internal resistance, and in hindsight this seems to have been one of the success factors for the Helsinki model to work.

Conclusions and the road ahead

Even with ten years of experience in embedding internationalization the University of Helsinki is not finished with the process, quite the contrary. It almost feels like it has reached a stage where the beginning is ending. Almost by definition, embedding internationalization is never complete. As the world and the operating environment of the University constantly change, new features keep being added to the internationalization agenda and the University needs to adapt and respond to these.

Looking at any given statistic, the University of Helsinki may not be the most internationalized university in the world. But what sets it apart from many other higher education institutions is that it is not restricted in its internationalization efforts by the size and scope of its international office. The understanding that internationalization is the responsibility of everyone has quite clearly spread at the University; no longer can anything and everything that could be labelled "international" be considered the responsibility of only a limited number of dedicated experts.

What are the next challenges to be faced, then? If the end of the beginning of embedded internationalization has been reached, where is the process taking us next? One of the most obvious challenges will be language, and especially the English language. The increasing numbers of international academic staff, currently at 20 percent, and students require the University of Helsinki to pay close attention to issues related to integration. And the extent to which information and services are provided in English is not a simple thing to resolve, especially because the University also has two official languages, Finnish and Swedish. On one hand, the University has the strategic aim to be included among the top-50 universities in the world, and this will require even more international faculty and students on campus, not because of any ranking indicators, but because without having the absolutely best talent available the strategic goal will remain unfulfilled. But on the other hand, if the numbers continue to grow at the present rate, the University will have to reconsider the balance between different languages, whether related to teaching or to services. At the moment a revision of an institutional language policy is underway.

Another significant challenge will be to achieve better coordination and synergies between international activities of research and teaching. Until recently these have followed slightly different paths at the University of Helsinki, but one topic, which will require the coordination between the two to be improved, is the establishment of so-called strategic partnerships. As most universities, the University of Helsinki has numerous international agreements and in an effort to have more effective internationalization new kinds of deeper and broader partnerships are being envisioned. And according to current thinking, these would not only have research or educational components but rather both.

The idea of embedded internationalization is already well-established at the University's central level. But there remains a lot to do in other parts of the organization, especially at the level of faculties. Currently they each have one or two administrators dedicated to internationalization and except for a few positive examples to the contrary, these international coordinators often have to work alone and without the full support of the rest of the faculties' staff. One opportunity for changing this is related to a recent reorganization of the University's doctoral education. Four new doctoral schools have been established, and it is quite evident that they will have to embrace internationalization in order to fulfill their mission to produce world-class doctoral education and graduates. Again, if the University is to reach its strategic goals, the whole organization needs, quite clearly, to be involved and feel ownership of internationalization.

In a 2011 article, Uwe Brandenburg and Hans de Wit provocatively announced that the end of internationalization is imminent and suggested that a post-internationalization age may be near (Brandenburg & de Wit 2011a). From the perspective of an institution which follows the embedded internationalization model it is easy to share some of the writers' ideas, especially concerning the fact that internationalization should be seen as a means and not an end in and by itself. However, the idea that internationalization should be somehow at an end does not seem very likely. Universities need to adapt to an ever-changing operating environment, where the internationalization agenda seems to be expanding day by day. By looking at internationalization more broadly and embedding it in the core activities and their support functions, universities are able to face the various challenges in a uniform and consistent way.

Notes

1 http://www.helsinki.fi/strategy/
2 http://www.helsinki.fi/intstaff/
3 http://www.leru.org
4 http://www.helsinki.fi/international-staff-exchange/
5 http://www.helsinki.fi/opettajienakatemia/eng/index.html
6 http://www.eaie.org
7 http://www.helsinki.fi/international

Chapter 10

Strategic internationalization in Sweden

The cases of Lund University and Blekinge Institute of Technology

Hans Pohl and Andreas Göthenberg

This chapter covers two case studies of internationalization at Swedish universities. In an introductory section, the higher education system in Sweden is briefly characterized. Thereafter two sections follow dealing with the cases of Lund University and Blekinge Institute of Technology. Finally, discussions and conclusions follow.

Introduction

Sweden, with approximately 9.5 million inhabitants, is located in Northern Europe. In 2012, there were 47 higher education institutions in Sweden. Like most developed small countries, Sweden has a lot of international collaboration in research (Glänzel 2001). Figure 10.1 shows that the share of international collaboration has been comparatively high with a growing trend.

Sweden offers high-quality higher education with a good average rank but no universities in a top-ten position in global rankings. In terms of research, the citation impact increases, compare Figure 10.2. Field-weighted citation impact (FWCI) is an indicator of mean citation impact, and compares the actual number of citations received by an article with the expected number of citations for articles of the same document type (article, review or conference proceedings paper), publication year and subject field.

In 2010, the Higher Education Act was amended to introduce application and tuition fees for citizens outside the European Economic Area and Switzerland. Higher education institutions were required to charge tuition fees to these students covering the full costs (Swedish National Agency for Higher Education 2011). Even though this change had been discussed for a while, the implementation generated turbulence and discussion. Partly as the number of scholarships available was far lower than the number of international students before the reform, there was a significant drop in the numbers. For example, free-mover students from countries outside the European Economic Area and Switzerland decreased by 79 percent (Swedish National Agency for Higher Education 2012).

STINT, the Swedish Foundation for International Cooperation in Research and Higher Education, was set up as an endowed independent foundation by an act of the Swedish Parliament in 1994. The mission of STINT is to enhance

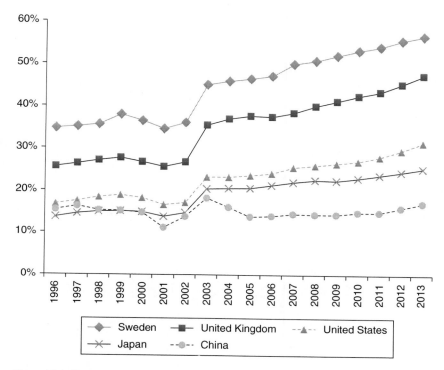

Figure 10.1 Share of international publications for selected countries. (Adapted from SciVal® database, Elsevier B.V., http://www.scival.com downloaded on April 2, 2014.)

the quality and competence of Swedish higher education and research through international cooperation. STINT offers Swedish academia a portfolio of various grant and scholarship programs.

One of STINT's experiences in over 15 years of promoting internationalization has been a keen demand for funding for individual researchers to conduct international projects. Almost all funding from STINT has been used for these types of activities, even though there was an aim to foster a more institutional type of international collaboration. A study of university presidents' positions in terms of internationalization revealed them to be quite interested, albeit weak in terms of actual management power and ambition to drive institutional change, particularly as related to forging international research collaborations and institutional partnerships (Göthenberg *et al.* 2012).

In the light of this, STINT's Strategic Grants for Internationalization program was launched. Its aim was to contribute to the renewal and development of internationalization strategies at university level. The first call closed at the end of March 2012. Out of 47 theoretically eligible university presidents, 20 submitted

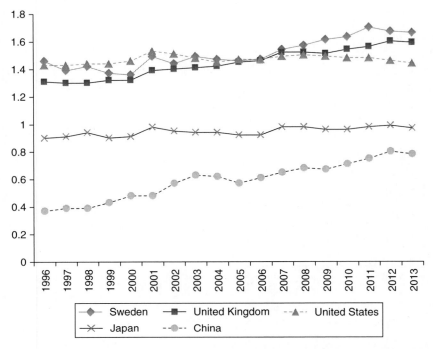

Figure 10.2 FWCI for selected countries. (Adapted from SciVal® database, Elsevier B.V., http://www.scival.com downloaded on April 2, 2014.)

a total of 31 proposals. The proposals were reviewed by an international panel of internationalization experts and in June 2012, five applications were granted funding. In the following two sections, two of these five strategic initiatives are described and related to the institutional internationalization vision and strategy.

Lund University and Swedish Excellence Seminars

Basic facts about Lund University

Lund University is a comprehensive higher education institution with 47,000 students and some 7,200 faculty and staff. It was founded in 1666 with the main campus in Lund in southern Sweden. In terms of publications and citations, Lund University is number two in Sweden. In a global perspective, it ranked number 71 in QS World University Rankings 2012 and 82 in Times Higher Education World University Rankings 2012 (Lund University 2013). Following the tuition fee reform, the share of international students starting at Lund University decreased from 34 to 31 percent between the years 2010 and 2011 (Swedish National Agency for Higher Education 2012).

Table 10.1 Lund University's international research collaborators

Institution	Country	Co-authored publications	Field-weighted citation impact
University of Copenhagen	Denmark	1,273	3.17
University of Aarhus	Denmark	651	3.05
University of Oxford	United Kingdom	611	4.98
University of Helsinki	Finland	541	5.15
Harvard University	United States	534	5.76
Imperial College London	United Kingdom	502	4.83
University of Cambridge	United Kingdom	498	6.46
Utrecht University	Netherlands	471	4.62
University of Bergen	Norway	470	4.05
Stanford University	United States	456	4.41

Adapted from SciVal® database, Elsevier B.V., http://www.scival.com (downloaded February 21, 2014).

In 2010, the construction of the synchrotron radiation facility MAX IV Laboratory began, and the world's most powerful neutron source ESS is also under construction in Lund as a European research facility. Lund University is Sweden's most active participant in EU framework programs. In Table 10.1, the top-ten international research collaborators during the period 2009–2013 are presented. FWCI for Lund University was 1.80 for the same period and all most prolific international collaborations have significantly higher FWCI. The share of international co-publications was 56.4 percent.

Internationalization vision and strategy

In the introduction of the internationalization policy of Lund University, it is stated that the ultimate aim of internationalization is to enhance the quality of research and education and sharpen the competitive edge of the university. The overall vision for Lund University is "[a] world-class university that works to understand, explain and improve our world and the human condition" (Lund University 2012:4). This is a substantial shift compared to the previous vision that was to become one of the premier universities in Europe (Lund University 2007). Lund University has increased its ambitions and moved from a European to a global context.

Internationalization is one of the four strategies leading towards the goal with highest quality in education, research, innovation and interaction with society. It is stated that internationalization is one of the strengths of the university. Cross-boundary collaboration, diversity and mutual understanding are essential to meet the global societal challenges. Specific attention is given to recruitment of students: "In particular, we need to work to recruit students from countries outside Europe in order to achieve diversity among the students that better reflects the diversity of the world" (Lund University 2012: 8).

In the last available internationalization policy from 2007, three internationalization goals are presented for education, research education, research and administration. Lund University shall be an international environment with international perspectives integrated in all activities. It should prioritize long-term relations and strategic networks and continuously monitor and ensure the quality of the internationalization activities (Lund University 2007). These goals are detailed in an action plan (Lund University 2010).

In one external evaluation of the university's internationalization policy, it is stated that there is a need for a policy even though the ultimate goal is to integrate internationalization in all activities and processes. It is also emphasized that there is a need for a more pronounced leadership of the internationalization process (Rindefjäll 2010).

In 2013, the internationalization director position was created and a vice president/deputy vice chancellor for internationalization was appointed. Previously the responsibilities for student mobility and recruitment, and strategic collaborations were handled by different persons and the pro-vice chancellor represented the leadership of the university in internationalization issues.

Towards the end of 2013, the production of a new internationalization policy was initiated. The old one expired in 2011. Several aspects contributed to the late start; among them, there was a need to analyze the consequences of the tuition fee reform. It was also discussed to what extent research, entrepreneurship and innovation should be a part of the new internationalization policy. Current status is that the forthcoming internationalization policy will cover all missions.

As the strategic plan clearly includes internationalization issues, it was also discussed if there was a need for an internationalization policy or rather an updated action plan. An internationalization policy is being made following a bottom-up process with the ambition to have it decided in the fall 2014.

Geographically, the strategy of Lund University in 2007 was to expand the cooperation with the Middle East, South-East and Southern Asia and the Far East in addition to the continuation of already established long-term relationships with universities in Europe and North America (Lund University 2007). Since then, the geographical focus has gradually widened to include additional countries and regions such as Brazil and Latin America, Africa, and Indonesia. As indicated in Table 10.1, the main research collaborations are very much in the Anglo-Saxon world.

According to the internationalization director, the upcoming strategy at Lund University will encompass more marketing and student recruitment activities, in particular in relation to developing regions such as several countries in Africa. However, this increase will not be at the expense of other internationalization efforts. Diversity and the global classroom is another aspect that probably will be emphasized in the new strategy. The vice-chancellor has indicated a goal of 20 percent international students, which might be included as a long-term goal in the strategy. Today, Lund University has approximately 11 percent international students.[1]

Swedish Excellence Seminars

In March 2012, Lund University applied to STINT's Strategic Grants. The application described a project encompassing four Swedish Excellence Seminars, two in Brazil and two in Russia over a period of two years. The seminars were to be organized together with local Swedish embassies. Guests from the community, including industry representatives, education and research ministries, university partners, scholarship organizations, Swedish businesses active in these regions and other businesses with ties to Sweden would be invited.

The first day of each seminar would cover a presentation of Swedish higher education, Swedish excellence in education and research, a presentation of Lund University and some selected research findings with a focus on environment and sustainability. The second day would basically be an alumni gathering.

The purpose of the proposed project was to make Swedish higher education better known while also strengthening the university's international competitiveness and brand. Both countries were considered of great interest for the recruitment of fee-paying students.

The STINT reviewers were convinced by the application and the following quote is from one of them:

> Though limited in scope, the proposed activities are likely to have a high impact and multiple benefits for the University and its region. When I saw the title of the project, I was skeptical, but as I read the proposal I was impressed with its clever simplicity and innovative character. This is a high impact high visibility project.

The longer-term plans for the project according to the application were to engage in similar activities in further countries. It was also mentioned that discussions with Uppsala University about collaboration had taken place.

Results and lessons learned

At an early stage in the project, Lund University approached STINT to discuss a change from Russia to another country. It was agreed to replace Russia by Taiwan and China.

The first seminar took place in São Paulo, Brazil, in December 2012. The second was held in Taipei, Taiwan in October 2013. Both these seminars were organized close to the original concept outlined in the application. However, a number of additional activities were also carried out during the period in Brazil, among them three bilateral meetings with Brazilian universities (Jensen 2013).

After the successful first seminar in Brazil, Lund University invited other Swedish universities to join the second seminar (at their own cost). This second seminar was organized in November 2013 in conjunction with other events. One of them was a roadshow with eight Swedish universities within the framework of Science without Borders. Moreover, a Nobel exhibition was inaugurated by the King of Sweden, together with a large Swedish delegation. The Swedish Excellence Seminar included researchers and vice-chancellors from five Swedish universities (Eriksson 2013). In spring 2014, a fourth and, within this project, final seminar will take place in China.

Given the novelty of this type of activity for Swedish universities, a few things have been adjusted during the course of the project. One lesson learned was that long presentations by researchers during the seminars were not ideal. Instead, more interaction and dialogue would be more efficient to create new relationships and hands-on results. This led to a changed format of the seminar, with more emphasis on smaller meetings before, during and after the seminar days.

As already indicated in the application, Lund University was prepared to invite other Swedish universities to the seminars. This materialized in the November 2013 seminar in Brazil. All participating universities were very satisfied with this event and at the time of writing (February 2014), an even larger group of Swedish universities are investigating possibilities to collaborate in further seminars in selected countries.

The intensified activities in Brazil have already been recognized and during a large EU–Brazil meeting in Brussels in February 2014, Lund University was the only HEI forwarded by the European Commission as a good example of how to develop the collaboration with Brazil.

Blekinge Institute of Technology and international students "in real life" at BTH

Basic facts about Blekinge Institute of Technology

Blekinge Institute of Technology (BTH) is a young and small university in southern Sweden. It has 7,200 students and 500 staff and faculty members. Bachelors and masters level education account for two thirds of its activities. The total share of international students starting in 2010 was 49 percent. The following year when

Table 10.2 BTH's international collaborators

Institution	Country	Co-authored publications	Field-weighted citation impact
Trinity College Dublin	Ireland	22	1.26
University of Bern	Switzerland	16	4.72
Moscow State University	Russian Federation	16	0.51
University of Washington	United States	16	4.72
University of New South Wales	Australia	15	0.91
RAS	Russian Federation	13	0.16
Suranaree University of Technology	Thailand	10	0.16
Norwegian Institute of Technology	Norway	10	2.71
RAS – General Physics Institute	Russian Federation	10	0.31
Osaka University	Japan	9	0.89

Adapted from SciVal® database, Elsevier B.V., http://www.scival.com (downloaded February 21, 2014).

tuition fees applied the share decreased to 26 percent. The decrease in incoming international students was 63 percent (Swedish National Agency for Higher Education 2012).

In Table 10.2, the top-ten international research collaborators during 2009–2013 are presented with FWCI. FWCI for BTH was 1.32 for the same period. The share of co-publications with other countries was 43.1 percent.

Internationalization vision and strategy

BTH's current strategy for internationalization consists of an internationalization policy and an internationalization plan. The policy and the plan have not been updated or renewed for quite some time, as they were both decided in 2007. The current strategy was intended to cover 2007–2009, which means that there has been no strategy formulated for the time from 2009 (BTH 2007a, 2007b). However, a new internationalization strategy is intended to be decided in spring 2014.

Its values stipulate that all activities at BTH should be measured by international standards. Furthermore, all research should be planned and carried out in a multicultural and international environment. Finally, the policy says that BTH should have a strong international focus.

The fundamental goals for the internationalization work at BTH are academic quality, meeting employer demands, international solidarity and internationalization as a recruitment tool. More specifically, internationalization should be integrated in the education programs and should be a tool for enhancing the quality of pedagogy. All education and research should be connected to international state-of-the-art research. The education should provide education that corresponds to the demands of the international job market. The university should also develop along the intentions of the Bologna process and strive for a fair and sustainable development.

The internationalization plan is basically a description of the internationalization work and its priority actions. The main thought behind the internationalization work is that each action should benefit several of the fundamental goals that were set in the policy.

During 2007–2009 there was a specific priority on getting students, faculty and staff involved in international mobility and active recruitment of foreign students, but also development of programs and courses with an international focus, as well as an effort to increase the number of double degree programs and cultural diversity.

International students "in real life" at BTH

In late March 2012, BTH submitted an application to STINT's Strategic Grants. The proposed project addresses two main problems: the difficulty for many Asian students to adapt to Swedish teaching methods involving independent, goal and project oriented work, and the difficulty for Asian students to enter the Swedish job market. The project is a pilot that aims at assuring that students coming for studies at BTH from five partner universities in India and China will be better prepared and succeed in their studies. The project also aims at assuring that the students will come with realistic expectations on what they can expect from the university and on what is expected from them. Finally, the project intends to enable the students to be better prepared and more attractive for the Swedish job market.

The background to this project was the 2011 i-graduate's "International Student Barometer." The Barometer indicated for some universities, among them BTH, a low ranking regarding counseling and preparation for the job market. However, BTH also has a history and reputation for working closely with the surrounding society and industry. Its slogan: "In real life," refers to the purpose of the education—a career after graduation. Although BTH's reputation lives up to this goal, it was apparently not the case for the international students. BTH believes that there are various reasons for this:

- The Swedish education system is focusing on independent thinking and team work in a way that is quite different from the traditional way of conducting higher education in Asia, where the majority of BTH's international students are coming from.
- The fact that Swedish universities expect students to find information and job opportunities and that they do not provide support, such as delivering complete instruction and information packages, to the students the same way as Asian students are used to at home means that these students have been culturally disadvantaged. The consequences have been that the international, often Asian, students have entered universities in Sweden, BTH in particular, less prepared than their co-students.
- The international students also had expectations that did not match the reality. These students struggled with the independent study situation, as well as team- and goal-oriented work.

The project intends to address and change these issues. As BTH has a long experience collaborating with Indian and Chinese universities, including double degree programs, the project was aiming at realizing a pilot project with BTH's office at Shandong University at Weihai (SDUW) in China and The Society of Indian Alumni of Swedish-European Universities in India as operational partners. The partner universities: SDUW, Beijing University of Science and Technology, JNTU Hyderabad and Kakinada are beneficiaries of the project. The project consists of developing and carrying out a package of preparatory courses for students from these partner universities planning to study at BTH. The courses are carried out in a combination of campus-based meetings in China and India and net-based contacts between students and course leaders.

Results and lessons learned

The project has contributed to the strategic work at BTH and influenced the new international strategy, which will be decided during spring 2014. The first cohort of students, 50 students from India, who have been going through the preparatory course, has started at BTH and the teachers have noticed that these students are better prepared and have more realistic expectations. The meeting at JNTU Hyderabad targeted 144 students. At SDUW the course was given to 50 students. Also students from other partner universities to BTH, as well as students at SDUW that were not initially targeted, could join the course.

Another outcome of the project is that faculty and staff at BTH have been more exposed to international work and become more experienced in that. Also, the coordination with the offices in China and India has improved. The project has been appreciated by the students and the participating universities.

A lesson learned is that the university leadership's involvement has been crucial for the success. An addition to the project is that a crash course in Swedish has been offered to the students.

The new policy and strategy that will be decided during spring 2014 has been influenced by the project and will emphasize more on internationalization as a strategic tool for improving the quality of higher education and research and less on recruitment.

Discussion and conclusions

Two Swedish universities with rather different profiles were studied with a focus on their internationalization strategies. In particular, two projects within the program Strategic Grants for Internationalization were presented and discussed. Lund University, an old, large and comprehensive university, has carried out Swedish Excellence Seminars, a branding type of activity in Brazil, Taiwan and China. The success of this project lies to a large extent in the inclusive approach, allowing other Swedish HEIs to join. There is a high probability that this type of joint internationalization activities will continue after the period with external co-funding.

BTH is a small and young university with a focus on Applied IT and Innovation for Sustainable Growth. BTH's project targets internationalization at home and how to improve the results of incoming students from China and India. One expected long-term consequence of this project is an alumni network supporting the recruitment of new students from these countries. It appears as if the new students are better prepared when they arrive to BTH.

From these two case studies of strategically prioritized projects at Lund University and BTH it is clear that international branding is of specific importance. It is also apparent from these cases that there is an increased focus on international-student recruitment. With the increasing international competition among universities and the development of an international market for higher education it becomes necessary for the universities to brand themselves internationally. This is true for a large comprehensive university among the top 100 or so, like Lund University, as well as for a lesser-known university focusing on a limited number of disciplines, such as BTH. Obviously, the fact that the number of international students drastically dropped when tuition fees were introduced is yet another reason that international branding is important for Swedish universities. Whereas Lund University was among the universities in Sweden with the lowest drop in international students, the impact on BTH was very strong.

The importance of branding for universities in a small country like Sweden raises the question whether universities would actually benefit by collaborative branding abroad. On one hand, a collaborative branding strategy might reduce the visibility of an individual university. On the other, it increases the chances that the activities have an impact at all. It seems as if the example at Lund University has opened up for collaboration in branding. In fact, there is definitely an indication of a trend shift here, as the universities in Sweden previously have been reluctant to collaborate abroad.

As the entire Swedish higher education system is highly ranked internationally, according to Universitas 21, there might be specific opportunities for collaborative branding in Sweden. When collaborating, it could be argued that universities with different profiles should join their forces. Judging from the Lund University initiative, this is not the case as most of the participating universities in the joint workshop in Brazil belong to the top tier in Sweden.

In the case of Lund, specific countries have been prioritized in the strategy, which can be a limiting factor if the strategy extends over a longer time. Most universities appear to lack this type of geographical precision in the strategies. As a concentration of the efforts is necessary to have an impact, it appears good to select some priority countries or regions, and then preferably not the same countries as everyone else. But as the case of Lund University exhibits, there is a need for a regular update of the selected areas, in order to benefit from initiatives like the Brazilian Science without Borders program.

Both universities have rather old strategies, consisting of a policy and plan that were decided in 2007. Typically, the policy should preferably focus on values and goals of a strategic character whereas the plans should be more action-oriented and operative. This difference is not so clear in the documents from the universities and the plans were not updated regularly. The fact that international policies and plans are not updated regularly is interesting and a bit worrying. Are the plans used at all after they have been decided? Or are the listed activities too general in character? The interest in policies and plans for internationalization is clearly linked to the power allocation in the HEI hierarchy. From a bottom-up perspective, there is typically a limited interest in a central plan and policy that is relatively detailed.

At Lund University it was discussed if an internationalization policy is needed, or if the general strategic plan is sufficient. Apart from the fact that the strategic plan clearly includes internationalization aspects, this discussion also reflects the ambitions to embed internationalization in all activities, i.e. some type of comprehensive internationalization. When an international or global perspective is integrated in all activities on all levels, specific internationalization units might not be needed any more.

Note

1 This figure is smaller than the number international students starting at the university, as domestic students typically study during a longer period.

Chapter 11

Michigan State University

Origins and evolution of an institution toward a global frame

Dawn Thorndike Pysarchik and John K. Hudzik

Michigan State University (MSU) is a large public university with 49,300 students, 4,700 faculty and academic staff, 17 colleges, and over 200 academic programs, with an annual operating budget of $2 billion. Its main campus is a contiguous area of 5,200 acres with another 19,600 acres in research sites, land, and facilities throughout the state of Michigan. Its origin as the nation's first land-grant college was far more humble. In 1855 the first entering class occupied temporary buildings on land donated by the Federal government.

This Federal "land grant" was to fund the start of a new kind of higher education institution in the United States that was mandated to provide access to quality higher education for ordinary people, not just the elites. The potential for public universities to drive societal growth and development for the common good, especially when coupled to core values of access for all, quality, and practical service to communities, was novel for its time. So was the curriculum that sought to blend practical learning initially in agriculture, engineering, and applied sciences.

Although this land-grant institution originally had a local and national frame of reference, its core values and missions were no less relevant in a global frame. By 1873, students from Asia and the Middle East came to study agriculture. By 1900, 60 international students, from 5 continents, had studied at MSU. By the beginning of the twenty-first century, over 3,700 international students and scholars were in residence annually, and there were as many as 500,000 MSU alumni worldwide.

Immediately following World War II, MSU's international engagement became expansive and systematic. The institution was called upon to engage globally, initially in post-war redevelopment efforts, and then development efforts worldwide and through educational programs in host countries and on the E. Lansing campus. A visionary university president, John Hannah, inspired MSU's international engagement from the mid-1940s until 1968. Successive presidents sustained that leadership.

By the end of the twentieth century, if not before, MSU's institutional ethos was to view itself not only as a pioneer land-grant institution and a member of the American Association of Universities (the largest research universities in the United

States) but one defining itself in *both* local and global terms. Its published mission statement includes "to discover practical uses for theoretical knowledge, and to speed the diffusion of information to residents of the state, nation, and the world."

MSU increasingly acknowledges the co-dependence of global and local co-prosperities. In this local–global role, the institution contributes to a global intellectual network of ideas, talent, and discovery, which help to fashion these networks for mutual benefit. To this end, development of new intellectual networks and collective capacities that link local and global pathways of innovation become crucial. This is reinforced in statements by the current MSU President, Lou Anna K. Simon:

> The boldness to which we aspire is to acknowledge that the world is our arena and that cutting-edge knowledge coupled with global engagements change the world, the local community and the lives of individuals .... There is unprecedented potential for progress when colleges and universities work in collaboration with local, regional, and international partners. In short, at MSU our potential partners can be anyone and are everywhere in relationships that are inspired by and hold to our values and a capacity to create shared goals.
>
> (Presidential address to the university, quoted in
> Hudzik and McCarthy 2012, p. 2)

In the late 1990s, the Dean and Office of International Studies and Programs (ISP), with support from the President and Provost, convened a series of campus discussions to analyze new global realities and develop strategies to redirect MSU's historic strengths to systematically address these new realities. A vision of internationalization at MSU in the twenty-first century emerged, which included goals and strategies to achieve them in eight critical areas. This laid a foundation for a comprehensive approach to internationalization.

1   *Competence*: Enhance the international and global competence of MSU faculty, students, staff, and other stakeholders.
2   *Opportunity*: Further the educational opportunities that contribute to internationalization and globalization of the curriculum and students' educational experiences.
3   *Funding*: Diversify MSU's contract, grant, and endowment portfolio to increase funding for international programming.
4   *Leadership:* Position MSU as a leader in shaping and taking advantage of the impact of globalization and internationalization on higher education.
5   *Planning and collaboration:* Strengthen the MSU international community by improving collegiality, collaborative planning, and priority setting within ISP and with colleges, departments, and faculties.
6   *Advancement*: Extend MSU's international presence and image through improved communication, image building, and links with international alumni and friends.

7   *Diversity*: Enhance internationalization opportunities for diverse students, faculty, and staff.
8   *Outreach*: Extend MSU's land-grant tradition of outreach and service to incorporate international and global programming and perspectives that benefit Michigan citizens by preparing them to live and work in a twenty-first century global community.

These aspirations were intended to build on an already expansive institutional commitment to international engagement which, by the start of the twenty-first century, included sending nearly 2,000 students annually to study abroad, being engaged in as many as 70 countries on every continent with hundreds of inter-institutional partnership agreements, and over 20 internationally focused centers and institutes on campus. These provided an institutional foundation for a more strategic and comprehensive global engagement. Our core institutional values prompted a framing question to guide the effort: How should a major US public university align its unique strengths to meet the needs and demands of a global society and strengthen its commitment to improving the public good?

Toward comprehensive internationalization in the twenty-first century

In 2005–6, the Higher Learning Commission of the North Central Association of Colleges and Universities conducted its regular decennial reaccreditation review of the institution. MSU's president voluntarily added a "special emphasis" self-study, "Internationalization at MSU," which then became an element in MSU's re-accreditation. This resulted in a comprehensive review of all international/global activity on and off campus, and provided a snapshot of MSU's international/global strengths and gaps.

Following this, in-depth discussions began about comprehensive internationalization and how to link historic land-grant values to contemporary institutional missions via models that blend research and application efforts with institutional, local, and global interactions. New thinking emerged about how to focus MSU's scope and scale in strategic academic and research areas. At the same time, President Simon led the institution in reconceptualizing MSU's mission from one of land grant to "world grant" in nature. This was not a paradigm shift but rather a call to reject the false dichotomy of local vs. global and to think in terms of a seamless connection between the local and global scale of operations. An example of local–global intersection involved the convening of participants from Detroit, Hyderabad, Nairobi, Johannesburg, Amsterdam, and Singapore in the Global Innoversity in Detroit in 2013. This innovative sustainability initiative was to collaboratively explore new thinking about feeding large metropolitan populations around the globe. The overall goal was to "develop a program of food system innovation to promote local economic development, land recovery and food security" where each world region would use the collective expertise to develop and operate their own program while continually collaborating with the global network to encourage further innovation.

The world grant approach required a reexamination of MSU's structures, policies, and practices. This meant making strategic decisions about what would be discontinued, transformed, or added. New complementary resource structures were put in place to facilitate goal attainment. Some of the changes involved faculty hiring and support, international-student admissions and support, study-abroad development and implementation, strategic engagement of international alumni, alignment of domestic and international advancement strategies, faculty/student business support resources, among others.

Implementing strategic and comprehensive internationalization

MSU has had a traditional focus on study abroad, area studies, language studies, international-student and scholar enrollment, international research, and development assistance. As it conducted strategic audits of its programs and assets, it became clear that to accomplish comprehensive internationalization, MSU needed to be more strategically focused in these and in new areas. This required building on core strengths but also re-engineering efforts. Some of the re-engineered strategies included the following:

1 *Supporting MSU's faculty assets in international engagement.* The growing number of internationally engaged MSU faculty and staff (1,400) in the changing higher education landscape needed new types of support. ISP conducts annual faculty audits with college deans and chairs to identify gaps in key international/global programming and research areas. Once identified, ISP partners with colleges/departments to fund strategic faculty hires with support from the Provost's Office. Similarly, cross-college/department faculty positions that fill faculty gaps in core and newly emerging global priority areas also expanded. Faculty and curriculum development grants and travel support also were expanded. For the first time, international activity and outcomes was added to the faculty reappointment, promotion, and tenure form, both to signal its importance and to recognize and reward its value.

2 *External funding assistance.* With the challenge to increase external funding, the Office of International Research Collaboration (OIRC) was created within ISP. Priority assistance is given to faculty developing trans-disciplinary proposals that focus on MSU's global research priorities in food security, sustainable environment and development, health and nutrition, and education.

3 *International partners.* With a renewed dedication to strengthening committed relationships with its international partners, MSU moved to a model of fewer strategic partnerships but with deeper and more comprehensive relationships with each. Pilot strategic country/area international partnerships are underway in places such as China, Brazil, India, and Turkey.

4   *Expanding study abroad.* Study abroad is an historic strength of MSU and a central component of MSU's international portfolio. Despite its national leadership in study abroad, MSU determined it needed to reconceptualize its approach. A renewed commitment to study abroad campus-wide emerged, including greater diversity in engagement models inter-linked with university and college priorities. Linkage strategies include: leveraging (and supporting) faculty research, developing research-integrated study-abroad programs for graduate students, and increasing internship and service learning experiences. Over 50 of MSU's study-abroad programs engage students with local community projects where they are studying. An Institute of Research on Overseas Programs was established to study international exchange programs at American universities. This office supports efforts from among 200 active program leaders annually to participate in research projects, to write grant proposals, to develop and assess research projects, to publish in journals or present at conferences, and to support students' study-abroad research.

5   *The American semester.* This new program allows students who are enrolled in an undergraduate degree program at one of MSU's strategic partner institutions abroad to take courses at MSU as a complement to their undergraduate degree program. Students can transfer credits back to their home degree but are not eligible for a degree from MSU. Although a relatively new program, MSU hosted over 200 students primarily from Europe and Latin America during the past year.

6   *Student global competence and assessment.* An institution with a world grant mantra must be intentional about developing "global competence" in its students, faculty and staff. Global competence and liberal learning goals were developed with campus wide involvement. Assessment of these goals is underway.[1]

    Curriculum development initiatives are under way to strategically design program content that reflects the liberal learning goals and global competencies. For example, area studies centers and thematic institutes offer internationally-focused "specializations" and certificate programs to encourage undergraduate and graduate students to integrate an international component into majors in all colleges. For four years, MSU has administered the Beliefs, Events, Values Inventory (BEVI)—mapped to MSU's global competencies—to a representative sample of incoming freshmen, and then again during their senior year to determine if and in what ways they have become more globally competent.

7   *New research and business resources.* MSU has more than 60 years of experience working on development projects and international education programs. As a land-grant university, MSU's faculty, staff, and students work to strategically align with partners in public and private sector organizations, NGOs, governments, and other universities globally to study and respond to many of the world's most intractable problems. MSU has built an extensive network of long-term partners at African universities to provide technical

assistance and build capacity in the areas of education, agriculture and food security, human and veterinary medicine, business, gender and development studies, and engineering, as well as in the core academic areas of arts, humanities, and physical and social sciences. Countries of engagement in Eastern and Southern Africa include Tanzania, Kenya, Ethiopia, Zimbabwe, Malawi, and South Africa. Reflecting this commitment, MSU has been a top producer of Ph.D. dissertations on Africa and its development.

Funding for externally sponsored programs comes primarily from federal agencies, state agencies, industry, associations, and foundations. MSU was awarded $117,000,000 in external funding for international projects that cover every world region in 2013. MSU averages approximately $15 million annually in administering USAID-funded programs, with an additional $25–$35 million of development assistance funded by other donors. MSU is one of seven US universities that partnered with the MasterCard Foundation on a $500 million African Scholars program to educate the next generation of African leaders. MSU received the largest grant because of its historical and sustained commitment to Africa. Other significant international grants received for flagship programs include: USAID's Higher Education Solutions Network ($25 million); several Bill and Melinda Gates Foundation grants ($10 million); USAID's BHEARD agricultural research capacity-building program ($7.3 million), among others.

8 *Fostering trans- and inter-disciplinary collaborations across the institution.* The diversity of MSU's international programming and its potential complementarity are assets, but fashioning more opportunities for collaborations involving a wider array of these assets is a key component of our strategic international vision. Leading the strategic thinking and implementation of internationalization across MSU is the centralized–decentralized constellation of more than 25 internationally focused units. Four such centers are US Department of Education Title VI funded national resource and language resource centers. Although some are located in ISP (e.g., area study centers), other international thematic centers are embedded in the colleges (e.g., business, education, engineering, gender, health, international development, and languages). Under the auspices of ISP, the Office of China Programs was established in 2005 to further MSU's long-term strategic plan to support academic, research, and economic development initiatives, along with global, national, and local strategic alliances in China.

Following on intensive self-studies and external reviews, the area study centers of Africa; Asia; Canada; Europe, Russia and Eurasia; Latin America and the Caribbean have strong ties to thematic international centers and institutes campus wide. These centers and other ISP units bring a new approach to comprehensive internationalization by facilitating cross-college and cross-region initiatives to create a global network of partner institutions and private sector organizations that can transcend geographic and disciplinary boundaries to help globalize education and solve some of the world's most pressing problems. This approach becomes critical in light of new funding practices and policies of funders (e.g., agencies, foundations, NGOs). Institutional priority and support is given to proposals for capacity building, and research and development contracts that build trans- and inter-disciplinary teams. Often, team-building is across major knowledge realms of the natural sciences, social and behavioral sciences, and the arts and humanities, and professional disciplines, which is the case in particular with more recent projects in several countries and locations in Africa.

9   *Expanded support for international students.* To respond to MSU's growing international-student population, the Office for International Students and Scholars expanded its international-student orientation programs and number of international-student organizations, created a new international coordinator/student advisor position for educational and cultural programming, hosted international coffee hours, and created an international-student essay contest. The local community has also mounted initiatives to assist international students to adjust to American life.

Other support initiatives include digital media and print publications. MSU produced or co-produced three China-focused films, which have been adopted by peer institutions and international education professional organizations. The MSU film production, *A Conversation with Chinese and American Students,* presents a candid conversation of two groups of MSU American and Chinese undergraduates who share their honest points of view. *The Dialogue* with accompanying MSU intercultural toolkit, an MSU/Crossing Borders Education co-production, depicts the challenges of intercultural engagement. An international advance screening was held during the 2013 International Education Week with over 10,000 viewers. The MSU film production, *Imported from China,* follows MSU Chinese undergraduates as they adjust to a new cultural and educational environment in the United States. Also, the School of Journalism created a series of intercultural guides that focus on different ethnic groups who are navigating life in the United States.

10   *Reconceptualized residence system.* With one of the largest university residential systems in the United States, MSU has redesigned its residence hall structure to accommodate diverse MSU students to see the world from global perspectives, learn by doing, explore new cultures, and live a healthy life. At the heart of this new Neighborhood structure are Engagement Centers with study lounges, game rooms, and other student services. New student intercultural aide positions foster interactions among culturally and experientially diverse students to promote an inclusive environment.

Outcomes of comprehensive internationalization at MSU

What are the results of a cross-disciplinary, cross-regional comprehensive approach to internationalization at a large world-grant institution? We present some highlights of these efforts. MSU was ranked in the top 100 world universities by Shanghai Jiao Tong, Times Higher Education, and Newsweek/MSNBC; and ranked 29th among the nation's public universities (*U.S. News & World Report* 2014). MSU is ranked fourth nationally for study-abroad participation and with nearly 6,800 international-student enrollments, MSU ranks ninth nationally. MSU ranks sixth as an all-time producer of Peace Corps volunteers. MSU is one of seven institutions globally to be part of USAID's Higher Education Solutions Network, which seeks to develop answers to global development challenges. It is also one of a small set of universities selected to participate in the Fulbright-affiliated Hubert H. Humphrey Fellowship Programs. MSU's internationalization efforts were recognized as a 2006 recipient of the Senator Paul Simon Award for Campus Internationalization and a 2005 recipient of the Goldman Sachs Foundation Prize for Excellence in International Education.

Lessons for the future of MSU's continuing international engagement

The need to advance the public good is a challenge for universities worldwide. The response needed is to build domestic and global partnerships and networks of institutions that share in the common values of quality, inclusiveness and access, and connections in service to communities.

MSU's president and others at MSU speak frequently about the intersection of education, research, and engagement and its potential to address local and world challenges. Just as any public university that pursues a research-intensive mission feels obligated to succeed in ways that the academy defines, so must a land-grant institution pursuing a world-grant ideal to meet the needs of diverse communities and clientele—whether they be far from home or at home. This requires maximizing core values rather than maximizing revenue and return on investment. A key strength of the world-grant ideal is to make a positive difference for the "have nots" as well as the "haves." The tide of prosperity rises with an increase in the proportion of the latter.

Building institutional culture

Successful world-grant comprehensive internationalization requires an institutional culture that provides over-arching drive, purpose, and sustainability. A succession of campus conversations at all levels of the institution over several decades reinforces and reinvigorates the MSU culture for internationalization. The driving culture for world-grant internationalization defines missions, values, and service in interconnected local, national, and global terms. It is not seen as an add-on responsibility but rather as a commitment to integrate global perspectives into the fabric of curricula and of institutional research and community engagement missions. It encourages the involvement of everyone. It is pervasive in institutional messaging and it is a broadly shared vision up and down the institution, and throughout the campus community about the necessity of effectively engaging and linking the local and the global.

To respond to these new global realities, MSU's leadership recently realigned MSU's top international position from Dean of International Studies and Programs (ISP) to Associate Provost and Dean of ISP. This landmark step signals a new era in global leadership at MSU and recognition of the centrality of "international" to the future of MSU. In accepting this new position, Steve Hanson spoke about the importance of alignment in the components of all international programs (strategy, vision, themes, relationships, etc.) as being critical to the success of comprehensive internationalization at MSU.

As with any unknown, we face challenges. Among these are the need to develop new evidence-based metrics that validate the value added of global engagement of institutions. The metrics need to focus outward, measuring outcomes and impacts on clientele both near and far. Some metrics, though, need to focus inward to assess outcomes and impact within the institution. Similarly, we need evidence-based documentation of new models of public university engagement in a borderless world that combine resources and efforts with the private sector, NGOs and other higher education entities globally. This includes easier means for building and working in networks, both formally and informally, and in virtual networks, to tap the collective assets of institutions with common values in pursuit of the world-grant ideal.

Note

1 MSU's goals in these areas can be found at http://global.undergrad.msu.edu/userfiles/file/LLG__GC_combined_table.pdf

Chapter 12

Internationalization of higher education—the Nanyang Technological University story
Perspectives and experience from the Lion City

Bertil Andersson and Tony Mayer

Background

1989 was a key year in World history with the fall of communism and the end of the Manichean division of the World resulting from the Cold War. Francis Fukayama coined the phrase "The End of History" to indicate we had entered a new era with a single dominant superpower—the USA (Fukuyama 1992). Of almost equal significance, and less visibility, the discussions under the General Agreement on Tariffs and Trades (GATT) were moving towards the establishment of the World Trade Organization in 1995. This started the process of globalization which has moved with an ever gathering pace over the past 20 years. At the same time, the "unseen" revolution in communication and information was occurring so that life is now unthinkable without mobile communications and internet access plus social media becoming ubiquitous, especially with the young generation. Naturally, academia has not been able to avoid being influenced by these historical events of major magnitude. We now live in a "global village" with instant information, global and easy physical communications, and the ability to source whatever we like from wherever we choose. Academia involving education and research is no exception.

At the end of the last century and into the twenty-first century, we have seen the effect of the rapid rise of Asia out of general poverty. Much remains to be done to alleviate poverty but the generality is true. With this development, peoples' aspirations change and there is a greater desire for more education to the highest levels. Governments have responded to this need and across the whole continent, we are seeing a huge increase in investment in higher education and research, not least in Singapore. To take advantage of this investment, we have seen the recruitment of foreign or foreign-trained talent. This manifests itself in the recruitment of young as well as established teachers and researchers from across the globe accompanied by the return of local people who had developed their careers in Europe or North America. It is globalization at work. One has to couple the changes in economic development in Asia with the huge human capital and young talent reservoir that exists in many of this continent's countries. Everywhere in Asia there are young populations eager to learn and develop their skills.

The results of this desire and the investment by governments across the continent are apparent. Already we see several Asian universities enter the top ranks of world universities. Similarly, the growth in research investment as measured by GERD (percentage of GDP devoted to research and development) shows the determination of Asian nations to invest not only through public money but also through private sector investment.

Against this global background we turn to the situation in Singapore which provides an interesting case study of Asian development and an example of planning development anchored in the concept of the "knowledge-based economy" driven by a government committed to this policy.

The development of research and the university sector in Singapore has been truly impressive starting from the low base, inherited from its earlier colonial period and immediate post-colonial period until Singapore's expulsion from Malaysia in 1965.

Singapore was founded by Sir Stamford Raffles of the East India Company in 1819 as an *entrepôt*—a role which it still has today (it remains one of the largest container ports in the World) providing a considerable part of its national income. It has evolved into a multicultural, cosmopolitan and diverse society with Malay, Chinese, Tamil, and English as the official languages—the latter being the language of government, business, and administration and the principal medium of education.

Research has been a major instrument of policy within Singapore to achieve its aim of being a leading first-world nation. Starting from a low base of 0.2 percent GERD in 1965, Singapore aims to reach 3.5 percent GERD in 2015 of which two-thirds will come from the private sector. Thus, research is a major instrument of policy within all parts of government. This level of investment puts Singapore into a small, elite group of knowledge-based economies—the "small, smart countries" comprising the Nordic countries, Israel, and Switzerland, all with a GERD level above that of the benchmark USA level of 2.5 percent.

The history of universities in Singapore started with a Medical School established in 1905 which evolved into what is now the National University of Singapore (NUS). The Chinese-medium Nanyang University was founded in 1955 and later merged with the predecessor of NUS to form the present university. In 1981, the Nanyang Technological Institute was created with the aim of training engineers. This eventually became the Nanyang Technological University (NTU) in 1991, later broadening its base into the present institution as a more comprehensive establishment but still with its main focus in modern engineering. However, it was not until 2005, with the granting of autonomy to the universities in Singapore, that NTU moved from its vocational education role into a research-intensive university in the Humboldtian tradition, from which it has gained its present reputation. The granting of a charter in 1991 coincided with

Singapore's major push forward in science and technology with the establishment of the Agency for Science and Technology and Research (A*STAR) and the initiation of five-year planning cycles for R & D. Accompanied by generous budget settlements this resulted in Singapore's transformation into a knowledge-based economy still with a commitment to retain a significant manufacturing sector. The initial investment established A*STAR as a major research institution. Then in 2005 Singapore really rose rapidly in the "world league" when it took a quantum leap in research funding, pushing NTU into its research-intensive direction. Based on the new National Research Foundation, which channeled funding to the university sector, this has underpinned the success of both NTU and NUS. This has also been coupled with the creation of new universities, notably the Singapore Management University (SMU) in 2000 and the Singapore University of Technology and Design (SUTD) founded in 2009.

Research and academic success has to be founded on a first-class general school and junior college educational system and this is a priority area for the government. The school system is envied throughout the World with teaching being regarded as a high status career. The OECD Programme for International Student Assessment (PISA) shows Singapore ranked second in the world in mathematics and reading, third in science, and top in problem-solving tests. In Singapore, all teachers undertake their training through the National Institute of Education (NIE), a part of the Nanyang Technological University (NTU). At the higher education level, 23 percent of the cohort of eligible young people enter tertiary education and the aim is to increase the size of the cohort to 40 percent by 2020. There has been an expansion of the university sector to meet this demand with the growth of both two major universities, NUS and NTU, plus SMU and SUTD and the establishment of two vocational training universities. These are the Singapore Institute of Technology (SIT) established in 2009 and the Singapore Institute of Management University (SIM University) for adult learning. Both work with international partner universities.

What is particularly distinctive about universities in Singapore is their strong international character, unlike most universities elsewhere. This is in part due to the geographical and economic position of Singapore and its relatively small population base. In NTU this attitude to international recruitment is not only the norm but it is the expectation resulting from a broad international outlook of its leadership and the "intellectual leavening" that this imbues throughout the institution. It is also seen in the make-up of the student body with 20 percent of undergraduates coming from outside the country, 60 percent for all graduate students and up to 80 percent of PhD students originating from elsewhere. These are remarkable figures in comparison with Europe and North America and other parts of Asia. NTU is also conscious of the need to try to drive up its figures of local PhD recruitment. This is a special challenge in what is a materialistic society when undertaking a PhD may not be seen as a "pathway to riches." Overall NTU (both the student body and faculty) is predominantly an international university in a national setting.

Singapore encourages internationalism within its university leadership with three out of the four major universities being led by non-Singaporeans from Belgium, Sweden, and the USA. This contrasts strikingly with the situation in most countries in Europe and North America. In other words, the search for talent is worldwide and not constrained only to Singapore.

Milestones

In terms of its history, 2006 was a critical year in the development of NTU as this is when its Board of Trustees (BoT) put a new academic structure in place with colleges headed by Deans reporting to a Provost to drive the reform process. Bertil Andersson, formerly Chief Executive of the European Science Foundation, a former Chair of the Nobel Chemistry Committee and Rector of Linköping University (Sweden) was appointed as NTU's first Provost with a mandate to turn NTU from a mainly teaching institution into a research-intensive establishment.

The Board of Trustees is itself rather atypical in that while the majority of the NTU Board are Singaporeans, it has members originating from the leaderships of ETH Switzerland, Imperial College London, and Stanford University, USA.

While NTU underwent a major reform, which was a necessity as the university changed direction, it took place within an environment of vastly increased funding for the universities. In the old Swedish saying "if it rains gold coins, it is the poor man who has no bucket." The task of reform for NTU was to create the "bucket" and so have the means for consolidating reform and building on this new base. Taking this forward, NTU has now advanced to become a globally competitive research university with a World-wide reputation.

Over the last 10 years NTU has become more comprehensive in its disciplinary coverage with an eminent and highly ranked business school, the NIE (see above), the Rajeratnam School of International and Strategic Studies—a graduate school akin to the Brookings Institution, Washington DC and Chatham House, London, and with new Colleges of Science and Humanities, Art and Social Sciences (which also embraces media and design studies). In this respect, the combination of arts and humanities with technology is particularly exciting. However, engineering, in all its aspects, remains at the core and provides exciting interdisciplinary interactions with the other subjects. NTU has established Singapore's third medical school, the Lee Kong Chian School of Medicine, which is a joint collaboration between NTU and Imperial College London—a specific and very fruitful example of international collaboration and is the first overseas "footprint" by Imperial College. Together, both universities combine technology, life sciences, and medicine in a new inter-disciplinary approach. Furthermore, taking advantage of new pedagogies and technologies, this joint operation has put both institutions into a forefront position as a medical teaching initiative.

During this period NTU has made a spectacular leap in terms of university rankings (41st in QS World University Rankings and 76th in the equivalent) and is now ranked number two in the world in terms of institutions less than 50 years old and is well established within the top 50 of all universities (QS World University Rankings). No university has changed its status so dramatically as has happened in NTU. Not only have its overall rankings improved but the impact of its research in terms of its research value as measured by citations has also shown a similar spectacular change. According to Thomson Reuters, NTU's research is shown to be the most impactful of the Asian universities; it has also risen dramatically in the *Nature* publication index. This is a major achievement for an engineering institution. It is both the level of achievement reached and its speed—the "kinetics of change" that is most noteworthy. In terms of impact, NTU was behind all its main regional rivals in 2004 and yet in only seven years it passed them all, including the sharply rising NUS, to become the top-ranked university in Asia in terms of its research impacts. This is spectacular for the speed with which NTU has achieved this position and the trend is continuing. It should be noted that NTU and NUS now occupy the two top spots in the Thomson-Reuters InCites for Asia which is no mean achievement for a country the size of Singapore.

How has this been achieved?

This unprecedented success has been due to a number of factors of which internationalization has been at its heart, especially in terms of its overall recruitment strategy.

This reform of NTU started with the faculty. A change in tenure rules provided an opportunity for a rigorous review of all faculty, conducted in accordance with the top level of best practice. This difficult exercise resulted in approximately one-fifth of faculty reviewed not achieving tenure. This meant that only the most research active with the greatest potential were retained. It also provided a unique opportunity for new recruitment. In the first four rounds of review between 2007 and 2010, nearly 800 faculty were considered for tenure of whom 58 percent were confirmed, 23 percent of the cases were deferred for further review pending improvement against targets and with the remainder (19 percent) not achieving tenure. This created a unique recruitment opportunity and was a major signal of intent to the whole institution.

An international recruitment followed with senior academics joining NTU from prestigious universities around the world. These included a USA National Academician, Fellows of the Royal Society, and other leading academic figures from universities around the world. Based on such personalities, NTU has been able to nucleate new top-level research groups. There is also a highly international component in other areas of the university leadership with one-third of School Chairs coming from outside Singapore, namely from Denmark, Germany, India, and Sri Lanka.

At the other end of the career spectrum, NTU has benefitted from the National Research Foundation's (NRF) Fellowship scheme, a derivative of the European Science Foundation's European Young Investigator awards, later the European Research Council's Starting Grants scheme. NTU was very successful in gaining a majority of the fellowship holders who chose NTU as their preference. These included three holders of these prestigious European awards for young investigators. In parallel, NTU has also introduced its own Nanyang Assistant Professor scheme with very attractive start-up conditions. This has regularly attracted more than 400 applicants annually from the most prestigious institutions around the world seeking some 10 posts available. This new recruitment at both senior and more junior levels was based on an international vision. With this global approach, NTU is one of the most internationally diverse universities in the world with some 70 percent of its faculty and research staff coming from outside Singapore and representing some 70 nationalities.

Another scheme which has been designed to attract leading researchers from around the World is the Research Centres of Excellence of which NTU hosts two out of the five established. The first to be established was the Earth Observatory of Singapore (EOS), which counts five NRF Fellows in its complement. The second is the Singapore Centre for Environmental Life Sciences Engineering (SCELSE), a ground-breaking initiative major "star" in microbial genomics. In fact, most faculty involved in these centres are drawn from outside the country— Australia, Europe, and North America.

A third aspect of international recruitment in Singapore is that it has sought to attract prestigious institutions to establish themselves in the country working closely with NTU and NUS. One example is in the medical area with the second and third medical schools being examples of this approach. We now have the Duke University/NUS medical school based on a small graduate intake and the third medical school developed between NTU and Imperial College London. Other institutions are established in Singapore including INSEAD—the Franco-Singaporean business school.

In addition to these special initiatives is a scheme to bring in major institutions to establish research activities in Singapore through the CREATE (Campus for Research Excellence and Technological Enterprise) initiative. The aim of this scheme is to provide a base for leading institutions from around the world to establish a project-based research presence in conjunction with the local universities (NTU and NUS). CREATE has been able to attract institutions such as the Swiss Federal Institute of Technology (ETH), Zurich, Massachusetts Institute of Technology (MIT), Technical University of Munich Technion-Israel Institute of Technology, Hebrew University of Jerusalem, Ben-Gurion University, Israel, University of California, Berkeley, Peking University and Shanghai Jiao Tong University (China), and Cambridge University.

New challenges and opportunities

NTU has led the formation of a new grouping of technological universities worldwide to provide a new forum where we can come together to discuss issues of common interest and also jointly take forward activities and policy positions which are best done at the international level. This is GLOBALTECH, the global alliance of technological universities which brings together NTU with the Indian Institute of Technology Bombay (India), California Institute of Technology (USA), Georgia Institute of Technology (USA), ETH Zurich (Switzerland), Imperial College London (UK), Technical University of Munich (Germany), Shanghai Jiao Tong University (China), and the University of |New South Wales (UNSW).

At the same time, NTU, as befits an engineering university, has to pay attention to the translation of research into intellectual property and economic development. In common with universities everywhere, there is encouragement for researchers at all levels from undergraduate to senior faculty to look at the economic potential of what they are doing, and we have support structures to maximize this effort through patents, licensing, and start-ups. However, alongside this, NTU sees great merit in developing close industrial research partnerships and encouraging researchers from industry to be present on campus, and we have encouraged such laboratories to be sited within the university as "Corporate Laboratories." Not only do we encourage collaborative research but we consider that joint supervision of PhD students is also a necessary "cement" for these relationships. In so doing we have now developed an impressive portfolio of partnerships with leading technologically based multi-national companies, in particular Rolls Royce, and also Bosch, EADS, BMW, Infineon, Lockheed Martin, Siemens, ST Microelectronics, Thales, and Johnson Matthey, to name just a few. Alongside these companies, we have also attracted units from the Fraunhofer Gesellschaft (Germany) and the CNRS (France) to locate within the university. Now there is much excitement in the development of a new science park being built immediately adjacent to the university to encourage the development of "green" and "eco" industry. The Nanyang Environment and Water Research Institute and the Energy Research Institute @ NTU—two of the pan-university structures that have been established—will become "anchor" tenants in this new industrial research development. It will also foster and by its existence encourage an even greater entrepreneurial sensibility in the university leading to more spin-offs. The Park also houses the Advanced Remanufacturing Technology Centre (ARTC). This is a concept developed and led by Rolls Royce in which it and other leading technology companies come together, working with a local university—in this case, NTU—and with other institutions (A*STAR), on a company program of industrial research.

What this demonstrates is that universities can develop very rapidly in their research activities and attract the very best people to join them from across the world. This has to be based on offering an encouraging environment and first-class infrastructure plus the availability of the best young brains backed with a determined and internationally orientated management. Naturally, this has to be supported with political will and investment by government. One does not need to wait 200 years to build first-class reputations once this right "mix" has been put in place. In a recent government quinquennial international panel review of NTU, Lord Ron Oxburgh, the former Rector of Imperial College and Chairman of Shell, said that he had never seen such a rapid advance in the development of a research intensive university anywhere as that over the past five years at NTU.

Concluding remarks

What we have demonstrated is the rapid upward trajectories of both Singapore and its universities, especially NTU coupled with a commitment to international-ism in the sense of both importing and using the best and most appropriate talent whatever its origin. NTU mirrors the Singaporean government in this respect. For example, this also occurs even in governance, so while NTU's Board mem-bership has an international component, so does the Singaporean government. In contrast, such a non-national membership was prohibited in Sweden until 2010. In Singapore, one of the highest policy-making levels in science and technology is the Research, Innovation and Enterprise Council, chaired by the Prime Minister and involving nine other Ministers, with another 13 members of whom 12 are non-Singaporeans. It is probably unique for such an important *national* policy committee to both include so many high ranking Ministers involved in research discussions and to have such an *international* membership. Similarly, the main equivalent of a research funding agency within the Ministry of Education has an American chair and a mainly non-Singaporean membership. In other words, Singapore has a tradition of drawing on the best brains and the best advice from wherever in the world.

What one sees in Singapore is a commitment to deliver a "high end" knowledge-based economy and which has taken place at a very rapid pace. Singapore is an exemplar of what is happening in Asia and it is difficult to see either Europe or North America matching the rapidity and success of such changes. While it is difficult for a super-tanker to change direction, what we see in Singapore is a super-tanker behav-ing with the characteristics of a speedboat.

However, although what one sees in Singapore is a commitment to interna-tionalization, this is very much embedded in the national structure and based on bilateral exchanges at both the personal and international level. Individual researchers may collaborate across frontiers and disciplines or belong to interna-tionally based research groups but, overall, the tradition is not one of belonging to international networks. Somehow the benefit of belonging to such networks is not fully appreciated.

However, we believe that NTU is an Asian success story and hope that it is also an inspiration to other Asian universities to follow similar paths. This is the result of the globalization of higher education and research—a trend that will continue and provide a global field on which we must all perform.

Chapter 13

Nelson Mandela Metropolitan University, Port Elizabeth, Eastern Cape, South Africa

Nico Jooste

NMMU in context

> [A]t the same time that international boundaries are both breaking down and being re-drawn, with serious consequences for higher education in the Third World, within South Africa major contestations are raging about the boundaries between institutions within the public system, and between public and private higher education. At this 'scrambled' moment of disappearing, emerging and possibly hardening of boundaries, it is difficult to tell which changes are contradictory and which could become complimentary.
>
> (Moja & Cloete 2001: 267)

This confused state of mind represented the South African Higher Education system at the end of 1994 and continued until early 2000. After apartheid and the end of the higher education isolation most South African universities had to begin a process of internationalization of the university, whilst the real focus was on rebuilding and transforming universities in an environment where major political and societal change was the real driver. The societal changes in which the South African universities had to operate are best described by President Nelson Mandela (1998) when he said:

> The greatest single challenge facing our globalised world is to combat and eradicate its disparities. While in all parts of the world progress is being made in entrenching democratic forms of governance, we constantly need to remind ourselves that the freedoms which democracy brings will remain empty shells if they are not accompanied by real and tangible improvements in the material lives of the millions of ordinary citizens of those countries.

Internationalization was thus not one of the priorities of South African universities in the era from 1994 to 2000, but one of the "complimentary" changes, as defined by Moja and Cloete (2001). Notwithstanding, the importance of internationalization and the reconnection with the world was seen as one of the urgent matters that, although not driven by government or any higher education system policy, needed the attention of higher education leadership. The internationalization of South African higher education was, however, fragmented and strongly reliant on the vision, leadership, and drive of particular universities. It is for this reason that the levels of internationalization of South African higher education institutions was, and still is, fragmented. Without the necessary leadership and institutional capacity that prevailed in South Africa just after 1994 under demanding conditions very few could actively participate in internationalization activities. It is for this reason that the concept of comprehensive internationalization was actively pursued by not more than twenty percent of the South African universities. These universities normally express their internationalization goals in the institutional strategic plans and policies as well as through the infrastructure provided to support the implementation of the internationalization of all facets of the institution.

The disparities within the South African system cannot be described in one or two paragraphs and as such it needs to be acknowledged that this chapter, being about the Nelson Mandela Metropolitan University (NMMU), is an example of the twenty percent that had the capacity to implement from the outset a strategy of comprehensive internationalization as relevant for a university in an emerging economy.

As if the external environment changes were not enough, at the same time a major restructuring of the higher education system was introduced that led to numerous institutional mergers with a view to correct the past injustices. This saw the establishment of a new South African university, Nelson Mandela Metropolitan University. It opened its doors on 1 January 2005, the result of the merging of the Port Elizabeth Technikon (University of Applied Sciences), the University of Port Elizabeth (UPE) and the incorporated campus of Vista University Campus in Port Elizabeth.

The NMMU brings together the best traditions of applied and fundamental university education and draws on more than a century of quality higher education, in a new kind of South African university, named a comprehensive South African university, which offers programs from diploma to PhD level.

Without the baggage institutional traditions of internationalization can bring, this new university could approach its international practices focused on its mission, vision, and goals. It expressed itself clearly in its Strategic Plan—Vision 2020, formally approved by the University Council in 2009—on the role of internationalization as a way to open discussion about the construction of an alternative cosmopolitan vision of the university. The mission of the NMMU highlights its international vision when it specifically refers to the following issues: to develop graduates and diplomats to be responsible global citizens capable of critical reasoning, innovation, and adaptability; and to engage in mutually beneficial partnerships locally, nationally, and globally to enhance social, economic, and ecological sustainability.

It further defines in Vision 2020 the relationship of the university to society as a series of interdependent and interrelated spheres, with first an essential linkage to the growth and development needs of the Eastern and Southern Cape. The constant interaction between the local and the global at all levels of knowledge activity, being it research or teaching and learning, has established an internationalization practice that is located in the local environment but that also provides the necessary connection globally in order to be both locally and globally relevant. It is for this reason that the NMMU's international vision recognizes that an internationalized higher education institution should be acutely aware of the current global setting that is still largely defined by different nations in the world. It should thus enhance the active, willing, and unrestricted movement across national boundaries of people and knowledge in processes of exchange. It further recognizes that internationalization is intensified by globalization, but respects and supports the idea of nationalities and the sovereignty of nations. It is this philosophy of internationalization that underpins the ideology and actions of comprehensive internationalization at NMMU. It further supports the South African Higher Education Department's strategic plan to advance the South African higher education system by positioning it globally in such a way that it becomes a preferred destination for international students and staff, particularly those wishing to pursue professional, postgraduate studies and research.

The road to internationalising the NMMU

The above has given a bird's eye view of the external factors that prevailed when the NMMU decided to embark upon a road to becoming comprehensively internationalized. (The internationalizing of the NMMU was a continuation of a process that started within the University of Port Elizabeth and is thus described as one process.) It also indicated that the NMMU developed a comprehensive understanding of internationalization and as such began a process to implement this vision. From the outset, the process of internationalization was guided and the necessary visionary support provided by the institutional structures that were responsible for the overall management of the university. The final decision to embark upon a process to internationalize the university was taken by the University Council (Board of Governors) in March 2000.

At the time that the decision was taken to begin the internationalization of the university, no structure existed that could implement the vision and as such the university decided to begin the process by appointing a senior person, the Senior Director—International Education (Senior International Officer). On 1 July 2000 the process of internationalization commenced, initially at UPE and then, since the merger in 2005, as part of the NMMU. The principles applied to make this an integrated process that would, from the outset, be inclusive, consultative, and transformational were founded on the understanding of the functioning of a South African University and as such built on the three management elements critical to the success of any new endeavor in this type of environment. These are institutional governance, leadership, and the provision of the necessary resources. Figure 13.1 indicates the relationship of the three management elements to the central management goal.

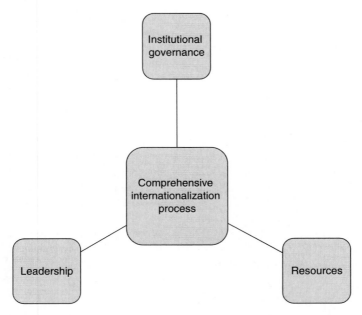

Figure 13.1 Relationship of the three management elements to the central management goal.

The internationalization of the NMMU is managed as a process and not as a single event. This involves the institution as a whole and not only some subsections. The successful implementation of internationalization strategies are, from time to time, measured against international best practices. During the 2010 International Colloquium a process of benchmarking amongst the NMMU's international partner institutions took place and was published for use by all participants (Jooste 2012).

The philosophy of comprehensive internationalization underpins the strategies developed to internationalize the university. Thus from the outset the focus has been on all aspects of the university and not on one activity e.g. student mobility.

The success of the NMMU in reaching its current level of internationalization in a relatively short time can be ascribed to the integrated manner in which the original process was planned and implemented. This relates to how the governance of internationalization was structured. The following is a short description of this aspect within the NMMU's governance model.

Governance

The internationalization of the university is overseen at senior management level under the guidance of the Internationalization Committee. The terms of reference of this committee are to:

1 Exercise governance over the NMMU's internationalization thrust.
2 Ensure that the required internationalization policies are in harmony with the NMMU's mission, vision, values, and strategic goals.
3 Develop and monitor the implementation of an internationalization strategic plan.
4 Assist in, monitor, and steer the integration of the process of internationalization in all spheres of the institution.
5 Recommend to the Finance Committee the annual budget of the Office for International Education.
6 Approve institutional student- and staff-exchange agreements.
7 Recommend institutional agreements for the approval and the signature.
8 Report to the University, Management Committee, and Senate on matters pertaining to internationalization.

The Internationalization Committee, as a committee of Management and Senate, consists of the following 18 members:

- the Deputy Vice-Chancellor— Research and Engagement (Chair Person);
- the Deputy Vice-Chancellor—Academic;
- the Senior Director: International Education;
- the seven Executive Deans of the Faculties;
- the Executive Director: Finance;
- the Registrar;
- the Dean of Students;
- the Dean: Teaching and Learning;
- the Senior Director: Centre for Planning and Institutional Development;
- the Executive Director: Human Resources;
- the Directors for Research Management and Research Capacity Developments;
- the Vice-Chancellor of the University, who is an ex officio member of this committee.

The above clearly illustrates that the Internationalization Committee is composed of and represents all senior managers of the university. The strategic oversight of internationalization is thus fully embedded in every facet of the university and therefore provides a structural framework where the university community can, at least once a quarter, have a focused look at the institutional international practices. This practice was established from the inception of the international endeavors of the university.

The comprehensive internationalization of a university like NMMU also requires that the interests as well as the sensitivities brought by internationalization and its inter-cultural dimension should further be represented when all the senior management committees of the university have their quarterly meetings. To ensure that the international dimension of the university is represented and enhanced, full membership of these committees is a requirement. Since the inception of the process of internationalization, the Office for International Education (OfIE) has been a full member of all these committees; the OfIE's function is not as an "observer" but as a full member and it can thus also add items to the agenda for discussion.

The Senior Director, or his nominee, is thus a member of the Senate Committees that oversee research, teaching and learning, quality assurance, risk and student life. One of the committees of the university that recommend academic matters as well as strategic managerial matters to the University Senate is the Executive Committee of Senate (ECS). Through the incorporation of the Senior Director as well as the Deputy Vice Chancellor Research and Engagement, the most senior line functionary of the OfIE, the strategic management and steering of internationalization is thus fully embedded in the governance structure of the university.

Leadership

The role of leadership—at all levels in the internationalization of higher education—has been discussed at numerous fora in the past. It was, however, recognized that to implement a strategy of comprehensive internationalization successfully at a relatively new university that had emerged from the apartheid past in a constantly changing environment, the dedication and involvement of a variety of leadership in the university would be required. As with the design of the governance model it was also recognized that the university leadership needed to be involved in the internationalization activities from the outset.

This is illustrated by the following extract from an article celebrating the NMMU's success in the international arena. The role of senior leadership is described as follows.

> The success of Nelson Mandela Metropolitan University's internationalisation endeavours is largely the result of visionary leadership. Vice-Chancellors have not only provided the necessary leadership but also created an essential focus on internationalisation that has supplied the institutional impetus for it to remain one of the focal areas that characterises the university.
>
> (Jooste 2013)

From the creation of the Office for International Education by Prof Jan Kirsten (2000) to the embracing of internationalization as a strategic priority of the newly created Nelson Mandela Metropolitan University in 2005, and then its inclusion as one of the strategic drivers within the Vision 2020 Strategic plan by Prof Derrick Swartz, internationalization has continually been integrated at all levels of the university. This strategic leadership of internationalization has therefore proven to be one of the most critical success factors in allowing for comprehensive internationalization to become part of the normal functioning of the university.

The above is illustrated in the paper delivered during the first international colloquium, hosted by NMMU, after the merger in August 2005, by the then Vice-Chancellor, Dr Rolf Stumpf. He indicated that internationalization requires the frequent attention of the Vice-Chancellor and the other senior line functionaries. Through this leadership arrangement the institution and the broader community, locally and globally, receives a message that internationalization is a strategic priority and that senior management is willing and dedicated to give time and strategic visioning effort to it. The level of knowledge and engagement of senior leaders is illustrated by comments made by Prof. Derrick Swartz during the international colloquium of 2010 (these colloquia took place with the "Family Week" every second year) when he provided his views on the future of higher education internationalization. His advice to the global higher education community was that:

> Internationalisation is in its early adolescence. The notion of internationalisation as it mutates and evolves into the future demands that we seek for meaning and create concepts to give us a better understanding of how to package better the world that is very bewildering. As this social movement is taking its course and its effect we want to give meaning to it and give labels, concepts, to describe it, and to give analytical tools to help us to understand our current practices better.
>
> (Swartz, quoted in Jooste 2012: 5)

The nurturing of leadership skills to understand the finer nuances of higher education internationalization was employed in a direct manner by exposing the faculty, especially the Deans, not only to international partners but also to those international occasions that provide a clear message about the different dimensions of internationalization. As such all Deans have visited the NAFSA or the EAIE conferences since 2005. This provided the university leadership with a definite message about the extent and impact of higher education internationalization on a university like the NMMU. The real success of the NMMU's comprehensive internationalization lies within the way the university leadership has over time engaged not only in the process but also with the reasons why it is being done. Through the constant leadership debate about this the strategies and direction are always relevant and current, a critical success factor used to evaluate the NMMU's success in internationalization.

Resources and organization

The third element in the successful implementation of any internationalization strategy is the allocation of the necessary resources. In this case this includes the provision for a management structure to implement the strategy as well as the provision of a funding model that is sustainable and will provide stability.

From the outset the university agreed to introduce a centralized model. Thus the OfIE was established with the clear mandate to strategically steer the university's internationalization strategy and policies. As a result, all the internationalization activities are managed and coordinated through the OfIE. A Senior Director manages the OfIE with an appropriate staff complement. The underlying management philosophy of this office is to provide a complete service to academic and administrative staff, international students, and international postdoctoral students. Since its inception the OfIE has grown to a staff complement of 22, consisting of the members shown in Figure 13.2 plus an English as a Foreign Language Lecturer. It is located in the International Centre that houses all the staff from where all services and other activities related to the university's internationalization are conducted. This structure not only supports the comprehensive internationalization strategies but also demonstrates our institutional commitment to internationalization.

This philosophy and practice has been in place for more than ten years at the NMMU. In 2009 the university commissioned a review of its internationalization practices. The review, conducted by an external higher education expert, was endorsed by the Internationalization Committee and approved by the University Senate. It endorsed our model of comprehensive internationalization and further recognized the fact that the internationalization practices at NMMU are a stable and permanent part of the university structure.

Keeping with its model of integrating the internationalization activities throughout the university, as part of the academic focus of internationalization, the emphasis of student mobility off the campus shifted to an Internationalization @ Home strategy and as such the Manager: Internationalization@ Home and Research works in close cooperation with all programs and schools on campus to develop a truly international campus.

Funding of internationalization is one of those critical drivers that can ensure success or failure if not thought through strategically. Within the South African university funding framework all universities are funded through three sources: first, through a governmental subsidy allocated annually and calculated through a specific formula, mainly based on student numbers; second, through student fees; and third, through funding raised by the university itself from external and other sources. Internationalization as such does not form part of the funding formula and in all cases universities need to "top-slice" their available budget to allocate financial resources to internationalization. The NMMU University Council at the inception of the OfIE decided that the international activities of the university should fund itself. As such, international-student fees are levied to fund these activities. The funds generated through international education activities of the university is thus earmarked to cover the annual operating budget of the OfIE as well as all the internationalization activities and any other activities that may be approved by the Internationalization Committee. The specific financial circumstances of universities in a developing environment with competing financial priorities coupled with a large number of students from poor financial backgrounds, force institutions to be innovative. In the case of the NMMU, most of its international activities initiated by the OfIE are thus funded through the

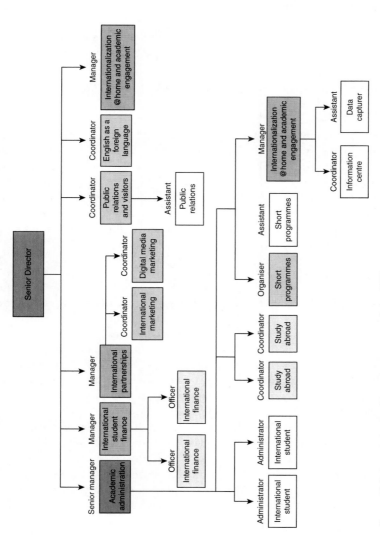

Figure 13.2 Internal capacity and structure of the OfIE.

fees generated through international students. Other activities such as international research projects are funded on a project basis through the normal budget process of the university.

Internationalization highlights

Although the comprehensive internationalization of the NMMU has provided highlights in all areas, the paragraphs below provide a glimpse of the highlights of the activities which have been most influential on the road to comprehensive internationalization. What will be discussed is the internationalization of the student body and management of international partnerships. The internationalization of the curriculum, the research practices, and outcomes, as well as bringing the benefits of internationalization to the local community are as important but not included in this study.

Internationalization of the student body

General principle

The university recognizes the value of a diverse international-student body. The OfIE manages the growth of international-student numbers in such a way that this diversity is enhanced. The broader university community is continuously informed about and exposed to the cultural diversity of international students. This is promoted through an International Week on campus as well as the frequent celebration of different international cultures. The university's rootedness to Africa and the varying cultures from the continent is also celebrated during the dedicated Africa Week in May each year.

Admission of international students

The general principle underlying the selection of international students is based on academic excellence. International students at under- and post-graduate level are selected on the basis of academic excellence and academic suitability for a particular program. The Office for International Education, in collaboration with the Centre for Access, Assessment and Research and Faculties, formulated admissions criteria for international students in accordance with the general principle described above and this is now the standard practice as approved by the University Senate and Council.

The admission of international students is administered in accordance with an enrolment plan for international students developed in cooperation with the Central University Enrolment Plan. The success in its internationalization practices in the student data presented doesn't tell the complete story. In 2001, when the internationalization process of the university commenced, it only had 127 registered international students. During the time of the merger in 2005 the number of international students grew to more than 1,200. The data presented

Table 13.1 International-student enrolments 2008–2012

Student type	2008	2009	2010	2011	2012
International	2,004	2,061	2,087	2,225	1,952
National	22,115	21,566	24,060	25,170	25,343
Refugees	13	12	9	16	11
Total	24,132	23,639	26,156	27,411	27,306

in Table 13.1 indicates a stable environment in which, notwithstanding the global economic crises in 2008, the OfIE maintained its student numbers. It also shows a substantial growth in post-graduate student numbers, especially from the developing world. The success of the internationalization of the university is also illustrated by the growth in the number of international students who graduate annually from the NMMU.

Although the institutional target of having 15 percent of its student body represented by international students is still not achieved, the current 9 percent do have a major impact on the development of a global learning environment on campus. With such a diverse student body, currently from 56 nationalities, the road towards comprehensive internationalization is well traveled and the end goal achievable.

Institutional partnerships

The NMMU developed its philosophy around institutional partnerships with a clear understanding that the knowledge society and its development assume mobility of all knowledge workers and as such an increase in mobility through networks. It is thus a prerequisite that international institutional and other partnerships should enhance its global reach and have a strategic impact on the academic activities of the university. One of the critical elements included in our evaluation of future and current partnerships is their ability to contribute to the transformation processes taking place if one is to develop a global learning environment on the campus. Institutional partners are thus encouraged to participate in joint projects, in teaching and learning as well as research, where innovative products emerge over time, resources are combined, and the relationship is as important as the product—expansive and ever-growing.

Institutional partnerships are managed and maintained through the Manager: International Partnerships. To manage and maintain these partnerships the University subscribes to the philosophy that all partnerships form part of a global network that should provide more than just individual benefits through each memoranda of understanding. The philosophy of partners connecting to each other via a network of individual partnerships is practiced through a bi-annual partnership week, also known as the "NMMU Family Week." All partners are invited to Port Elizabeth for a weeklong celebration of internationalization. The Colloquium, the highlight of the week, debates internationalization and its challenges amongst partners with the end result being a publication of the deliberations widely used in higher education internationalization debates.

The NMMU currently partners with 63 higher education institutions globally. True to its mission it has a number of longstanding and active partnerships in Africa and similarly longstanding and valuable partners in Europe and North America.

Conclusion

The NMMU's road to comprehensive internationalization is not complete but is rather an on-going process dictated largely by external factors shaping the South African and global environment. One of the lessons learnt over the past 14 years, however, is that it requires dedication, innovation, academic rigor, leadership, and stability to comprehensively internationalize a university. The success of the internationalization of a university such as the NMMU is driven by its close association to the academic mission, to educate students for work and for life, in such a way that they can be successful in their professions but also be leaders in developing a better world for all.

The greatest success of the comprehensive internationalization of the NMMU is that it is fully integrated in all aspects of its governance structure. The continuous engagement of academics and professionals in the institutional international activities has made internationalization largely part of the NMMU's life. It is, however, a process and its success is closely linked to the continuous management and steering of internationalization throughout the university. It is not a process that can be self-driven in an environment with so many other important competing interests.

Chapter 14

"Knowledge without borders"

Internationalization strategy at the University of Nottingham

Christine Ennew

Introduction

Within the UK, the University of Nottingham has variously been described as the country's "most international university," and the closest to a "truly global university." It is widely regarded as having played a pioneering role in the development of internationalization in UK higher education and the most visible manifestation of this is the University's two international campuses in China and Malaysia. This chapter provides an overview of the way in which the University of Nottingham has developed its international activity over time to build a strategic approach which genuinely seeks to deliver a comprehensive and broad-based approach to internationalization.

Any organizational strategy is necessarily contextual and an understanding of current strategic activity in the international domain must be conditioned by an understanding of both national and international context. Accordingly, the chapter begins with an overview of the evolution of the institution and its operating environment. The next section outlines the position of internationalization within the University's overall strategy and explains the principles that the University uses to guide its international activity. The subsequent section explores the components of the current internationalization strategy in greater details and highlights specific activities that have been undertaken in order to deliver in relation to specified aims. Finally, the chapter closes with a reflection on the effectiveness of the strategy itself, the challenges around managing delivery and future developments.

Conditioning strategy—understanding context

The way in which the University of Nottingham has developed its strategic approach to internationalization is very much conditioned by both the institution's own history and characteristics as well as by the nature of the external operating environment. Both could generate very significant discussion so the following paragraphs will focus on providing a summary overview of both.

This history of the University of Nottingham is one that is characterized by institutional mobility, partnership working, and an entrepreneurial spirit. Originally established in the city center in 1881, the University quickly outgrew its premises and in 1928 moved to a parkland campus on the edge of the city with financial support from one of the region's leading businesses, initiating a partnership which continues today. Subsequently linked campuses were developed in and around the city (Sutton Bonington, Jubilee, King's Meadow) and, subsequently, at a rather greater distance in Malaysia and China. The University also opened (in 1970) the first new medical school in the twentieth century. Almost 40 years later, Nottingham launched the first purpose-built new veterinary school to be opened in the UK in 50 years. The result of this activity is one of the UK's largest universities and one with one of the broadest range of subjects on offer to students.

International activity was evident at the University from its early days; high-profile international visitors were welcomed (including Professor Albert Einstein and Mahatma Gandhi), its researchers travelled to collaborate with scholars worldwide, and international students have been seeking out the University since the 1940s if not before. Perhaps not surprisingly, student choice of country was impacted by colonial and post-colonial relationships, and in the case of Nottingham, there were particularly strong ties to what were to become Malaysia and Singapore. But, like most other UK Universities, much of this activity happened organically; there was little in the way of proactive management—at least not until the 1980s—when a new policy environment prompted very significant changes in the way in which UK universities approached international activity.

A severe economic recession in the early 1980s led the UK Government to end the practice of subsidizing international students and require institutions to charge full-cost fees. Not surprisingly there was a strongly negative reaction to this development from international students, as well as from the universities themselves, particularly when further government funding cuts were introduced. Nottingham was one of the first universities to respond proactively to this changed environment; it recognized that if international students were still to be attracted to the University, there was a need to professionalize both recruitment and student support. And as a result it was one of the first to put in place a dedicated International Office.

Full-cost fees for international students inevitably had the effect of reducing the size of potential market compared to what it would have been with subsidized fees. As a result the 1990s were characterized by increased competition in recruitment and the development of innovative models to reach international students; it was the late 1980s and early 1990s that saw the emergence at scale of the models of transnational provision which are so widespread today. And of course as institutions moved from a pure "exporting" model, based around student recruitment, to more contractual models (twinning, articulation, validation, franchising), there was a compelling logic that would suggest that in an increasingly interconnected world, institutional mobility internationally could be a very effective alternative to the mobility of people (see Mazzarol *et al.* 2003 for a more detailed discussion of these "three waves of internationalization").

Broader policy agendas around institutional performance, especially in research, also contributed to the move towards an increasingly strategic approach to internationalization. International collaborations were recognized as an important indicator in assessments of research quality and funding to support international collaborations was growing; as a result an increasing number of UK institutions (Nottingham included) began to recognize the value of trying to actively manage the international dimensions of research activity as well as student recruitment.

In brief then, Nottingham as an institution appears to have something of an established disposition to look outwards and to innovate. Over the past 30 years it has seen some dramatic changes in the policy environment, primarily in relation to funding and performance measurement. These changes have significantly conditioned the way in which the University has managed and developed its activities in support of internationalization. These will be outlined in more detail below.

Internationalization strategy: an overview

The University's Strategic Plan 2010–2015 provides the context for the current articulation of the University's international ambitions. The Strategic Plan is structured around nine key themes, one of which is entitled "Global Reach." This particular section of the plan outlines the institutional vision with respect to internationalization as well as specifying key aims, objectives, and targets. A more detailed Internationalization Strategy ("Knowledge without Borders") sits below the overarching plan as a "supporting strategy."[1]

The starting point for the development of the institution's approach to internationalization is the overall University mission:

> At The University of Nottingham we are committed to providing a truly international education, inspiring our students, producing world-leading research and benefitting the communities around our campuses in the UK, China and Malaysia. Our purpose is to improve life for individuals and societies worldwide. By bold innovation and excellence in all that we do, we make both knowledge and discoveries matter.

Implicit in this mission statement is a recognition that internationalization is not an end in itself, but rather a means to enable the institution to deliver more effectively in relation to both education and research. There is a conscious focus in "Knowledge without Borders" on breadth of activity, recognizing the significance of broad-based and comprehensive approaches to internationalization (see, e.g., Hudzik 2011). The decision was also taken to formally specify the principles that would guide the internationalization process and while these were by no means unique to Nottingham, making a formal statement was seen to be of value in communicating institutional intentions to a broader audience both internally and externally. These principles were outlined as follows:

- *Reciprocity.* Internationalization is a two-way process; for the University to realise the full benefits of our global reach we must give as much as we get. We believe as a community that by working multilaterally rather than unilaterally we achieve more in terms of teaching, research and knowledge transfer.

- *Commitment.* Internationalization is an investment for the future and requires a long term commitment—to our students, to our staff, and to our partners globally.

- *Quality.* We seek to maintain the highest standards in all that we do. Although we are fundamentally a British institution, internationally we will always aim to be sensitive and relevant to local circumstances.

- *Social and environmental responsibility.* Knowledge is a public good and we recognise that we have a responsibility to generate and share knowledge for the greater good of society. As an educational institution operating on a global level, we are committed to educational capacity development in emerging economies, doing so in a way that is environmentally sustainable.

The overarching University mission, the underpinning role of internationalization, and the guiding principles provided a framework within which more specific activities could be identified and coordinated in pursuit of a range of specific aims. These are discussed in more detail in the next section.

The components of internationalization

The University's internationalization strategy is broadly defined and encompassing, with a long-term aspiration that internationalization is embedded across all relevant University activities. Key activities that would drive internationalization were identified as follows:

(a)   establishing an in-country presence;
(b)   international teaching partnerships and transnational education (TNE);
(c)   international-student recruitment;
(d)   student mobility;
(e)   staff mobility;
(f)   research;
(g)   knowledge transfer;
(h)   social responsibility and international development;
(i)   international alumni;
(j)   philanthropy;
(k)   an international curriculum.

An integral part of the analysis that underpinned the internationalization strategy was a mapping of activity by region focusing on both the current position and

Table 14.1 Scale and scope of current internationalization activity

	In-country presence	TNE partnerships	International students	Student mobility	Staff mobility	Social responsibility	Research	Knowledge transfer and business	Alumni	Philanthropy
N America			✓	✓✓✓	✓					
Latin America	✓		✓	✓				✓	✓✓	✓
Europe		✓	✓✓	✓✓✓	✓		✓			
MENA			✓✓				✓✓			
Africa		✓	✓✓						✓	
N & C Asia			✓✓			✓			✓	
South Asia			✓✓✓					✓	✓	
East Asia (excl. China)			✓✓✓	✓		✓	✓		✓	
China	✓✓	✓✓✓	✓✓✓	✓✓	✓		✓✓✓	✓	✓	
SE Asia		✓✓✓	✓✓				✓✓	✓✓	✓✓✓	✓
Malaysia			✓✓✓	✓✓	✓			✓	✓✓✓	✓
Australasia	✓✓		✓✓✓	✓✓✓	✓		✓		✓✓✓	✓

desired future developments. An illustration of this process is presented in Table 14.1, which contains the initial mapping of activity by broad region. Fundamental to this approach was a recognition that the University would not seek to deliver all activities in all regions. Rather the approach was to focus on activities that were most appropriate to a given region based on overarching institutional objectives and capacity aligned with identified opportunities. For each cell in the matrix, more detailed analysis was undertaken to map current activity and outline future plans. As an illustration, in relation to the activity "In-country presence," the mapping identified existing representative offices in Brazil, Mexico, Malaysia, and China, as well as campuses in Malaysia and China. Future plans highlighted that the University would not seek to develop additional campuses but would focus on the opening of additional offices in West Africa and India to support other activity in these regions (dominantly recruitment in Africa, alumni, dominantly partnerships and careers in India).

One feature of the evaluation of activity by region (as outlined in Table 14.1) was the dominance of international-student recruitment as an activity and the heavy emphasis on China as a region. International-student recruitment has dominated internationalization activity in most UK universities, and Nottingham has been particularly successful, as Figures 14.1 and 14.2 show. This analysis resulted in a conscious decision to seek opportunities to broaden activity and regional scope to develop under-represented areas and under-represented activities, where the institution had the necessary capabilities and where the right opportunities existed.

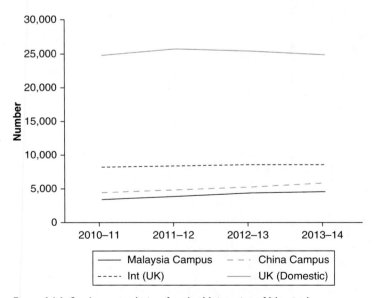

Figure 14.1 Student population for the University of Nottingham.

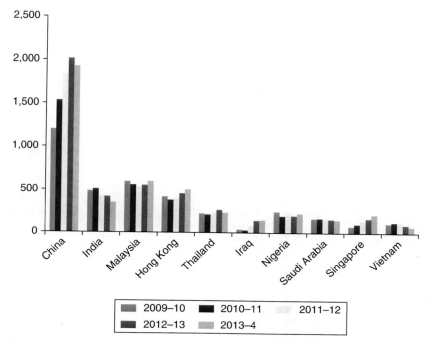

Figure 14.2 International student populations—main source countries.

The structural arrangements for delivery evolved over the period of the strategy. In broad terms, leadership for the strategy rests with the University Executive Board with an International Strategy Board having direct oversight. With respect to implementation, specific responsibility rested with a range of professional services functions, dominantly the International Office, but including other relevant functions such as teaching and learning, research, business engagement, alumni, and careers, as well as academic schools.

The University's Executive Board includes a Pro Vice Chancellor (Vice President) with specific responsibility for internationalization, supported by four regionally focused Assistant Pro Vice Chancellors (APVCs). In addition, the Provosts of both international campuses are members of UEB and other functional Pro Vice Chancellors (PVCs) have responsibility for the international components of their portfolios.

The overarching University Strategic Plan specifies a broad range of aims regarding internationalization. These appear across each of the plan themes, although are most prominent within the "Global reach" theme. "Knowledge without borders" takes these aims and explores delivery options in more detail. The following paragraphs outline these aims, organized by strategic theme and for each aim, there is a discussion of the actions that have been taken in pursuit of these aims.

Theme: global reach

Aim 1: Secure our achievement in establishing the two campuses in Asia, by fuller integration, coordination, and expansion, and taking advantage of all the opportunities associated with their success.

- Growth in student numbers and breadth of subject provision, development of significant research portfolios;
- development of major research focused initiatives in both China (Marine Economy) and Malaysia (under-utilized crops);
- development of growing range of summer school options at all levels to provide opportunities for student to enhance their understanding of Malaysia, China and the broader regions;
- growth in number of hosted conferences and meetings;
- enhanced integration across campuses in terms of internal structures and management arrangements; institutionalization of the "one University, multiple locations" model.

Aim 2: To magnify the international impact of our research and commercialization activities.

- Investment in more proactive leadership including the creation of the "Asia Business Centre," resulting in a significant growth in volumes of research output and size of research grant portfolios in both China and Malaysia;
- proactive targeting of key countries and institutions leading to a growth in international funding and international research collaborations via UK campus including in Europe, India, China, and Brazil;
- significant growth in commercial partnerships, particularly in China including a number of major funding successes. Associated development of Executive Education activity including a major partnership to deliver programs in banking and finance in China;
- establishment of an International Doctoral Innovation Centre in China; network of doctoral partnerships in Malaysia.

Aim 3: To expand student and staff mobility.

- Active promotion of student mobility opportunities—especially to China and Malaysia;
- development of Erasmus program for both study and work placements—creating one of the largest programs in the UK;
- active promotion of opportunities for staff to move between locations; creation of an inter-campus mobility fund to support his process;

Aim 4: To develop and enhance international teaching and research partnerships.

- The Universitas 21 network, of which Nottingham was a founder member, was identified as presenting particular opportunities for partnership development with similar institutions; Nottingham chose to engage actively in joint PhD initiatives as well as cross institutional teaching innovations;
- continued development of U-NOW open courseware initiative to facilitate sharing of teaching and learning resources internationally—and specifically with partner institutions;
- a systematic analysis of the partnership portfolio and market opportunities was used to guide future activity in this area. Specifically, existing partnerships were categorized according to the matrix outline in Figure 14.3. Four partner categories were identified as follows:

Standard-focused

The University has relatively large numbers of this type of relationship and small- scale partnerships tend to be characterized by relatively high costs for development and maintenance. Accordingly, recommended activity was:

- o Developments in this area focused on strategic priorities (in underrepresented subject areas and in regions which are attractive but underrepresented).
- o Focus on opportunities to expand existing partnerships in terms of either scale or scope.

	Scope: Focused (Dominant focus is a single activity in a single area)	Scope: Broad (Dominant focus is multiple activity or multiple areas)
Scale: Standard Numbers impacted relatively small	*Standard-Focused* Partnerships with a single clear focus impacting on relatively small numbers— e.g. a dual or joint award for limited student numbers in a given subject area	*Standard-Broad* Partnerships with a multiple foci impacting on relatively small numbers—e.g. an exchange agreement across multiple academic areas, or an agreement involving collaborative teaching, research links and staff exchange in a single academic area
Scale: Extensive Large numbers of individuals involved	*Extensive-Focused* Partnerships with a single clear focus impacting on relatively large numbers—e.g. a large scale undergraduate articulation teaching partnership	*Extensive-Broad* Partnerships with a multiple foci impacting on large numbers—e.g. a large-scale teaching articulation augmented by student and staff exchange and multiple research collaborations

Figure 14.3 The partnership portfolio matrix.

Extensive-focused

These partnerships are typically well established with a growing volume of activity. However, in many cases there is a high concentration of activity in specific academic area. Strategically, the focus of attention was:

- o Where partners have a broad range of academic activity, explore opportunities to broaden the partnership (into other academic areas and/or other activities).
- o For partners who are narrowly focused, monitor and where appropriate invest to maintain and develop.

Standard-broad

In these cases there is a range of activity taking place but at a relatively small scale. The breadth of activity is a clear strength, but the limited scale and geographic imbalance maybe regarded as weaknesses. Strategic priorities should be:

- o Build scale in key partnerships where there is identified willingness from both partners.
- o Broaden geographical spread by building on existing links.

Extensive-broad

This category was expected to be small, but clear opportunities existed to broaden existing partnerships in terms of range of areas or numbers involved:

- o A focus on both the development of existing partnerships and the creation of new ones in under-represented and priority areas worked effectively in terms of increasing the number and scale of teaching partnerships beyond the targeted level.

Theme: excellence in education

Aim 5: To establish the campuses in Asia as leading institutions within their regions, in terms of teaching quality.

- Development of subject portfolio in both locations, growth in student numbers, enhanced professional development capacity with a particular focus on teaching and learning (including provision of Post Graduate Certificate in Higher Education;
- Key developments included Arts and Humanities programs in Malaysia, broader range of engineering-focused programs in China, development of economics and environmental science in both locations.

Theme: world-changing research

Aim 6: By 2015 to achieve a research profile at our campuses in Asia in key areas comparable to that of the Nottingham campus.

- Strategic investment to pump-prime research activity in key areas across all three campuses including significant funding for PhD scholarships;
- strategic investment in research infrastructure to support existing research activity and underpin future funding initiatives;
- development of research training programs in both locations to support the development of research capacity.

Theme: university life

Aim 7: To enhance support for international mobility of students and staff. (See also Aim 3 above)

- Active promotion of full range of student mobility opportunities;
- development of tri-campus sporting competition to rotate across campuses on an annual basis;
- development of short-term mobility opportunities with a focus on volunteering work (for example, construction of a school in South Africa, growing number of medical related placements).

Theme: social responsibility

Aim 8: To be "good neighbors," in Nottingham, Ningbo, and Semenyih.

- Growth in volunteering activity including initiatives across a range of locations worldwide (work with Orang Asli community in Malaysia, school-based collaboration including students as volunteer teachers, diversity of student-led charitable initiatives).

Theme: sustaining excellence

Aim 9: Expand alumni engagement programs.

- Establishment of alumni offices at both international campuses;
- plans for the establishment of charitable foundations in a range of locations outside the UK to support international philanthropy;
- growth in the number of alumni associations in key locations worldwide— alumni led and university supported.

Key to delivery in relation to these aims has been the engagement of staff across the institution; while cultural change takes time it has become increasingly apparent that a growing number of staff do see the international dimension as embedded within their core activity. The supporting role of staff has been complemented by a willingness at institutional level to commit resource in support of existing and new international initiatives.

Challenges

Internationalization was and is a key component of an overarching institutional strategy that was designed to guide the development of the University of Nottingham over the period 2010–15. The central role given to internationalization reflects its importance as a source of differentiation for the University, with the two international campuses being of particular significance in this respect. Work on strategic direction for the next five years is well advanced at the time of writing. This will further refine and develop the University's international ambitions but will not change the fundamentals. Embedding and integrating internationalization across the full range of University activity will continue to sit at the heart of what the University does and will continue to be identified as a point of differentiation.

While the University has occupied a leading position with respect to internationalization within UK higher education, it continues to face a range of challenges with respect to the continued development of its strategy. These are not necessarily unique to either higher education or to internationalization, but are worth further discussion because they are a consequence of the particular approach that the University has adopted to developing a comprehensive internationalization strategy.

Structural

The approach being used by Nottingham seeks to integrate international activity across a range of functional areas. While an International Office has oversight of much internationalization activity (particularly that which is student related), significant responsibility for activities related to research, business engagement, philanthropy, and alumni rests with other professional service functions and with academic schools. This creates what is effectively a matrix structure with management and delivery involving a range of different groups within the institution. As with any set of activities that are structured in a matrix format, careful thought needs to be given to the ownership of an activity and coordination across interested parties.

Leadership

The matrix structure outlined above also gives rise to challenges around leadership and in particular, raises questions about how leadership responsibility is determined given the involvement of multiple different interest groups. Ultimately, the solution chosen combined distributed and dedicated leadership with a PVC (Internationalization) as the primary owner working collaborative with PVCs and senior managers in other key functional areas.

Managing conflicting objectives

With multiple, potentially conflicting objectives, a major challenge in developing a broad-based internationalization program relates to the allocation of scarce institutional resources in support of different activity in different regions of the world. The challenges that are apparent domestically are magnified when considering international scale activity.

Reconciling top-down and bottom-up

In developing its current and future internationalization plans the University has tried to put in place a set of strategic objectives and targets to provide a framework for decision making—to allow activities and opportunities to be tested against a pre specified set of desired outcomes. This offers the obvious benefit of trying to ensure a clear focus on delivery and reducing the risks of being distracted by opportunities that are not consistent with institutional plans. At the same time, every organization has to recognize that opportunities may arise that could not have been considered when a strategic plan was developed. Thus a major consideration within the management of internationalization has related to determining the right balance between focusing on top-down activity as specified in the overarching plan and responding to opportunities that emerge in a more bottom-up fashion.

These are challenges that will be familiar to many other Universities and indeed to many other institutions. Putting in place the appropriate decision making structures, multiple reporting lines and frequent meetings all play a role in addressing such challenges. And of course communication is key to ensuring appropriate coordination of activity.

Note

1 Available at http://www.nottingham.ac.uk/aglobaluniversity/documents/kwb-internationalisationstrategy-2011–15-v15(public).pdf

Chapter 15

Pontifical Catholic University of Rio de Janeiro

Internationalization, a well-assembled puzzle

Rosa Marina de Brito Meyer

In the international education arena, the Pontifical Catholic University of Rio de Janeiro has been recognized as one of the most successfully internationalized Brazilian universities. This general understanding was acknowledged by CAPES (Coordination for the Improvement of Higher Level Personnel) Brazilian Agency when it awarded PUC-Rio the "Most Successful Brazilian University in International Cooperation" in the year 2011. It hasn't been easy to achieve this position, though: many people worked hard on many fronts and program areas throughout more than six decades.

A pioneer among the Brazilian universities in creating a unit dedicated to international affairs, PUC-Rio celebrated the twentieth anniversary of its international office, the International Cooperation Central Coordination Office (CCCI) in 2012. Nevertheless, international collaboration did not start in 1992; a lot had been done before through varied initiatives of scattered faculty members, departments, and/or units, in a construction similar to assembling a puzzle. And more than 20 years later there is still much to be done.

We can divide PUC-Rio's internationalizing process into four phases: the incidental, the natural, the professional, and the strategic.

The incidental phase

The incidental phase dates to the mid-1950s. The first private university in the country, PUC-Rio was created in 1940 with the primary objective of standing out as an institution of academic excellence based on humanistic values. In 1951 the Federal government created the funding agency CAPES and launched a policy of funding the qualification abroad of third-degree professionals. PUC-Rio took advantage of this opportunity by sending large numbers of its faculty members for their MAs, MSCs, and PhDs in the most prestigious universities in the world. This movement allowed the development of joint research and the exchange of visiting professors, mainly in the STEM fields, thus giving the university an initial international visibility. Most of these visiting professors were renowned senior scholars in their fields, among them some Nobel Prize laureates.

In the 1960s and 70s, the highly qualified faculty body created some of the earliest graduate programs in the country; this kept the scientific production intense and consequently maintained the relationship with researchers from abroad. By having had the chance to study abroad, the graduate professors advised their students to do the same.

In 1969 another pioneer action became the starter of student exchanges: the offering of Portuguese as a Second Language certificate classes, called "Portuguese for Foreigners." These courses were attended mainly by visiting professors, and eventually international students on campus and international residents in Rio de Janeiro. Among some of the prestigious students who learned Portuguese in our classes we feel honored to be able to highlight the famous Dr. Albert Sabin, the Polish American medical researcher and scientist best known for having developed the oral polio vaccine. The existence of such classes resulted in PUC-Rio being approached by a number of US universities that already taught the language and needed a destination for their students to have an immersion experience. The University of Texas at Austin and the University of Arizona were the first to send groups of students in the month of July a few years in a row. The success of the short-term summer courses led some other US and European universities to propose long-term exchanges. As a consequence, the Portuguese for Foreigners regular courses for credit started being taught during the academic terms and no longer on winter and summer breaks only. Among the very early exchange programs we can mention the ISEP (International Student Exchange Program), a Georgetown University initiative that gathered mostly Jesuit universities around the world.

All these exchanges involved very small numbers of students both ways, but they represented a promising start. The presence of international students on campus already gave our campus a singularity not found in any other Brazilian university, and of course stimulated our Brazilian students to pursue the same experience.

These were the main movements towards the internationalization of PUC-Rio until the late 1980s: qualification of faculty members abroad, joint research—most of the time among professors only, not celebrated in MOUs or other types of agreements—reception of groups of international students for immersion in Portuguese, student exchanges, reception of visiting professors and the presence of our professors abroad as visiting professors too. Motivated by external demand and individual *ad hoc* initiatives, these activities were not created, organized, planned, or managed by any specific unit: they could start within any department or by the wish of any professor or due to some unexpected circumstance. In short, they represented the incidental phase of PUC-Rio's opening its doors to the world.

The natural phase

As a natural consequence of the success of these different actions, three major international institutions approached PUC-Rio in 1991 with the proposal of establishing long-term student exchanges involving larger numbers of participants: the University of California EAP (Exchange Abroad Programs) and Brown University from the United States; and the Ecole Supérieure des Sciences Economiques et Commerciales (ESSEC) from France. PUC-Rio understood then that it was about time to give a more centralized attention to a process that seemed inevitable: the university's internationalization.

This sequence of facts led the internationally minded Vice-President for Community Affairs at the time to create PUC-Rio's international office, then called "International Programs Office," in 1992. He advocated so passionately for international affairs that soon he chose to leave the position as Vice-President in order to dedicate himself fulltime to this cause. This was the start of the second stage in the internationalization process, the natural phase.

The office was conceived with an identity profoundly related to student exchanges and therefore it had the word "exchange" (*intercâmbio*) in its Portuguese name: "Coordenação Central de Intercâmbio Internacional" (CCII). And with such an office, internationalization naturally grew in a new scale during the 1990s and the first decade of the twenty-first century.

During this period, the President, then Fr. Jesús Hortal, a Spanish Jesuit priest internationally experienced and thus highly internationally minded, included the item "internationalization" in the main documents of the university, presenting it as one of its primary goals for the near future. And most important of all, internationalization was defined as a tool for academic enrichment, not for financial growth. As a consequence, soon the CCII was moved from the Office of the Vice-President for Community Affairs to the Office of the Vice-President for Academic Affairs, the Provost.

In January of 1996 I was invited by the Provost to take the responsibility of the area as Associate Vice-President for Academic affairs in charge of International Programs and consequently Head of the CCII. As an Associate Professor in the Linguistics and Portuguese as a Second Language fields, I was only slightly familiar with the area of International Education and confess having taken over the office without experience on what had to be done. But with the steady support of our internationally minded President and the Provost, I understood that the first action had to be related to assuring the university's presence in the International Education arena. Therefore I started to represent CCII and thus PUC-Rio at various forums and conferences: the national FAUBAI (Brazilian Universities International Affairs Assistants Forum) and international ones like NAFSA (Association of International Educators) and EAIE (European Association for International Education). Through these international forums' workshops and sessions I was able to understand the field in a global context and to obtain professional training; international education wasn't—and still isn't—an academic or professionalizing area of study in Brazil.

Personal relationships played an important role in this process. Building professional relationships with people who, like me, were in charge of international affairs in their universities and also like me were very pragmatically experiencing (new) ways to improve their units and internationalization was crucial. Together we attended workshops and sessions, working breakfasts and luncheons, work receptions and parties: the routine was hectic, but the feeling of mission accomplishment compensated it.

By the late 1990s the number of students exchanged had grown dramatically. New exchange destinations in new countries were offered to PUC-Rio students; special services were created in order to better receive the international exchange students; many agreements of many different types and with institutions from the most different regions of the world were signed. An expanding number of international scientific events took place on campus than ever before. And because of these facts, the number of the international office's staff members had to grow accordingly. And they too started to participate in international education conferences abroad.

In the early 2000s, the university was on its way to deepening its international partnerships. It was able to offer to its partners a wide range of areas of cooperation: graduate programs in all areas of study on campus, most of them highly ranked by CAPES (Coordination for the Improvement of Higher Education Personnel, a Federal Government funding and graduate programs evaluation agency); a strong program of undergraduate research; a successful company incubator where international students could work as interns; steady collaboration with some of the main national and multinational companies; and a renowned excellence in many fields of study on campus. PUC-Rio firmly headed toward an ever deeper internationalization.

Student exchanges were our internationalization start-up activity, but now international activities began to broaden. New initiatives had the objective of extending the successful experience with student exchanges to deeper academic collaboration: the creation of thematic international chairs. The Antonio Vieira High Studies Chair in Portuguese Studies funded by the Instituto Camões from Portugal was inaugurated in 1998; the Fulbright Commission in Rio de Janeiro was hosted on our campus in 2000; the High Studies Chair in American Studies funded by Fulbright was created in 2003; and the Confucius Institute funded by the Hanban from China was inaugurated in 2011. All these international chairs, as well as other ones created in other phases, are fully active, bringing distinguished scholars to our campus and sending some of our most prominent researchers abroad yearly.

In 2002 CCII celebrated its tenth anniversary. As a consequence of the increase in the amount and diversity of responsibilities, the office's name was changed to International Cooperation Central Coordination Office (CCCI). The substitution of the word *exchange* with the word *cooperation* sent a clear message to the university community: the international office was not in charge of student exchanges only; all international affairs should be submitted to/ managed by this office. That was the beginning of the professional phase.

The professional phase

During the first decade of the 2000s, new initiatives took place based on an explicit professionalization and service-to-clients policy. This policy determined that CCCI's staff must exhibit key professional characteristics: professional qualification; high quality of services; dedication to students; loyalty to partners; and availability to PUC-Rio's professors and/or units that requested support. And it determined also that these principles should be achieved through a specific set of parameters: assistance to all; integration among ourselves, with our partners and with students; safety at all times; and, most of all, academic focus. Observing professional standards, maintaining professional attitude, pursuing professional outcomes: this was the new rule.

As a consequence, many new trends emerged in the student exchanges area, and new exchange programs were designed and offered: Double Degree programs, mainly with European universities; FIPSE-CAPES projects in different fields of study; a set of scholarships offered to low-income PUC-Rio students for them to be able to participate in exchanges; language immersion short-term exchange programs for PUC-Rio students to immerse in languages abroad during their Brazilian vacations and thus acquire language proficiency for a long-term exchange. Existing programs such as the Portuguese as a Second Language intensive courses were improved and enlarged; courses taught in English started to be offered so as to allow non-Portuguese speakers to study at PUC-Rio; customized summer programs were brought to our campus by US, European and Latin American universities; special services for international students were improved and very unique ones were created—like the hiring of a police detective to give them emergency support for any need; among others.

Innumerable official visits to partner university campuses were made for the staff to have better understanding of the other countries' university context. At the same time, the number of visitors from abroad who came individually or in delegations—groups of students, researchers, teachers, administrators, diplomats, etc.—increased in an exponential way.

Consequently, the CCCI staff grew to meet this increase of responsibilities and activities and had to be reengineered. The position of Deputy Associate Vice-President for Academic Affairs in charge of International Cooperation was created because one faculty member only was not able to cope with the busy agenda anymore. Internal biannual professional development seminars were created in order to assess recent activities and to plan for the following years. Responsibilities were reassigned, new positions were created, new and more qualified people were hired. And still, a friendly and warm environment was maintained in the office's headquarters always and the team worked in harmony and with a collaborative attitude in spite of any difficulties that might occur. PUC-Rio has been very lucky with such a dedicated and efficient staff supporting its process of internationalization.

A larger number of CCCI staff members than before were sent abroad to participate in international conferences, attending workshops and sessions, meeting with partners from around the world, being strongly exposed to the English language, and thus acquiring better professional skills. A professional development program was created so as to allow staff members to attend graduate courses and/or to participate in language immersion courses abroad. And here we must present our appreciation to the State University of New York (SUNY) at New Paltz that generously hosted some of CCCI's staff in their ESL summer courses. Because of this fact, added to the presence of many staff members and interns who went to SUNY as exchange students, Dr. Bruce Sillner, Dean of International Programs at SUNY New Paltz, jokingly noted that CCCI was the "SUNY Rio" office. We just loved it and keep repeating it today.

With the same spirit of collaboration, PUC-Rio hosted many partner universities' staff members in its Portuguese intensive courses without charge. We taught Portuguese to partners from Argentina, Germany, Canada, and the United States, among other countries.

PUC-Rio's visibility also enlarged considerably. As the only Brazilian university to be represented at NAFSA and EAIE conferences for more than 10 years, PUC-Rio proved that it took international cooperation very professionally and because of this image—a real one—it became the reference institution for Brazilian university in the international education community. When for the first time the Brazilian government funded a Brazilian universities booth at NAFSA in Washington D.C. in 2008, the organizers invited us to speak at the reception, publicly recognizing and highlighting the fact that PUC-Rio had been the pioneer Brazilian university at NAFSA for a long time.

The outcomes of all these efforts are remarkable. Compared with the 1996 figures, we now host more than 1,300 international students on campus and send around 400 abroad per year, an increase of almost 2,000 percent (see Figure 15.1). The CCCI team encompasses 23 people—2 faculty members, 13 staff members, 5 interns, and 3 minor interns—and 2 external collaborators, an increase of almost 800 percent. And we have 319 valid agreements signed, an increase of around 400 percent.

The CCCI team usually attends 8–10 international conferences abroad and receives at least 120 visitors yearly; we are always invited to join governmental delegations of Brazilian universities abroad. PUC-Rio's President is constantly invited to participate as keynote speaker in countless academic, political, and cultural international events. The number of national and international awards, prizes and distinctions received by professors, undergraduate and graduate students, and the university itself every year is remarkable.

Nevertheless, it would be unfair to assign CCCIs successes to its team only. Little of our success would have been possible without:

- higher leadership—President, Provost, and Vice-Presidents—that allowed us to work appropriately for the benefit of the university community as a whole;
- the mention of the importance of the university's internationalization in every document, strategic plan, annual report, etc.;

PUC-Rio students abroad

PROGRAM	1996	1997	1998	1999	2000	2001	2002	2003	2004	2005	2006	2007	2008	2009	2010	2011	2012	2013
Regular courses	23	32	37	78	52	49	97	115	122	143	170	156	181	236	243	233	223	166
CsF																	67	127
Double degree						5	9	14	29	36	32	30	61	48	44	48	39	46
Short term										20	44	98	131	91	80	141	105	89
Total per year	23	32	37	78	52	54	106	129	151	199	246	284	373	375	367	422	434	428
Main destinations	France, USA, Portugal, Spain, Germany, England, Italy, Mexico, Australia, Canada																	

International students at PUC-Rio

PROGRAM	1996	1997	1998	1999	2000	2001	2002	2003	2004	2005	2006	2007	2008	2009	2010	2011	2012	2013
Regular courses	57	77	73	87	123	144	226	267	214	244	390	433	466	499	623	553	627	779
Double degree						7	10	5	5	12	17	18	8	10	8	7	12	19
Intensive courses	8	40	32	33	42	16	97	80	69	172	177	183	184	244	274	305	341	344
Customized									10	38	49	136	122	96	66	247	171	324
Internships																6	29	13
Total per year	65	117	105	120	165	167	333	352	298	466	633	770	780	849	971	1,118	1,180	1,479
Main nationalities	USA France, Portugal, Spain, Germany, China, Norway, Mexico, Canada, England																	
Total of exchange students per year (PUC-Rio and intl. students)	88	149	142	198	217	221	439	481	449	665	879	1,054	1,153	1,224	1,338	1,540	1,614	1,907

Figure 15.1 Numbers of students sent abroad and international students on campus, 1996–2013.

- PUC-Rio's trust in CCCI's work and support of CCCI's initiatives at all times;
- the possibility of hiring staff every time that a new project or the growth of existing programs required it;
- providing adequate office space;
- financial independence—CCCI is a self-supported office; the reasonable freedom of decision-taking;
- and most of all the encouragement and recognition at all times.

Of course we must also appreciate the core role of our partners in this process. As we usually say in presentations and speeches, we have a large number of very good partner universities and a select group of sister universities—which we prefer to call our "friend universities," because friends are chosen. These are institutions where we made friends who we can always count on, no matter what happens, and this is the most precious accomplishment of all for us Brazilians: to turn a (strictly) professional relationship into a (deeply desirable) personal one. It is probably in these institutions that we found some of our best international partners and friends, and this closeness is precious within the Brazilian culture. It is always a moment of joy to meet with them at a conference or a partner university family meeting in some far location somewhere in the world. They are the priceless gift that we from CCCI gained as a reward for our hard work.

Coincidently with the CCCI's twentieth anniversary, at the moment when we were ready to celebrate our accomplishments and when the best of professional quality seemed to have been reached, our new President presented us a very welcome challenge: he chose PUC-Rio's internationalization as one of the two priorities for his mandate and therefore asked us to lead an Internationalization Committee with the objective of building an internationalization strategic plan.

So after a seminar with the university leaders enriched by the presence and contribution of Ms. Rita Moriconi, Education USA's Southern Cone Reac, this Committee was established and worked hard for two years towards the creation of PUC-Rio's "International Agenda" in analogy to PUC-Rio's "Environmental Agenda" that was successfully launched in 2009. The International Agenda was released in December 2012, inaugurating a new moment in PUC-Rio's internationalization: the strategic phase.

The strategic phase

PUC Rio's International Agenda establishes that becoming a fully international institution should be the general objective of the new and strategic internationalization process of the university. As such, it should, for example: be capable of receiving international people as regular students by offering a full range of classes taught in English; of graduating professionals able to efficiently work in other countries; of building an cross-culturally friendly environment on campus;

of hiring staff and faculty members who speak only English; of providing lodging for visitors and visiting fellow researchers; among other recommended initiatives.

CCCI anticipated the beginning of this strategic moment by launching, in April 2012, the PUC-Rio website in English, an essential instrument for any university that wishes to call itself international. Also, it is rewarding to testify that some of the activities recommended by the International Agenda are already being implemented, like English and Chinese classes that have been offered to staff members free of charge.

But there is still much to be done in the years to come. PUC-Rio's internationalization process is at a strategic moment under new leadership. Ideally CCCI will help the university to spread the internationalization process out more evenly among its various units as well as more deeply in all levels of the academic and administrative community. It will be important for the university to keep the forward momentum under new leadership. Launching the next phase of the International Agenda would be an important step forward, as would the establishment of a university-level International Affairs Committee to advise CCCI. Through the effective continuing implementation of the International Agenda, PUC-Rio will be able to maintain its leadership in Brazilian higher education.

Chapter 16

Internationalization at the University of Queensland

An institutional journey

Anna Ciccarelli and Janey Saunders

A great deal has been written about the role of internationalization at the institutional level: from purpose and strategy to effective whole of university approaches. This chapter will outline The University of Queensland's approach to comprehensively internationalize the university and will offer reflections on successes and challenges. This should be read against the backdrop of Australian internationalization context, which is defined by a large inbound international-student program, significant academic engagement in the Asia Pacific region, and a strong commitment to expand the outbound mobility experiences of Australian students. This commitment, whilst intrinsically motivated by institutional priorities, is also strongly promoted through governmental priorities such as The New Colombo Plan 2014 program, a signature initiative of the Australian Government which aims to lift knowledge of the Indo Pacific in Australia and strengthen people-to-people and institutional relationships, through study and internships undertaken by Australian undergraduate students in the region (DFAT 2014).

A university with global reach

The University of Queensland (UQ) is the largest and most comprehensive university in Queensland with more than 46,000 students including an international-student population of 11,000, from 134 nations, and more than 200,000 alumni worldwide. UQ is a leading research intensive university and consistently ranks in the top 100 according to major university ranking systems and has won more Australian Teaching and Learning Council Awards for Teaching Excellence than any other in Australia (Shanghai Ranking Consultancy 2013; Times Higher Education 2014; Quacquarelli Symonds 2014; National Taiwan University 2013).

The University's strategic framework is focused on the core pillars of learning, discovery, and engagement. In 2010, the responsible senior officer leading the University's international portfolio, the Vice President International, sought to frame, position, and embed internationalization goals and objectives in each of these pillars, putting internationalization at the core of the University's teaching, research, and engagement mission. This approach challenged a previously fragmented approach that prioritized internationalization predominantly as the business of international-student recruitment with only tokenistic focus on mobility and internationalization of the curriculum as well as global research relationships and global engagement agendas. UQ's reframed approach was to formulate an outward-looking global strategy coupled with comprehensive internationalization objectives that shaped the internal settings and culture. These were designed to optimize UQ's contributions to global higher education and strengthen its capacity to forge strategic partnerships with people and organizations across higher education, research, industry, government, relationships, philanthropy, and alumni.

"Comprehensive internationalization" (CI), as defined by John Hudzik (2011) was used to frame the broad approach because it was compatible with UQ's mission, ethos, goals, and approach. Hudzik defines CI as "a commitment, confirmed through action, to infuse international and comparative perspectives throughout the teaching, research and service missions of higher education" (p. 6). This connects directly with the notion that internationalization should add value and strengthen the core mission of the university, rather than be the passion of the committed few; that is, it should be deeply useful to the university achieving its core goals in a globalized higher education system.

Internationalization at UQ is a whole of university responsibility, strategically driven by the Vice President/Deputy Vice-Chancellor International as the Senior International Officer. In 2009, the University commissioned a review of UQ perceptions and practices in internationalization (Green and Mertova 2009). The reviewers engaged in an extensive audit, including consultation with both academic and institutional leaders and wider faculty to ascertain strengths and areas of improvement for UQ in this area. Out of this review, targets for mobility, international staff, internationalized curricula and language learning, international research partnerships, and collaborative programs were developed. Measuring tools for many of these areas continue to be strengthened and UQ's strategic plan includes dedicated internationalized key performance indicators across its three pillars.

The resulting UQ Framework for Comprehensive Internationalization encompasses initiatives, policies, and programs under five interconnected target areas.

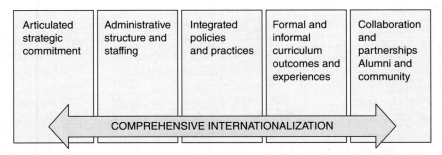

Figure 16.1 UQ's Framework for Comprehensive Internationalization. (Adapted from Center for Internationalization and Global Engagement 2012.)

These are represented diagrammatically in Figure 16.1 and will be addressed in further detail throughout this chapter.

I Articulated strategic commitment

UQ's comprehensive internationalization (CI) strategy was explicitly articulated and positioned, by the Vice President International, with governing council, academic senate, and with faculty as an issue of strategic importance. This signaled the beginning of a top-down strategy of internal engagement and organizational change that sought to connect with faculty priorities. The CI strategy promoted a University-wide approach to the development and integration of international, intercultural, and global perspectives in institutional policies, programs, and initiatives. By comprehensively internationalizing its campuses, student experiences, and formal and informal curricula, UQ seeks to embed intercultural and global perspectives into learning, research, and service cultures. UQ's commitment to students extends beyond graduation, as it continues to prioritize ongoing relationships with alumni, who live and work in more than 160 countries.

It would, however, be fair to say that the focus was very much on internationalizing the teaching and learning mission. This is reasonable given the scale of the teaching enterprise with over 9,000 graduates per annum. The internationalization of the research mission in a research-intensive University such as UQ, which ranks the top 100 or top 50 of any of the four major ranking systems, is by its very nature a different process, requiring less input and effort but nevertheless vital in terms of integrating the internationalization of research endeavor into the outward-looking global strategy. A strong partnership with the VP Research ensured that the global strategy was led by key research relationships, thus contributing to important international research outputs. Internationalizing the engagement, or service, mission was a much more nascent proposition given the state of global alumni and philanthropic engagement.

Nevertheless, while each of the three pillars was distinctive in nature and developmental stage, the shared touch point for the VP International was to develop a shared and inclusive narrative in partnership with the senior leaders of each pillar. While as the following section will show, some of this was achieved by leveraging formal governance structure, much was the result of informal influence and internal partnering. This will go some way to explaining the dominance of effort in the teaching and learning arena outlined in this chapter.

2 Administrative structure and staffing

In order to support internationalization goals at UQ, the institution employs a hub-and-spoke model, which includes a large central portfolio under the VP/Deputy Vice-Chancellor International, which focuses on: global engagement strategy; managing the large international-student program and related marketing, admissions, government compliance, and reporting requirements; provision of English language pathways and services for international students; managing international relationships, from due diligence to signed agreements. The international portfolio allocates strategic funds in excess of 1.5 million AUD annually towards internationalization initiatives and programs particularly supporting English language development and outbound mobility across the university.

As mentioned previously, a critical factor in comprehensively internationalizing the University was internal collaboration and partnership between the UQ's international portfolio and other central, whole of university portfolios and faculties and schools or departments. The success of these partnerships reflects a top-down and bottom-up model which allows international strategy to drive and coordinate operations but also capture and reflect emerging trends, as experienced on the ground and at the frontline, as it were, to inform strategy. This is a necessary attribute of managing internationalization within organizations, taking the view expressed earlier that internationalization must serve the core mission of the university rather than become a self-referential endeavor.

One of the most successful and strategic internal partnerships was with the advancement portfolio, which was at the same time building its local and global community outreach. Serving alumni globally served both portfolios and the Global Leadership Series, provide an opportunity for UQ alumni, parents, community members, and friends to engage with the University's academic leaders in discussions of global significance, such as food security, climate change, sustainable development, and peace and conflict. This proactive and committed work of the University's staff, students, community, and external partners is instrumental in translating UQ's global strategy and internationalization goals from words into action.

Additionally, all faculties have dedicated staff to focus on internationalization outcomes, including student recruitment, development of internationalized programs and research partnerships, promotion of awards, development and monitoring of faculty internationalization plans, which cascade down from the University's internationalization strategies.

UQ's global strategy and internationalization agenda was embedded in the annual celebration of teaching and learning through keynote speakers and workshops, thus positioning internationalization as an integral part of the core teaching and learning program.

3 Integrated policies and practices

UQ's approach has been both "top down" and "bottom up" in promoting comprehensive internationalization across the institution. Rather than jumping headlong into signature projects or activity for the sake of it, a deliberate strategic decision, responsive to emerging trends and national and state governmental priorities and incentives, was made to focus strongly on framework issues and to revise relevant policies and procedures, in order to engage and drive behaviour, and by building a committee structure to ensure collective leadership, decision-making, and endorsement of internationalization priorities and strategies. Establishing these foundations, through policy frameworks and governance structures, has mainstreamed internationalization across the University's central structure, academic faculties, and schools and provided the underpinning for the growth of sustainable programs and projects. The core mechanism was to mainstream internationalization and global strategy goals, objectives, and outcomes into the University's annual planning and review processes. This ensured governing endorsement as well as legitimacy.

Transforming strategy into action has been an important focus of CI practice at UQ. UQ faculties and schools include internationalization goals and targets supported by plans and dedicated internationalization focused staff and teams. Internationalization occurs across the key areas of teaching and includes the implementation of student and staff national and overseas mobility through exchange, as well as leadership in community engagement both within Australia and overseas. Many Faculties and Schools have Internationalization Committees to oversee and audit internationalization, in research and curriculum, and all report on internationalized themes such as overseas enrolments, student exchange numbers, and delivery of UQ degree programs overseas. Furthermore, initiatives in these areas are centrally supported through outbound mobility programs that foster studying abroad.

4 Formal and informal curriculum outcomes and experiences

Internationalization of the curriculum

"Internationalisation of the curriculum is the incorporation of an international and intercultural dimension into the preparation, delivery and outcomes of a program of study" (Leask 2009, p. 209). As a higher education institution, UQ focuses on preparing students to take up leadership roles in an increasingly globalized workforce. As part of this, the internationalization of its curricula has been a key focus for the University. Collaborations with leading national and international scholars in this field have provided leadership and strong intellectual direction in this area.

UQ's Internationalization of the Curriculum@UQ Framework is based on key frameworks developed by Professor Betty Leask, La Trobe University (Leask 2012a), and Dr Wendy Green, UQ Teaching and Educational Development Institute (TEDI) UQ. UQ's framework promotes a three tiered approach which presents Aims, Approaches and Outcomes to support Internationalization of the Curriculum within the Institution. Details of the approach are presented in Figure 16.2.

The importance of outbound mobility

UQ offers its students the opportunity to gain international experiences via an array of exchanges and internships. Through internships, many UQ students have assisted communities around the world while also benefiting from unique overseas experiences. With exchange partners in 39 countries including leveraging UQ's membership of the global consortia of institutions "Universitas 21"network, UQ

AIM

UQ provides all students with a broad, internationally relevant education that prepares them to thrive in diverse and global communities. UQ provides a learning environment characterized by:

OPPORTUNITY AND CHOICE
The UQ Advantage delivers learning experiences distinguished by opportunity and choice: opportunity to gain international experiences and develop global and inclusive perspectives, and choice among flexible pathways toward highly valued academic qualifications.

INTERCULTURAL COMPETENCIES
Students engage with diversity and develop intercultural understandings and communication skills.

GLOBAL ORIENTATION
Research-led curricula are informed by international perspectives of the discipline.

EDUCATING LEADERS
Leadership development in the context of future societal, environmental, economic and global challenges is expressed through the Graduate Attributes and Student Charter.

APPROACH

UQ adopts a comprehensive approach to internationalization of the curriculum which occurs through opportunity and choice in the formal and informal curriculum.

THE FORMAL CURRICULUM
Internationalization of the formal curriculum is embedded and relevant to core disciplinary content. It addresses the needs of all UQ students:

- globalized content
- cross-cultural perspectives on disciplinary knowledge
- pedagogy for teaching linguistic and culturally diverse classes
- opportunities for international and intercultural experiences.

Beyond the core degree programs, enrichment and specialist programs can further strengthen the internationalized experience within the formal curriculum. These programs include:

- concurrent diplomas in Language, Music and Global Issues
- a degree in International Studies.

THE INFORMAL CURRICULUM
The UQ Advantage Award program promotes co-curricular participation through leadership and student mobility experiences such as service learning, internships, exchange and volunteering across three core categories:

- global and cultural engagement
- research and entrepreneurship
- social responsibility and leadership.

The UQ Career Advantage PhD Program provides innovative curricula in the areas of:

- higher education practice and leadership
- research innovation, translation and commercialization
- global collaborations.

OUTCOMES

UQ's internationalized curriculum approach strives to educate graduates of the highest calibre.

KNOWLEDGE AND SKILLS
UQ graduates will have a critical knowledge and disciplinary competence relevant to local and global contexts and on issues of professional, political, environmental and social significance.

COMMUNICATION
UQ graduates will be able to demonstrate intercultural communicative competencies within diverse settings.

ETHICAL AND SOCIAL UNDERSTANDING
UQ graduates will be responsible, global citizens and they will be able and willing to engage with issues of equity and social justice and sustainability.

Figure 16.2 Internationalization of the curriculum at UQ.

aims to have a quarter (currently at 17 percent) of its undergraduate students study overseas during their degrees. UQ provides opportunities for students to travel overseas during their UQ program through a number of internally branded programs which very much include research degree students.

Funding support for student exchange

In 2013, UQ provided 475,000 AUD to 302 students to support their participation in an exchange. This funding was made available through a combination of central, faculty, and government scholarship schemes. The vast majority of scholarship and grant recipients had a Grade Point Average (GPA) above 5.4 out of 7 point scale. UQ also works closely with the Australian federal government to facilitate student access to the OS-HELP loan scheme. In 2013, 408 loans were processed (an increase of 11 percent from 2012) totaling 2,433,779 AUD. Just fewer than 55 percent of UQ Abroad students took advantage of an OS-HELP Loan to support their overseas study.

With the release of the federal government's New Colombo Plan, there will be continued opportunities and funding to increase student mobility to Asia through semester exchange and short-term study programs as well as clinical placements. Furthermore, an increasing number of partners have begun offering short-term programs that coincide with UQ semester breaks, which will provide a wider range of options for students from all discipline areas (Gallagher 2013).

5 Collaboration, partnerships, alumni, and community

The entire UQ community is enriched by its relationships with international partners. These partners are universities, governments, and institutions that share our commitment to addressing issues of global importance and preparing future leaders. As part of an evidence-based approach to international collaboration inclusive of joint degrees, broad student mobility, student exchange as well as joint research projects and publications, and alumni; UQ developed a Partner Engagement Framework (PEF) (University of Queensland 2014b), which evaluates international University relationships, particularly in research co-publications and collaborations with more than 200 global partners in identified priority regions and countries. The PEF was born out of a directive to determine "Who are UQ's most highly engaged partners and how do we know? How could we apply a data informed and evidence based approach to this issue?" (Ciccarelli and Kennett 2013). The framework, accessible through a dashboard interface, measures international collaboration across 13 indicators of learning, research and staff, including mobility sponsorship, alumni, joint publications, and funded research programs, to name a few. This allows UQ to identify areas of strength, potential future engagement, and where further development is required to maximize the mutual benefit of these partnerships. Additionally, the newly developed Country

Engagement Framework (CEF) looks at the university's relationships in a much broader fashion, incorporating links with governments and government agencies, research institutes, and sponsoring bodies, as well as university partners.

Tools such as the PEF and CEF inform UQ's global strategy and have facilitated successful initiatives such as the University's USA engagement strategy, which was successfully launched in partnership with the advancement portfolio with the opening of an office in Washington DC and the establishment of The University of Queensland in America Foundation, which received more than 10 million AUD in its first year. The University has also opened an office in Jakarta in 2014 to support research, education, and alumni activities and increase engagement with industry partners in what is a country of strategic importance to Australia.

Moreover, in keeping with global trends to work in consortia to achieve shared vision and outcomes, UQ has leveraged its membership of the Australian Group of Eight (Group of Eight 2014), a coalition of leading Australian universities, intensive in research and comprehensive in general and professional education, to develop international agreements and internationalized learning and research opportunities with:

- China 9 (C9) research universities C9 includes some of China's leading research-intensive universities, which have been selected by the Chinese Government to receive intensive funding for investment in world-class research infrastructure and staff.
- European Molecular Biolog Laboratory (EMBL): EMBL is Europe's life sciences research flagship and the highest performing research institution (based on analysis of citation data).
- Council of Rectors of Chilean Universities UNIVERSITAS 21 global consortium of leading research intensive and comprehensive universities.

These partnerships have facilitated a number of collaborative internationalization achievements, including joint research and teaching programs.

One area of tremendous potential involves the university's capacity to challenge its conventional means of presenting curriculum and to engage newer technologies and pedagogical practices that are less resource intensive and dependent on soft funding sources to succeed. UQ's recent partnership in the edX consortium with founders Harvard University and the Massachusetts Institute of Technology is one example of the university embracing an opportunity to provide another dimension to internationalize the student experience through online technologies (University of Queensland 2014a). The University has also developed several targeted internationalization initiatives, such as the Bachelor of International Studies in which foreign language studies and overseas experience is compulsory and the shared Universitas 21 Diploma in Global Issues; a great example of shared global curriculum which serves to link academics globally, to broaden students' knowledge of cultural and world issues and also prepare them for a career in a global workforce.

In the area of social change and global responsibilities, UQ's work with its partners in international development and capacity building continues to grow with recent achievements including more than 400 short-course participants from 50 developing countries through AusAID-funded training programs, achieving transformational outcomes for the participants' local communities across Africa, Asia, and the Pacific.

Reflections: critical success factors

Success in these important areas of implementing a comprehensive approach to internationalizing a University, its programs and culture, is predicated on two critical, but not exclusive, factors which made a significant difference: a holistic and integrated approach, and recognition and reward.

A holistic and integrated approach

Establishing and articulating a holistic institutional approach to internationalization required an intentional strategy that aligned with and exploited the nature of UQ. The rationales for internationalization needed to align with the objectives of a research intensive globalized university educating a large body of Australian and foreign students all of whom would work in intercultural, globalized settings.

A critical success factor in establishing and maintaining internationalization as vital to strategy and practice at UQ was the establishment of the Global Strategy Sub-Committee, reporting directly to the University's Senior Management Group, chaired by the Vice-Chancellor. This included Deputy Vice-Chancellors Academic, Research, and International, and other key leaders across the University. Reporting to this peak committee as a core member meant that internationalization was a highly visible and integrated part of UQ's governance architecture. As mentioned, it was the reference group for the development and "ownership" of key frameworks such as the PEF and CEF. It ensured mainstream reporting for planning outcomes and directions for the University's' global and internationalization strategies. It gave internationalization gravitas and relevance well beyond the international portfolio and facilitated cross-university partnerships and collaborations on seed projects and sustainable programs.

Engaging key institutional leaders and representatives through key and mainstream governance committees and processes served to bring the internationalization agenda in from the periphery of the University to the core. Equally important was having the international portfolio leader as a core and key contributor, alongside faculty and institute leaders, to important University-wide academic and management committees.

One of the main failures of many approaches to comprehensive internationalization is the failure to engage in relevant central and governing/executive committee work composed of the broader academic collegium, thus ensuring that the broader internationalization agenda, ethos, and values are communicated, debated, shared, and embedded.

Maintaining leadership and focus for institutional internationalization changes as university priorities shift, is challenging. A data-informed and evidence-based approach, such as the inclusion of mobility, publication, collaboration, teaching and learning measures, and key performance indicators served to bring the same level of rigor, scrutiny, and accountability to international work that is routinely applied to teaching and research. Mainstreaming the annual review and reporting of internationalization achievements also serve to build shared ownership, pride, and recognition. This also contributed to embedding internationalization into strategy as well as seeing it as a useful and shared responsibility across the leadership of the University.

Recognition and reward

UQ translates its strategy into action by rewarding exceptional endeavors in internationalization through various high-level awards for staff, students, and alumni. Some of these annual rewards include the Vice-Chancellor's Awards for Internationalization, International Alumnus of the Year awards and Alumni Equity and Diversity Awards.

The Vice-Chancellor's Awards for Internationalization (University of Queensland 2013) recognize individuals and organizational units that have shown leadership in areas that further UQ's internationalization. The categories of awards include academic and professional staff projects; internationalization of the curriculum; promotion of overseas mobility for staff and students; and partner and student participation in internationalization promotion and or expansion. The quality and diversity of the 50 nominations UQ received in 2013 across all the categories are strong indicators of the outstanding and innovative work being undertaken throughout the University.

Concluding remarks

As de Wit (2010) and others comment, internationalization means different things in different national and institutional contexts and it is not an end in itself, but must contribute to guiding universities in collaborating, competing, and being successful in a highly globalized system of research, education, and engagement. At UQ, a comprehensive internationalization approach came to be seen as serving and contributing to the University's mission of relevant global research, educating professionals, and engaging with a distributed and globalized alumni community. The approach will continue to be judged not only by particular internationalization achievements but more importantly to its utility in serving the broader strategic and globalized agenda of the University of Queensland.

Chapter 17

Connecting internationalization to university vision
The Swinburne experience

Melissa Banks

Introduction

Consistent with national trends, and in line with institutional priorities, international engagement at Swinburne University of Technology has reached a scale and level of maturity that positions the University for more sustainable and meaningful international engagement that secures Swinburne's place in the world now and well into the future. The global and national tertiary education sector is undergoing great change. Australia's universities must position themselves for sustainable and viable international engagement within the context of increased national and global competition, shifts in the world's financial power towards Asia, contracting public funding, and disruptive innovation in digital technologies that are challenging traditional constructs of higher education.

Swinburne is a publicly funded Australian University located in Melbourne. Established in 1908 and achieving university status in 1992, Swinburne today is a progressive, world-ranked, modern university. In 2012, coinciding with wholesale university reform, Swinburne introduced a whole-of-university International Engagement Strategy and Framework. This was a significant change to how internationalization was defined, executed, and resourced in Swinburne. Two years later the strategy continues to be refined but some outcomes and lessons learned are shared in this chapter.

The national context

Australian universities face great adjustment with a complex array of monetary, policy, and technological challenges necessitating innovation and change. Beginning with a major review of the system in 2008[1] other policy shifts include formation of a national regulator (TEQSA)[2] and political and diplomatic reorientation towards Asia with release of the Asian Century White Paper[3] and the advisory paper Australia—Educating Globally.[4] Public funding for the tertiary system continues to contract and universities are under more pressure to commercialize research outputs as research funding declines (except in health). There is increased focus on STEM (science, technology, engineering, and mathematics) disciplines and Australia's aging population (median age up from 33.0 years in 1993 to 37.3 in 2013) is also changing participation in Australia's higher education system (Australian Bureau of Statistics 2013).

Looking forward, the review of the demand-driven higher education system[5] and an independent review of higher education regulation[6] is likely to result in further change. Competition domestically and globally is intensifying with more providers entering the sector particularly via online platforms. The advent of online content, delivery, communication, and assessment options including Massive Open Online Courses (MOOCs) are transforming accessibility, participation and the nature of tertiary education, and may compete with or complement traditional on-campus learning.

International education in Australia is receiving more political consideration than ever before with a proliferation of Federal and State government committees and international education/international-student strategies, and numerous student visa and skilled migration policy reforms. For the foreseeable future there will be continued growth of global student mobility with modest increase in numbers coming to Australia, particularly in the higher education sector, continued internationalization of curriculum and the student experience, growth in cross-border education with increased utilization of technology, growth in international and domestic research collaborations, and continued growth in outbound staff and student mobility.

Institutional challenges

As a federally funded public university, Swinburne is not immune to the changes and challenges facing Australia's higher education system. Consequently, significant organizational and structural changes are in motion. Commencing in 2012, the reform agenda has seen the closure of two of Swinburne's campuses and expansion of the main campus in Hawthorn with consolidation of all higher education provision there. Following the Federal government decision in 2008 to align higher education funding with student demand, Swinburne created Swinburne Online through a public–private partnership with Seek Ltd. Today full degree programs are delivered to over 5,000 students wholly online.

Throughout all this change and disruption the University's senior leaders have redefined Swinburne's vision for the future. In early 2013, following a series of visioning workshops with one hundred of the University's senior leaders, the University released its blueprint for the next seven years—Swinburne's 2020 Plan. Swinburne's vision is clear and ambitious: "By 2020, Swinburne will be Australia's leading university of science, technology and innovation" (Swinburne University of Technology 2012).

International engagement is a core enabling component of the University's vision and 2020 Plan:

Our reputation and impact as an engaged university will be amplified by fostering productive, mutually-beneficial relationships that create solutions to challenging problems. We will be public spirited, providing a trusted source of expertise and thought leadership in science, technology and innovation. Our global impact will be enhanced through our international engagement in education and research and opportunities to enhance the mobility of our students and staff.

(Swinburne University of Technology 2012, p. 4)

The International Engagement Strategy and Framework provides the context and rationale for institutional internationalization which is spearheaded by a suite of high-reputational, multi-dimensional relationships with institutions, governments, and industry in the communities in which Swinburne engages. Developed in parallel with the University's 2020 vision, the International Engagement Strategy and Framework emphasizes institutional sustainability through engagement and collaboration and adopts a rationale-driven approach to partnerships and how these will facilitate related objectives in the recently released Teaching and Learning Strategy, and the Research and Development Strategy.

The International Engagement Strategy and Framework

The International Engagement Strategy and Framework heralds a shift from what previously was fundamentally a two-dimensional approach to international education characterized by inbound and outbound student flows, to an institution-wide research-led approach to international engagement. It provides a rationale-driven, proactive model for the pursuit of collaborations with selected partners in strategic locations. It incorporates a taxonomy for engagement which defines and incorporates multiple modes of engagement that can be customized according to the desired engagement model adopted with each partner. The classifications include:

- *Reputational relationships*—these are high-value, multi-disciplinary, multi-faceted, whole-of-university partnerships with high-performance universities and research centers.
- *Collaborative research agreements*—these typically originate at researcher to researcher level and involve a specific academic department or research center only. They may develop into reputational relationships.
- *Educational relationships*—these involve mainly program, staff, and student mobility through joint curricular development, dual or joint degree arrangements, credit transfer or articulations, joint staff development, and student and staff mobility.
- *Commercial relationships*—the primary objective of these arrangements is to generate income and/or establish pipelines of prospective students for study at Swinburne campuses.

Each classification has a unique set of objectives and rationale, perceived benefits both for Swinburne and our partners (at home and abroad), a set of metrics by which agreements and partnerships will be measured and tracked, and partner selection criteria. A governance structure has been formed and is outlined below.

Key actions to get underway

The development and implementation of the International Engagement Strategy and Framework began with a review and audit of the University's existing international activity in terms of the geographic locations of research partners and how this aligned with the nations from which research students originated. Destinations of outbound students and how these aligned with the location of educational or transnational education (TNE) relationships and the countries of origins of inbound students were also examined.

The audit of international engagement identified a misalignment. Outbound mobility and research activity was heavily centered on Europe and the United States, while educational relationships and inbound mobility were mostly centered in Asia. A core aim of the International Engagement Strategy and Framework has been to achieve a greater alignment in international engagement activity. Essentially this requires a range of research relationships to be built in Asia, as well as broadening and deepening existing quality educational relationships across a range of engagement activities. Not coincidentally this re-orientation towards Asia coincided and complemented emerging government policy concerning Australia's engagement in Asia. Swinburne has proactively identified preferred partners in priority locations such as China, India, Malaysia, and Singapore. This involved mapping teaching and research areas against prospective partners to ascertain alignments, and identifying existing researcher-to-researcher relationships. Prospective research partners were selected on the basis of their alignment with Swinburne's research priority areas and research capacity. To facilitate and activate collaborations, a model for partnered PhDs, customizable for each partnership, was developed.

A cross-disciplinary reference group consisting of experienced and engaged faculty representing higher education, vocational education and Swinburne College provided a critical source of input and perspective. All policies, processes, and governance related to international partnerships were reviewed and updated. The aim was to improve coordination and collaboration whilst respecting separation of management and academic aspects of partnerships, ensure long-term viability of partnerships, reduce risk and ensure regulatory and contractual compliance, develop measures of outputs and outcomes, recognize and share examples of good practice, improve and standardize partner communications and engagement, and develop a toolkit of resources to support Swinburne faculty to foster existing and develop new agreements. This remains work in progress.

An internationalization forum was conducted to signal a significant shift in the internationalization mission in the University. The forum was enriched through attendance and contributions of invited international and national internationalization experts and all senior University academic and professional staff were invited. A draft strategy was written and socialized through various interest groups, road-tested with University Executive, and presented at the annual senior leader's forum prior to implementation.

Strategy implementation

International engagement at Swinburne is managed on both an organizational and committee structure level (Figure 17.1). Both levels work together from both

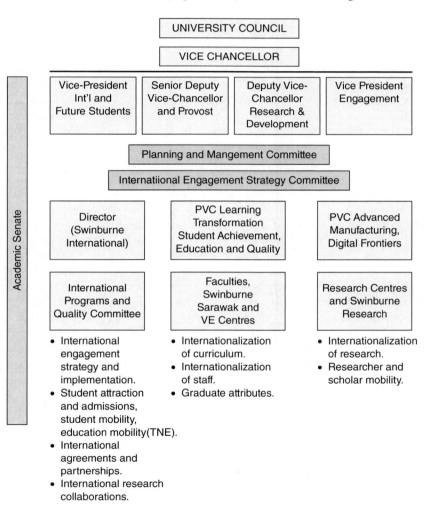

Figure 17.1 Implementing internationalization at Swinburne.

top-down to bottom-up to comprehensively manage all aspects of the university's international engagement.

The Vice President International and Future Students is ultimately responsible for international engagement and is supported by the Director of Swinburne International who has specific management responsibility for outbound mobility, inbound student recruitment and admissions, boosting international research engagement, international educational partnerships, and management oversight of TNE agreements.

Internationalization of the curriculum and staff is driven on multiple fronts within academic departments and faculties and with leadership and support from the Pro Vice Chancellor Student Advancement and targets in the Teaching and Learning Strategy. Ultimate responsibility for internationalization of curriculum and staff rests with The Senior Deputy Vice Chancellor and Provost.

The Deputy Vice Chancellor Research and Development is responsible for internationalization of Research. The Pro Vice Chancellor International Research Engagement, the Pro Vice Chancellor Advanced Manufacturing and Pro Vice Chancellor Digital Frontiers support the DVC R&D in driving research advancement both internationally and domestically within their respective fields. Each faculty has an Associate Dean Research and Engagement who provides leadership and support to individual researchers and research centers on international research engagement.

The International Engagement Strategy Committee (IESC) and the International Programs and Quality Committee (IPQC) provide a governance framework and are tasked with debating and agreeing priorities and strategy and for ensuring that international engagement plans and activities are developed, implemented and monitored ensuring University targets are met.

Academic Senate has oversight of the University's academic curriculum and quality assurance. The Senate accredits courses of study, develops policy in relation to academic programs, and monitors academic and research quality and standards. The Senate reports to University Council—the University's governing body. Regular reports are provided by academic departments, the Vice President International and Future Students and the Pro Vice Chancellor and Chief Executive Swinburne Sarawak campus to the Senate in relation to TNE programs, international-student admissions and progression, and international-student life.

The University's Governance Framework outlines Swinburne's policy structures and processes that guide how decisions are made in the University. A key objective of the governance framework is to distinguish the corporate governance function of University Council from the academic governance function of the Academic Senate. The University is currently rationalizing its policies and streamlining work instructions but at the time of writing there are several policies that govern our international activity at Swinburne.

Before and after—progress to date

International research engagement

Previously, international research engagement was not an integrated component of the University's internationalization strategy. There was no strategy for collaborative international research connections, individual researchers and research center staff were unassisted and under-supported, and there were inconsistent approaches to partner engagement and support. Contractual agreements did not always gain appropriate approvals and potentially posed risk to the University, there was no sharing of contacts and partners across disciplines, and often research relationships became inactive once the specific research project concluded.

Today there is a clear plan for growth with the International Engagement Strategy and Framework being a key enabler for realizing the objectives and targets in the Research and Development Strategy: 2013 to 2020. Through collaborations with high-performance international research organizations the Research and Development Strategy aims to secure Swinburne's position in global university ranking systems and Excellence in Research for Australia (ERA) rankings, enhance Swinburne's ability to attract high-quality research staff and students, and expand capacity and attract research grants in select disciplines.

New research partnerships in China and India developed under the strategy have developed collaborative projects that have attracted funding. By 2013 funded projects with partners in India and China had grown by 120 percent and 350 percent respectively. Research staff exchanges are occurring, annual joint conferences have been conducted, and joint research centers with partners in both countries are under consideration. Partners are citing Swinburne publications more frequently and joint papers are being written and published. Swinburne is attracting more research students. In 2013 commencing international research enrolments grew by 36 percent against negligible national growth (Austrade 2014). Swinburne invested 10.1 percent of international-student fee revenue in international research scholarships in 2013, well above the national median of 7.8 percent (Olsen 2013a).

Internationalization of curriculum, staff, and students

Internationalization of the curriculum and the student experience was not coordinated across the University and tended to be driven at academic departmental level. This now has a dedicated academic lead. The Learning and Teaching Strategy: 2013 to 2020 seeks to expand Swinburne's reach and accessibility through online education and enhancement of accompanying study and support services for students from diverse backgrounds and geographic locations; and create globally aware learners through inclusion of course relevant global issues into each teaching course and embedding international experiences in all courses.

Previously the University had limited student and staff exchange agreements in Asia yet at the time of drafting the International Engagement Strategy and

Framework there was a discernible shift in federal diplomatic and policy dialogue towards Asia. The strategy has positioned the University to take advantage of Australian Government funding schemes such as The AsiaBound Grants Program and New Colombo Plan[7] schemes promoting Australia's position and engagement in the region. Today the University is aiming to have 50 percent of outbound students undertaking an international study experience in Asia (coming from 26 percent in 2012) (Olsen 2013b).

Education collaborations are providing opportunities for student and staff exchanges, virtual mobility through joint projects and interactive classrooms, and curricula innovation and internationalization. Dual-degree program agreements are expanding and enrolments in TNE programs are growing once again following a period of rationalization of educational partnerships. A particularly interesting example of international educational collaboration is the Swinburne Design Factory. Student project groups work across borders and in cross-disciplinary teams to collaborate on challenging externally sponsored projects with other members of the Design Factory Network including Aalto University in Finland, Tongji University in China, and Duoc UC in Chile. This faculty-led initiative is a good example of multinational educational engagement and is strengthening and evolving to incorporate elements of research collaboration.

Swinburne's international branch campus

The opportunities afforded by having a campus in Asia were largely untapped, the most obvious examples being low levels of student and staff exchanges, lack of curricular enrichment across campus programs, little or no interactivity across classrooms even though the same programs were offered in Melbourne and Sarawak. Swinburne had no University-level agreements with Malaysian universities. Today Swinburne Sarawak remains largely autonomous but is an active member of the International Engagement Strategy Committee (IESC), Sarawak is now the first default destination for outbound exchange for students from Melbourne campuses, and caps on semester-long exchange have been removed.

Research engagement with Sarawak is a core element of international engagement. The Melbourne–Sarawak Research Collaboration Scheme is an internal competitive research grant program funded by the Vice Chancellor and administered by Swinburne Research. The Scheme has a total funding commitment of 7 million AUD. The primary aim of the Scheme is to support existing research collaborations between Swinburne Melbourne and Swinburne Sarawak at all stages of development, with a view to extending and strengthening those collaborations and expanding research-led engagement opportunities.[8]

Lessons learned

Two years since launching the International Engagement Strategy and Framework the vision remains largely intact, although the execution is under constant refinement.

The development of Swinburne's International Engagement Strategy and Framework coincided with substantial institutional and national higher education reform. Arguably this provided an environment that was receptive to new initiatives and approaches but extensive structural changes have resulted in new or changed players and stakeholders. More staff than ever before are involved in international engagement. Some staff were quick and willing to participate; others were less inclined and/or needed support. This is still work in progress but some of the initiatives adopted include cross-cultural communications training, cultural briefings, and development of online resources and tools to support and assist faculty engagement. The next step is to explore how the University's reward and recognition system and hiring strategies can further facilitate faculty engagement.

The creation of an Engagement Division responsible for industry and community engagement provides opportunities to expand our partnerships to industry and community partners domestically and abroad. The expansion of some academic disciplines, particularly in allied health and law, provides scope for new and different partnerships.

Some reputational and research partnerships have activated quickly, while others have been slow to develop, emphasizing the need to consult and collaborate with Swinburne's research community. Gaining the trust, cooperation, and commitment of the research community was fundamentally linked to the success of the strategy. Some were and remain suspicious, were reluctant to share their research contacts and/or thought the University was forcing them into arranged partnerships.

Swinburne has adopted an integrated approach to internationalization, as distinct from a centralized approach. Responsibility for achieving objectives and targets are shared across administrative, academic, and research units and embedded in faculty and administrative unit plans. Swinburne International consults each faculty to formally agree on international engagement priorities and strategies and track progress against agreed objectives and targets. The Teaching and Learning Plan has set ambitious targets for fostering internationalization of the curriculum, staff, and the student experience. Shared objectives and targets are ensuring a cross-institutional approach is adopted in which roles and responsibilities are defined and shared strategies are developed and implemented.

Reconceiving and realizing the value of the Sarawak campus in positioning the University in one of the fastest-growing regions of the world is an essential aspect of the University's long-term engagement in Asia. Building respectful relationships with counterparts across campuses and including senior Sarawak staff in strategy development and partner engagement is work in progress.

Other forms of cross-border activity such as expansion of online delivery to international students and transnational education delivery in countries in the Asia Pacific region will also be considered in the next update of the University's International Engagement Strategy.

Swinburne has developed focused, deeply rooted and multi-dimensional engagement with a few selected partners who share our values, competencies and ambitions, in localities that are of strategic long-term value. We are pursuing deeper focused engagement in specific locations such as China, India, Malaysia, Singapore, and Brazil, for example, whilst maintaining existing active relationships with partners in North America and Europe.

Measures of impact are necessarily long-term so output measures are useful in tracking progress. Some of the measures tracked by Swinburne include: access rates to outbound mobility; proportion of outbound study experiences undertaken in priority locations (including at Sarawak); and indicators of educational engagement with selected partners such as growth in dual degree arrangements or virtual curricular exchanges, staff exchanges, growth in joint PhD enrolments, and growth in joint publications. Other measures include growth in citations of Swinburne authored articles, improved ERA rankings and maintenance of Swinburne's position in global university ranking systems, and growth in research grants from offshore funding agencies. Each engagement classification has its own unique success measures and various output measures are reported to University Council and University Executive several times per annum.

The strategy continues to be refined and adjusted but the rationale and objectives remain largely intact. It is in the execution of the strategy where flexibility and adaptability along with a good dose of patience has been necessary.

Notes

1 Review of Higher Education (commonly referred to as The Bradley Review) was undertaken by an independent expert panel led by Emeritus Professor Denise Bradley AC. The report was released by the Australian Federal Government December 2008 and can be viewed at: http://www.innovation.gov.au/higheredu-cation/ResourcesAndPublications/ReviewOfAustralianHigherEducation/Pages/default.aspx

2 The Tertiary Education Quality and Standards Agency (TEQSA), established in 2011, was one of the key recommendations from the Bradley Review. TEQSA is an independent statutory authority responsible for regulation and quality assurance of Australia's higher education system. For more information see http://www.teqsa.gov.au/

3 Australia in the Asian Century White Paper was released by the Australian Federal Government in October 2012. It provides a roadmap for the whole of Australia—governments, industry, unions and the broader community—and the opportunities and challenges Australia faces in engaging in the region through to 2025. The report can be viewed at http://www.asiaeducation.edu.au/verve/_resources/australia-in-the-asian-century-white-paper.pdf

4 Australia Educating Globally is an advisory paper from the International Education Advisory Council. Released in February 2013 the paper considers the opportunities and challenges facing international education in Australia in the Asian century and contributes to the Federal Government's five year strategy for the international education sector. The report can be viewed at https://aei.gov.au/IEAC2/theCouncilsReport/Documents/Australia%20%e2%80%93%20Educating%20Globally%20FINAL%20REPORT.pdf

5 In 2012 limits on funding bachelor degree places in Australian universities were lifted. In November 2013 the Minister for Education, the Hon Christopher Pyne,

appointed a review panel to look at and make recommendations in relation to the demand driven funding arrangements. The report, released 13 April 2014 can be accessed online at http://education.gov.au/report-review-demand-driven-funding-system

6 In May 2013 the Australian Federal Government commissioned a review of higher education regulation. The report proposes significant change to the size and scope of TEQSA and seeks to reduce regulatory burden. It can be accessed online at http://www.innovation.gov.au/highereducation/Policy/HEAssuringQuality/Documents/FinalReviewReport.pdf

7 Developed by successive Australian Federal Governments in the wake of the Asian Century Whitepaper, The AsiaBound Grants Program and New Colombo Plan (NCP) both provide scholarships and grants to Australian students undertaking study experiences (and internships in the case of the NCP) abroad in Asia. Further information is available online https://aei.gov.au/International-network/Australia/AsiaBound/Pages/AsiaBound-Grants-Program-Guidelines.aspx#ProgramOverview and http://www.dfat.gov.au/new-colombo-plan/

8 More information about the Sarawak Research Collaboration Scheme is available online at http://www.research.swinburne.edu.au/grants-contracts/funding/internal-grants/ms.html

Chapter 18

Pathways to comprehensive internationalization

Connecting CI concepts and strategies with the institutional case stories

John K. Hudzik

This chapter is not intended to be a substitute for reading the institutional case stories in Part II of this book. Within each case story is a rich blending of institutional history and context as well as an understanding of environmental drivers and motivations for internationalization. The evolution of thinking and practice toward institutionalized CI is on display in each.

The purpose of this chapter is to link key points made in the first seven chapters of this book to examples from the institutional case stories, highlighting particularly both similarities and diversity in institutional pathways to CI. It is a sampling rather than an exhaustive replay of the case stories. As case authors individualized their stories within a general framework, not every case highlights each key point. Highlighting relevant examples will be sufficient to provide an introduction to both commonalities and diversity, as well as to underscore the idiosyncratic nature of higher education institutions in their approaches to CI.

None of the case stories gives a sense that the institution has "arrived"—that is, having fully achieved a vision for comprehensive and strategic internationalization. To the contrary, the sense is one of unfolding stories in an evolving twenty-first century context. This is consonant with views expressed at several points earlier in this book that CI is a journey, not a destination that is necessarily ever reached. There is also a hint in some of the case stories that the journey has elements of fragility and is dependent on continuing leadership and commitment. A reading of all the stories shows the complex interplay of institutional history, traditions, twenty-first century environment, goals, motivations, and internal and external drivers toward CI. Each case is a means to understand how the weaving of many factors has produced individualized institutional tapestries of CI.

Key issues and examples from the cases

Chapter 1 underscored that internationalization is not a homogenous concept, nor is comprehensive internationalization engaged in a uniform way by higher education institutions because of diversity in institutional missions, starting points, environments, and histories. The eleven institutional stories embedded in the ten case chapters amplify diversity in approach and taking individual pathways to CI. Nonetheless, there is also an underlying commonality of aspirations relating to CI which can also be seen across the eleven institutional cases.

Mission connection is paramount

Beloit College approaches comprehensive internationalization through its principal mission of undergraduate liberal arts education. Swinburne University of Technology and Nanyang Technological University give attention in their CI approaches to instruction, research, and cross-border partnerships in the context of their historical roots as institutions of science and technology, and although both advance global perspective, they also link as a matter of priority to their world region. Nelson Mandela Metropolitan University's (NMMU) approach to CI emerges from the context of an institution which was the product of recent mergers, post-apartheid, and with missions relating to those of a university in an emerging economy. The twenty-first century origin of NMMU in a radically new national environment allowed a fresh start at internationalization for both institution building and nation building purposes.

Although it can be argued that most of the case institutions think and act widely in mission and programmatic terms on internationalization, the University of Queensland and Michigan State University (MSU) are examples of institutions (both large and complex in mission and programmatic terms) that tend to see their strategic planning for internationalization in wide, deep, and complex ways, and as pushing this complexity out to a global frame: defined as "global reach" by UQ and "from land grant to world grant" by MSU. Both Queensland's and MSU's approaches explicitly connect to all core missions—the "core pillars of learning, discovery and engagement." The University of Nottingham's story also calls explicit attention to such a global frame and across all missions. Nottingham's institutional mission statement highlights that, "our purpose is to improve life for individuals and societies worldwide."

The quality driver

The case institutions explicitly or implicitly view CI as a means to enhance quality in meeting missions. Some examples: The Pontifical Catholic University of Rio de Janeiro's (PUC-Rio) historic mission is to base "academic excellence on humanistic values" in all that it does; this led PUC-Rio initially to engage internationally as a means of faculty and staff development, and now continuing that objective by becoming a "fully international university" across its missions. Lund views CI as essential to enhancing quality in research and education missions and improving global position in these. The University of Helsinki likewise sees a core connection between quality and its international engagements (particularly those within the EU) and for meeting institutional goals to rise in global stature. Nanyang views internationalization as core to its drive to advance institutional quality and achieve a very high global position as an institution, and these in turn advance both the reality and perception of Singapore as a first-rank, high-quality contributor to knowledge-based economies. At Nottingham international collaborations came to be recognized as an important goal as well as indicator of research quality. Lund's introduction to its internationalization policy states that the "ultimate aim of internationalization is to enhance the quality of research and education ...." Blekinge Institute of Technology sees "the fundamental goals for internationalization [to include] academic quality ...."

Mission inclusion

In several cases (e.g., Helsinki's) there is recognition that CI while having begun relatively narrowly with mobility, or with faculty and staff development as in PUC-Rio's case, the sense across all the cases is a pushing out of internationalization to cover all institutional missions (e.g., from mobility to education more broadly, and beyond to institutional research and synergistic collaborations across missions). In the case of Swinburne the objective is to align its teaching and research partnerships and to move from "a two-dimensional approach to international education characterized by inbound and outbound student flows, to an institution-wide research-led approach to international engagement." Connecting CI to priority institutional missions and looking for synergies in actions across missions as CI is engaged, is a key aspect of CI as discussed in Chapter 1 and is generally reflected in the institutional case stories.

Commonalities of aspirations

Also in Chapter 1 it was suggested that institutions pursuing CI would be likely to share the pursuit of several common aspirations: (a) mainstream access; (b) expand staff and departments contributing to it; (c) build synergies across missions; and (d) integrate CI into core institutional missions. To varying degrees and in varying ways the case institutions pursue these commonalities as a part of their internationalization efforts. Examples: Helsinki's core strategy of "embedded internationalization" is clearly an effort to move the work of internationalization into and throughout the institution (to mainstream and integrate throughout)—it simultaneously seeks to mainstream access as well as widen the circle of those who contribute. Queensland's "whole of the university" strategy for CI not only makes explicit its intention to mainstream participation and access, but also to expand responsibilities to play a role in delivering it. Nottingham's list of key "components of internationalization" is an encyclopedia of aspirations to ensure that "internationalization is embedded across all relevant university missions and activities."

PUC-Rio, as it moves into its "strategic phase" of internationalization, clearly seeks to mainstream and widen contributions in its objective to "spread the internationalization process out more evenly among [PUC-Rio's] various units as well as more deeply in all levels of the academic and administrative community." As an indicator of NMMU's interest in pursuing all four of the common aspirations above, its "Internationalization Committee" is composed of the senior leadership of all academic and service entities in the institution. This is similar to the strategy at MSU involving all the academic deans as well as heads of key support units as full partners in institutional CI. In all of these examples, one can see elements of mainstreaming, spread of responsibilities, and integration of CI into the expectations for behaviors throughout the institution. Nanyang's commitment to the four common aspirations shows itself in many ways, but particularly through faculty reform and internationalization which includes the global recruitment of faculty. At Lund the ultimate goal is to "integrate internationalization in all activities and processes." Integration is implicit and mainstreaming of access and responsibility explicit in Blekinge's values, "that stipulate that all activities should be measured by international standards. Furthermore all research should be planned and carried out in a multicultural and international environment." Swinburne's new internationalization strategy also embraces the four common strategies, but perhaps among the most significant change element is research engagement of the institution's internationalization strategy—spreading to incorporate all institutional missions and integration throughout all sectors of the institution are key components in addition to widening access and participation.

Institutional and environmental drivers of CI

In Chapters 1 and 2 the importance of environmental trends and drivers of CI were underscored. The case stories reflect the influence of the environment on directions of CI. In several, national policies and priorities have shaped institutional directions toward CI. For Nanyang, Singapore government priorities to build a world-class internationally connected education system to drive Singapore's knowledge economy and its continued development was a prime factor, along with funding. At Queensland and Swinburne, government policy to build and protect quality higher education connected to the region and globally (reflected in a 2012 white paper and a 2013 advisory paper on "international education in Australia in the Asian century") reinforced robust institutional approaches underway at both institutions.

At Helsinki (and with Finland joining the EU) the University expanded its connections across teaching and research missions to contribute to building country connections outward. Lund and Blekinge, and many other Swedish institutions have been aided by STINT, an independent Swedish foundation established by act of Parliament which actively encourages and funds innovative projects expressly to advance more comprehensive internationalization of Swedish institutions in research and teaching. At PUC-Rio, it was a government-sponsored staff quality improvement effort (CAPES) that funded an effort labeled "qualifications abroad third degrees." PUC-Rio's international engagement began with it and laid the foundation for ongoing cross-border professional development and teaching collaborations, growing into its current phase of strategic internationalization.

Many of the case stories show institutions responding to changing global higher education capacities, and changes in regional influence or importance. This seems clearest with revised CI institutional strategies in response to the growing position and higher education capacities in Asia: e.g., Swinburne, Nanyang, and Nottingham.

In other instances there may be a more subtle environmental influence at work in institutional movements toward CI. While the Federal Title VI program to fund area and language development has been highly influential in advancing the internationalization of hundreds of US institutions, the MSU and Beloit cases highlight the influence of "responsibility" to become locally, nationally, and globally engaged as an institution—to be responsive to environmental realities and needs at home and abroad. For decades Beloit has accepted a responsibility, "that students would understand the interrelationships and interdependence of aims and aspirations of the nations of the world …. more fully aware of man's common store of knowledge and thought." At MSU, and consonant with its land grant values, it, too, has for decades seen an obligation for the institution to view itself, "as a resource for the state, nation and the world." At NMMU a principal internal and external driver is to enhance the institution's role to advance an emerging economy in a global environment.

At times the policy environment can be a shaper of change through less than salutary means as was the case with Nottingham when the UK Government ended subsidies for international students (the same being the case in Sweden). Nottingham is described as having a relatively established disposition of looking outward as a part of institutional ethos. But "dramatic changes in the policy environment, primarily in relation to funding and performance measurement" have conditioned how the institution now retains its traditional outward look but manages its internationalization differently and more strategically.

The I³ of CI

It is striking that all the cases, some more explicitly than others, share aspects of a common strategy in moving from less to more strategic and comprehensive forms of internationalization. In all we see forms of an "*integrated, institutionalized internationalization*" (I³) taking hold. Examples include Helsinki where "embedded internationalization" can be seen as a synonym for "integration" as well as for "institutionalized" internationalization. Moving to "imbed" is not to displace responsibility but rather to spread it throughout along with expectations of results to be produced throughout. At Beloit the integrated approach meant involving the entire institution, as was becoming the case in Europe through, for example, internationalization at home. At Swinburne "integrated" is taken to be in contrast to "centralized" with "responsibility for achieving objectives and targets shared across administrative, academic and research units and embedded in faculty and administrative unit plans." MSU's strategic planning explicitly incorporates an integration of its core institutional values into a world or global frame of reference and to "think in terms of a seamless connection between local and global ...." At Queensland, the meaning of "integrated" has both horizontal and vertical dimension: "UQ's approach has been 'top down' and 'bottom up'.... and mainstreamed internationalization across the University's central structure, academic faculties, and schools ...."

Environmentally inspired organic to institutionalized CI

There is a thread that runs through many of the cases that internationalization began organically and then progressed to more "managed" and institutional versions. This is most clearly stated in the cases by Nottingham: "... like most other UK Universities, much of this [international] activity happened organically; there was little in the way of proactive management—at least not until the 1980s—when a new policy environment prompted very significant changes in the way in which UK universities approached international activity."

Even a casual reading of the rest of the cases will lead to the conclusion that "from organic to institutionalized" characterizes the march toward CI, and in each case, various mixes of environmental factors from policy, to financial issues, to a complex array of rationales and motivations such as those discussed in Chapter 3, were responsible for the advent of institutionalized and managed CI.

Resources

Discussed as one of the key enabling conditions for CI in Chapter 4 and then in detail in Chapter 7, resources for CI are not only strategically and operationally important, they are also important agents of change. While a detailed consideration of resource issues was not possible within the confines of space allotted for the cases, important points surrounding resources emerge and reinforce core points in Chapters 4 and 7. First, all case institutions appear to be employing a strategy of dual-purposing resources (see Chapter 7). Embedded and integrated internationalization is inherently connecting CI to existing resources found in established programs, faculties, and academic and service units. There are aspects of dual purposing implied or explicit across substantially different types of institutions: e.g., Beloit, Queensland, Helsinki, and PUC-Rio.

Other aspects of "resources" surfaced as drivers of change, initially in a less positive way as happened with the end of subsidies for international students at Nottingham, Lund, and Blekinge. The result for each institution was its having to develop more pro-active and strategically integrated approaches to attract international students (now on a fee-paying basis). Access to additional resources from abroad, particularly for research, is conscious strategy associated with CI at all of these institutions but very explicit as examples in the cases of MSU and Nanyang. However, there is little if any evidence in any of the cases that CI is a strategy principally for purposes of revenue enhancement. At the same time several institutions view CI as a means for making the institution more entrepreneurially competitive.

As argued in Chapter 3, to be entrepreneurial or not as a part of internationalization is an unnecessary dichotomy; a balancing of motivations (some revenue and some linked to core institutional values and missions) is possible and appears as a relevant strategy in a number of the cases.

Multiple points of leadership

A key enabling condition identified in Chapter 4 is that leadership for CI cannot come only from the international office. NMMU's Internationalization Committee is a good example of expectations of widespread and multiple points of leadership being engaged. A similar kind of multi-office leadership matrix appears at work at Swinburne, Queensland, and MSU to name a few examples; multiple points of leadership are inherent in Helsinki's "embedded" model. Returning for the moment to notions of "shared CI aspirations" raised earlier in this chapter, the cases demonstrate a proclivity toward not only expanding involvement of all academic and administrative entities in the work of CI, but to set expectations of contributions from each. Further, there are implied expectations of these other entities not only contributing to international activity but in each case proactively engaging (thereby leading) aspects of CI. While this is not explicitly stated in all of the institutional case stories, there is reason to believe it is a widespread expectation nonetheless.

Organization and structure

Chapter 4 discussed, among other topics, the nature of organizing structures to support CI, and suggested that strictly top-down organizational structures would probably not be too successful for CI purposes. Indeed, the great majority (perhaps all) of the institutional cases appear to avoid strictly top-down models for organizing support for CI. Initial impetus and macro-level strategies may originate centrally as described by Queensland, but as several institutional cases including Queensland make explicit or at least imply, "bottom up" and a "matrix" structure begin to form once action for CI begins to mature. The Helsinki model gives the appearance of being the most decentralized among the case institutions.

As noted by authors of the Queensland case, continuing involvement of a high-level management group in setting global institutional strategy has been important as part of its matrix of leadership, organization, and support. Nottingham appears to be the clearest example of a matrix-style organization for internationalization but with some challenges, as noted in the last section of this chapter. Besides Queensland, other obvious examples of matrix organizational design with variations include Swinburne and MSU. The matrix can take many forms, including, for example, at NMMU, where the Office of International Education has full membership on all key institutional standing committees and the NMMU case authors underscore the importance of internationalization being fully integrated throughout the governance structure of the institution.

The common core features of structure and organization in the cases, again some more explicit than in others, appear to include aspects of central coordination and advocacy via a senior international officer of some type; expectations of responsibilities for CI programming devolved broadly across academic and service units; and in most instances an over-arching philosophy or aspiration of the entire institution having access to and being involved in the delivery of aspects of internationalization. This last point translates to a kind of multidimensional "mainstreaming" aimed simultaneously at: (a) widening access; (b) widening responsibilities and contributions to CI; and (c) encompassing all core institutional missions. Each of these aspects of mainstreaming, but particularly the underlying devolving of responsibilities for CI, is likely to be very significant agents of change in organization and structure.

Dialog and culture building

In Chapter 4 one of the most important macro-level strategies for building a strong culture of support and active engagement across the institution in CI is wide and deep campus dialog for that purpose. Among the strongest examples in the case studies of such dialog, some repeated periodically during times of update are MSU, Swinburne, Queensland, and Beloit. One can view NMMU's involvement of all levels and aspects of governance as a form of on-going dialog. The rest of the case stories as written are less than explicit about the nature or extent of such dialog. But perhaps some assumptions can be made: for Helsinki the discussions are likely to occur within the decentralized "embedded" environments. But as pointed out in Chapters 4 and 5, it is difficult to imagine a CI approach without some degree and level of institutional dialog about it. Nonetheless, the core point is that there appears to have formed strong support cultures for internationalization, probably at all of the case institutions, which have permitted their continuing movement toward CI.

Remaining challenges

It is probably fair to state that a tipping point seems to have been reached at most of the case institutions such that turning back from more comprehensive and strategic internationalization has a low probability. At the same time, as with any broad-based institutional initiatives, a challenge will be in maintaining momentum, particularly in continuing to renew and update institutional commitment to internationalization. MSU has gone through several stages of renewal over the last several decades, and perhaps one could describe a portion of the periods in between as consolidation. Periods of consolidation and refinement following periods of rapid change are not unusual in organizations and one should not ignore the challenges of mature enterprise being resistant to further change as discussed in Chapter 5. If one takes at face value the scope and complexity of change underway at, for example, Swinburne, Queensland, Nanyang, and others, it will be interesting to watch for the scale and scope of continuing evolution of CI and its possible inter-mixing with periods of consolidation. The allied issue probably for all is whether momentum for CI can be sustained over the long run even with leadership change which is an issue that arose at the end of the PUC-Rio case story.

Looking at the specific challenges identified in the case stories, there is an interesting array of matters on the horizon at each institution. A sampling of these include the following. Among Nanyang's concerns is to balance and rationalize modes of cross-border collaborations involving individual faculty behaviors, institutional bilateral partnerships, and institutional network memberships and collaborations. Helsinki identifies the challenge of imbedding internationalization further into the faculties and better coordinating and finding synergies between teaching and research. Authors of the two Swedish institutional cases worry that institutional strategic plans are not being regularly updated and wonder further if this is a sign that the strategic plans for internationalization are not being used. The authors also wonder whether central institutionalization units are needed if internationalization is fully embedded in academic and support units. Also, does this imply that bottom-up is more valuable in terms of prompting practical CI action?

Authors of the Queensland case raise a number of potential challenges or factors critical for continuing success. Among them is whether CI can continue to effectively evolve and relate to the overall institutional priorities and goals of a research intensive institution. The Queensland case also highlights the key issue raised in Chapter 6 regarding the importance of documenting impacts and outcomes. Specifically, the authors highlight the importance and implied challenge of

> A data-informed and evidence-based approach, such as the inclusion of mobility, publication, collaborating, teaching and learning measures, and key performance indicators served to bring the same level of rigor, scrutiny, and accountability to international work that is routinely applied to teaching and research.

Similarly, the Beloit case author focuses on the challenge of showing results and outcomes, but to do so under the potential complication of seeing internationalization as a process, not a product.

Nottingham raised the on-going challenges of reconciling top-down and bottom-up and potentially conflicting objectives and clarity of leadership associated with matrix models. This reflects the point made in Chapters 4 and 5 that although matrix organizations provide greater flexibility and ability to combine assets for specific purposes, they can create discomfort or worse in situations intolerant of ambiguity.

In sum

The case stories and the concepts, trends and related issues raised in the first seven chapters of this book offer a view of the internationalization of higher education institutions that is taking root in strategic and comprehensive ways globally. There is clearly substantial diversity in how comprehensive internationalization is made operational by institutions of varying types, shaped and individualized in terms of their varying missions, size, location, starting points, and preferred institutional modes of operation. Internationalization of higher education institutions has been evolving in concept and in practice, and there is little doubt, if any, that practice and possibly the concept of comprehensive internationalization itself will continue to evolve in response to changes in higher education and the nature of higher education institutions. Clearly, the global environment continues to evolve and develop in ways that are only partially predictable with any degree of certainty.

There is a wide range in the degree of international engagement among the large number of higher education institutions that exist globally, perhaps 15,000–18,000 institutions of varying kinds. The degree of institutional internationalization and engagement across these institutions ranges from little or none to institutionally complex and ubiquitous. Yet, the trend toward wider and more comprehensive and strategic international activity across core missions of teaching/learning, research/scholarship, and service/engagement is encompassing a widening circle of institutions and would seem irreversible in the realities of a twenty-first century environment.

Bibliography

Aerden, A., De Decker, F., Divis, J., Frederiks, M., de Wit, H., 2013. Assessing the internationalisation of degree programmes: experiences from a Dutch-Flemish pilot certifying internationalisation. *Compare: A Journal of Comparative and International Education* 43, 56–78. doi:10.1080/03057925.2013.746562

Alexander, B.G., 2013. *Analysis of OECD Report "Trends Shaping Education 2013"* [WWW document]. URL: http://blogs.ubc.ca/etec522sept13/2013/09/09analysis-of-oecd-report-trends-shaping-education-2013 (accessed 7.28.2014).

Altbach, P., 2010. The state of the rankings [WWW document]. *Inside Higher Ed.* URL: http://www.insidehighered.com/views/2010/11/11/altbach (accessed 10.16.14).

American Council on Education (ACE), 2012. *Mapping Internationalization on U.S. Campuses.* Center for Internationalization and Global Engagement, ACE, Washington, DC.

American Council on Education (ACE), 2014. *ACE/FIPSE Project on Assessing International Learning* [WWW document]. URL: https://www.acenet.edu/news-room/Pages/ACEFIPSE-Project-on-Assessing-International-Learning.aspx (accessed 4.5.14).

American International Recruitment Council (AIRC), 2014. *Who We Are—Overview, Mission, Vision, Governance, Quick Facts* [WWW document]. AIRC: About the American International Recruitment Council. URL: http://airc.worldsecuresystems.com/about-airc (accessed 4.15.14).

Anderson, J.Q., Boyles, J.L., Rainie, L., 2012. *The Future Impact of the Internet on Higher Education: Experts Expect More-Efficient Collaborative Environments and New Grading Schemes; They Worry About Massive Online Courses, the Shift Away From On-Campus Life.* The Future of the Internet. Pew Research Center, Washington, DC.

Arum, J., Roska, J., 2011. *Academically Adrift: Limited Learning on College Campuses.* University of Chicago Press, Chicago, IL.

Arum, S., Van der Water, J., 1992. The need for a definition of international education in U.S. universities, in: Klasek, C. (Ed.), *Bridges to the Future: Strategies for Internationalizing Higher Education.* Association of International Education Administrators, Carbondale, IL, pp. 198–203.

Association of Public and Land Grant Universities (APLU), 2011. *The Voluntary System of Accountability* [WWW document]. URL: http://www.voluntarysystem.org (accessed 4.20.14).

Austrade. 2014. International Student Enrolement Data – Australia – YTD December 2013 Standard Pivot Table, Canberra, Department of Foreign Affairs and Trade Australian Government. URL http://www.austrade.gov.au/Education/Student-Data/2014/Pivot-Tables (accessed 4.14.14).

Australian Bureau of Statistics, 2013. 3101.0 *Australia's Demographic Statistics, June 2013.* [WWW document]. URL: http://www.abs.gov.au/ausstats/abs@.nsf/Products/3101.0~Jun+2013~Feature+Article~Population+by+Age+and+Sex,+Australia,+States+and+Territories+(Feature+Article)?OpenDocument (accessed 4.13.14).

Australian Education International, 2013. *International Student Enrollment Data, Table 23: Higher Education Enrollments and Commencements by Nationality and Level of Study for December 2013.* Australian Government, Canberra, Australia.

Australian Government, Department of Foreign Affairs and Trade (DFAT), 2014. *About the New Colombo Plan* [WWW document]. URL: http://www.dfat.gov.au/new-colombo-plan/about.html (accessed 5.19.14).

Australian Universities International Directors Forum (AUIDF), 2013. *AUIDF Benchmarking 2012.* (Unpublished.)

Balogun, J., 2001. Strategic change: introduction. *Management Quarterly* 10, 2–11.

Balogun, J., Hope Hailey, V., 2004. *Exploring Strategic Change, 2nd ed.*, Exploring Corporate Strategy series. Prentice Hall/Financial Times, Harlow, UK.

Bandura, A., 1977. *Social Learning Theory.* Prentice Hall, Englewood Cliffs, NJ.

Bandura, A., 1986. *Social Foundations of Thought and Action: A Social Cognitive Theory.* Prentice Hall, Englewood Cliffs, NJ.

Banks, J.A., 2004. Approaches to multicultural curriculum reform, in: Banks, J.A., McGee Banks, C.A. (Eds.), *Multicultural Education: Issues and Perspectives.* Wiley & Sons, Hoboken, NJ, pp. 242–264.

Banks, M., Olsen, A., Pearce, D., 2007. *Global Student Mobility: An Australian Perspective Five Years On.* IDP Education, Canberra, Australia.

Barker, R.A., 2002. *On the Nature of Leadership.* University Press of America, Lanham, MD.

Barnard, M., Stoll, N., 2010. *Organisation Change Management: A Rapid Literature Review* (No. Short Policy Report No. 10/01). Centre for Understanding Behavior Change, Bristol Institute of Public Affairs, University of Bristol, Bristol, UK.

Barnett, R., 2013. *Imagining the University: New Studies in Critical Realism and Education.* Routledge, New York.

Bartlett, C.A., Ghoshal, S., 1990. Matrix management: not a structure, a frame of mind. *Harvard Business Review* 68, 138–145.

Beck, K., 2012. Globalization/s: reproduction and resistance in the internationalization of education. *Canadian Journal of Education* 35, 133–148.

Beelen, J., 2011. Internationalisation at home in a global perspective: a critical survey of the 3rd global survey report of IAU. *Globalisation and Internationalisation of Higher Education, Revista de Universidad y Sociedad del Conocimiento (RUSC)* 8, 249–264.

Beerkens, E., 2013. Why the university as we know it will still be here in 25 years, in: de Wit, H., Hunter, F., Johnson, L., van Liempd, H.-G. (Eds.), *Possible Futures: The Next 25 Years of the Internationalisation of Higher Education.* European Association for International Education (EAIE), Amsterdam, pp. 44–47.

Beerkens, E., Brandenburg, U., Evers, N., van Gaalen, A., Leichsenring, H., Zimmerman, V., 2010. *Indicator Projects on Internationalization: Approaches, Methods and*

Findings. (A report in the context of the European Project "Indicators for Mapping & Profiling Internationalization" (IMPI).)

Beloit College, 1960a. *Blueprint for the Future—An Expanded View.* Morse Library Archives.

Beloit College, 1960b. *How Broad is Outlook?* Editorial. The Round Table, March 30.

Beloit College, 2002. Internal document, Office of International Education.

Beloit College, 2014. *International education mission statement* [WWW document]. URL: http://www.beloit.edu/oie/international_education/mission/ (accessed 5.19.14).

Bennett, C.A., Lumsdaine, A.A. (Eds.), 1975. *Evaluation and Experiment: Some Critical issues in Assessing Social Programs.* Quantative Studies in Social Relations. Academic Press, New York.

Bennett, D.C., Cornwell, G.H., Al-Lail, H.J., Schenck, C., 2012. An education for the twenty-first century: stewardship of the global commons. *Liberal Education* 98(4), 34–41.

Biddle, S., 2002. *Internationalization: Rhetoric or Reality* (ACLS Occasional Paper No. No. 56). American Council of Learned Societies, New York, NY.

Blekinge tekniska högskola, 2007a. *Internationaliseringsplan vid Blekinge tekniska högskola* [Plan for Internationalization at Blekinge Institute of Technology]. Karlskrona, Sweden.

Blekinge tekniska högskola, 2007b. *Internationaliseringspolicy vid Blekinge tekniska högskola* [Internationalization Policy at Blekinge Institute of Technology]. Karlskrona, Sweden.

Bloom, B.S. (Ed.), 1956. *Taxonomy of Educational Objectives: Handbook I. Cognitive Domain.* David McKay, New York.

Blumenstyk, G., 2009. *In a Time of Uncertainty, Colleges Hold Fast to the* Status Quo [WWW document]. The Chronicle of Higher Education. URL: http://chronicle. com/article/In-a-Time-of-Uncertainty/48911 (accessed 10.16.14).

Brandenburg, U., 2013. *Internationalisation Without values? A Response.* Presented at the ACA 20th Anniversary Conference, Academic Cooperation Association (ACA), The Hague, June 9–11.

Brandenburg, U., de Wit, H., 2011a. The end of internationalization. *International Higher Education* 62, 15–16.

Brandenburg, U., de Wit, H., 2011b. *Has International Education Lost Its Way?* [WWW document]. The Chronicle of Higher Education. URL: http://chronicle. com/blogs/worldwise/has-international-education-lost-its-way/28891 (accessed 1.1.14).

Brandenburg, U., de Wit, H., 2012. *Higher Education is Losing Sight of What Internationalisation is all about* [WWW document]. *The Guardian.* URL: http:// www.theguardian.com/higher-education-network/blog/2012/apr/02/internationalisation-labeling-learning-outcomes (accessed 4.29.14).

Brandenburg, U., Ermel, H., Federkeil, G., Fuchs, S., Gross, M., Menn, A., 2009. How to measure the internationality and internationalisation of higher education institutions: indicators and key figures, in: de Wit, H. (Ed.), *Measuring Success in the Internationalisation of Higher Education.* European Association for International Education (EAIE), Amsterdam, pp. 65–76.

Brandenburg, U., Hudzik, J., Ota, H., Roberston, S., 2013. From innovation to mainstream and beyond: the unfolding story of internationalisation in Higher

Education, in: de Wit, H., Hunter, F., Johnson, L., van Liempd, H.-G. (Eds.), *Possible Futures: The Next 25 Years of the Internationalisation of Higher Education*. European Association for International Education (EAIE), Amsterdam, pp. 63–78.

Brewer, E., 2013. *Faculty Development: Does It Matter to Internationalization?* Presentation drawing on a 2012 survey of Beloit College participants in international faculty development activities.

Brewer, E., Leask, B., 2012. Internationalization of the curriculum, in: *The SAGE Handbook of International Higher Education*. Sage, Los Angeles, CA, pp. 246–265.

British Council, 2012. *The Shape of Things to Come: Higher Education Global Trends and Emerging Opportunities to 2020*. British Council, London, UK.

British Council, 2013a. *Culture at Work: The Value of Intercultural Skills in the Workplace*. British Council, London.

British Council, 2013b. *MEGATRENDS: The Future of International Education*. British Council, London.

Brooks, J.S., Normore, A.H., 2010. Educational leadership and globalization: literacy for a glocal perspective. *Educational Policy* 24, 52–82. doi:10.1177/0895904809354070

Burwell, F., 2011. *George Collie Dreams of an International College* [WWW document]. Fridays with Fred. URL: https://www.beloit.edu/campus/news/fwf/ (accessed 5.19.14).

Campbell, D.T., Stanley, J.C., Gage, N.L., 1963. *Experimental and Quasi-Experimental Designs for Research*. Houghton Mifflin, Boston.

Carlecrantz, G., 2012. *Swedish Excellence Seminars: An application for Strategic Grants from STINT*. Lund University, Lund, Sweden.

Castells, M., Muller, J., Cloete, N., Badat, S. (Eds.), 2001. *Challenges of Globalisation: South African Debates with Manuel Castells*. Maskew Miller Longman, Pinelands, Cape Town.

Center for Global Education, 2014. *Impact of Study Abroad on Retention and Success* [WWW document]. GlobaledResearch.com: Study Abroad Research Online. URL: http://globaledresearch.com/study-abroad-impact.asp (accessed 4.7.14).

Center for Internationalization and Global Engagement (CIGE), 2012. *Mapping Internationalization on U.S. Campuses: 2012 Edition*. American Council on Education, Washington, DC.

Chao, R.Y., 2014. GLOBAL: the ongoing and future crisis in higher education. *University World News* No. 302, January 10, 2014.

Chemers, M.M., 1997. *An Integrative Theory of Leadership*. Erlbaum Associates, Mahwah, NJ.

Childress, L., 2009. *The Twenty-First Century University: Developing Faculty Engagement in Internationalization*. Peter Lang Publishing, Frankfurt, Germany.

Christensen, C., Eyring, H., 2011. *The Innovative University: Changing the DNA of Higher Education from the Inside Out*. Jossey-Bass, San Francisco, CA.

Ciccarelli, A., Kennett, G., 2013. Do partnerships advance internationalisation? *University World News* No. 284, August 24.

Clark, B.R., 1998. *Creating Entrepreneurial Universities: Organizational Pathways of Transformation*. Pergamon, New York.

Collie, G.L., 1924. *Outline college plan for fusing of all races; Beloit professor believes courses for foreign students here, with co-operative and scientific study of racial problems would aid world peace*. New York Times, NY.

Committee of the Corporation and the Academic Faculty, 1828. *Reports on the Course of Instruction in Yale College* [WWW document]. URL: http://www.yale.edu/terc/collectiblesandpublications/specialdocuments/Historical_Documents/1828_curriculum.pdf (accessed 5.19.14).

Cook, T.D., Campbell, D.T., 1979. *Quasi-Experimentation: Design and Analysis Issues for Field Settings*. Houghton Mifflin, Boston, MA.

Council and House of Representatives of the Territory of Wisconsin, 1846. *Beloit College Charter* [WWW document]. URL: http://www.beloit.edu/~libhome/Archives/beloit/charter.html (accessed 4.13.14).

Cuthbert, D., Smith, W., Boey, J., 2008. What do we really know about the outcomes of Australian international education? *Journal of Studies in International Education* 12, 255–275.

Dale, R., 1999. Specifying globalisation effects on national policy: a focus on the mechanisms. *Journal of Educational Policy* 14, 1–17.

Daquila, T.C., Huang, S., 2013. Introductory editorial for a special theme of the *Journal of Studies in International Education*: Internationalizing higher education in Southeast Asia—government and institutional responses. *Journal of Studies in International Education* 17, 624–628. doi:10.1177/1028315313502982

de Ridder-Symoens, H., 1996. Mobility, in: de Ridder-Symoens, H. (Ed.), *A History of the University in Europe: Vol. 2. Universities in Early Modern Europe*. Cambridge University Press, Cambridge, UK.

de Wit, H., 1995. *Rationales for Internationalisation of Higher Education*. Universiteit, Amsterdam.

de Wit, H., 1998. *Rationales for Internationalisation of Higher Education* [WWW document]. Polytechnic Institute of Viseu. URL: http://www.ipv.pt/millenium/wit11.htm (accessed 4.20.14).

de Wit, H., 2002. *Internationalization of Higher Education in the United States of America and Europe: A Historical, Comparative, and Conceptual Analysis*. Greenwood Press, Westport, CT.

de Wit, H., 2010. *Internationalisation of Higher Education in Europe and Its Assessment, Trends and Issues*. The Accreditation Organisation of the Netherlands and Flanders (NVAO), Amsterdam.

de Wit, H., 2011a. *Trends, Issues and Challenges in Internationalisation of Higher Education*. Centre for Applied Research on Economics & Management, School of Economics and Management of the Hogeschool van Amsterdam, Amsterdam.

de Wit, H., 2011b. GLOBAL: Naming internationalisation will not revive it. *University World News* No. 194, October 23.

de Wit, H., 2012. *Assessing Internationalization of Degree Programs—a Dutch–Flemish Pilot* [WWW document]. Inside Higher Ed. URL: http://www.insidehighered.com/blogs/world-view/assessing-internationalization-degree-programs-%E2%80%94-dutch-flemish-pilot (accessed 4.29.14).

de Wit, H., 2013. Internationalisation of higher education, an introduction and the why, how and what, in: de Wit, H. (Ed.), *An Introduction to Higher Education Internationalisation*. V & P, Milan, Italy, pp. 13–46.

de Wit, H., Hunter, F., Johnson, L., Van Liempd, H.-G. (Eds.), 2013. *Possible Futures: The Next 25 Years of the Internationalisaton of Higher Education*. European Association for International Education, Amsterdam.

de Wit, H., Knight, J. (Eds.), 1999. *Quality and Internationalisation in Higher Education*. OECD, Paris.

de Wit, H., Merkx, G., 2012. The history of internationalization of higher education, in: Deardorff, D., de Wit, H., Heyl, J., Adams, T. (Eds.), *The SAGE Handbook of International Higher Education*. Sage, Thousand Oaks, CA, pp. 43–59.

Deardorff, D.K., de Wit, H., Heyl, J.D., 2012a. Bridges to the future: the global landscape of international higher education, in: Deardorff, D., de Wit, H., Heyl, J., Adams, T. (Eds.), *The SAGE Handbook of International Higher Education*. Sage, Thousand Oaks, CA, pp. 457–486.

Deardorff, D.K., de Wit, H., Heyl, J., Adams, T. (Eds.), 2012b. *The SAGE Handbook of International Higher Education*. Sage, Thousand Oaks, CA.

Deardorff, D.K., Psyarchik, D.T., Yun, Z.-S., 2009. Towards effective international learning assessment: principles, design and implementation, in: de Wit, H. (Ed.), *Measuring Success in the Internationalization of Higher Education*. European Association for International Education (EAIE), Amsterdam, pp. 23–38.

Deardorff, D.K., van Gaalen, A., 2012. Outcomes assessment in the internationalization of higher education, in: Deardorff, D.K., Wit, H. de, Heyl, J. (Eds.), *The SAGE Handbook of International Higher Education*. Sage, Thousand Oaks, CA, pp. 167–189.

Delgado-Marquez, B., Hurtado-Torres, N., Bondar, Y., 2012. Internationalization of higher education in university institution rankings: the influence of national culture. *Journal of International Education and Leadership* 2, 1–17.

Duderstadt, J.J., 2009. *Current Global Trends in Higher Education and Research: Their Impact on Europe*. Presented at the Dies Academicus 2009 Address, Universitat Wien, Vienna, Austria.

Earl, S., Smutylo, T., 2001. *Outcome Mapping: Building Learning and Reflection into Development Programs*. International Development Research Centre (IDRC), Ottawa, Canada.

Eckel, P., Green, M., Hill, B., 2001. On Change V. *Riding the Waves of Change: Insights from Transforming Institutions*. American Council on Education, Washington, DC.

Editorial, 1960. *How Broad is Outlook?* Beloit College Roundtable, March 30.

Egron-Polak, E., Hudson, R., 2014. *Internationalization of Higher Education: Growing Expectations, Fundamental Values*. IAU 4th Global Survey. International Association of Universities, Paris.

Engberg, D., Green, M.F. (Eds.), 2002. *Promising Practices: Spotlighting Excellence in Comprehensive Internationalization*. American Council on Education, Washington, DC.

Epstein, E.H., 1994. Comparative and international education: overview and historical development, in: Husen, T., Neville Postlethwaite, T. (Eds.), *The International Encyclopedia of Higher Education*. Pergamon, Oxford, UK.

Eriksson, P., 2013. *Spännande besök i Brasilien* [Exciting visit to Brazil] [WWW document]. URL: http://lundarektorerna.blogg.lu.se/spannande-besok-i-brasilien (accessed 4.11.14).

Erkkilä, T., Piironen, O., 2013. Shifting fundaments of European higher education governance: competition, ranking, autonomy and accountability. *Comparative Education*, 1–15. doi:10.1080/03050068.2013.807643

Ernst & Young, 2013. *Hitting the Sweet Spot: The Growth of the Middle Class in Emerging Markets*. EYGM, UK.

Estermann, T., Pruvot, E.B., Claeys-Kulik, A.-L., 2013. *Designing Strategies for Efficient Funding of Higher Education in Europe*. European University Association, Brussels, Belgium.

European Commission, 2013. *Communication from the Commission to the European Parliament, the Council, the European Economic and Social Committee and the Committee of the Regions: European Higher Education in the World*. European Commission, Brussels, Belgium.

Forum on Education Abroad, 2012. *Bibliography of Outcomes Assessment Studies in Education Abroad (October 2012)* [WWW document]. URL: http://www.forumea.org/research-outcomes-reviewsypnosis2011.cfm (accessed 3.22.14).

Fukuyama, F., 1992. *The End of History and the Last Man*. Free Press, New York.

Galbraith, J.R., 2008. *Designing Matrix Organizations that Actually Work: How IBM, Procter & Gamble, and Others Design for Success*. Jossey-Bass, San Francisco, CA.

Gallagher, J., 2013. 2013 *Global Mobility and Internationalisation Report*. University of Queensland, Brisbane, Australia.

Glänzel, W., 2001. National characteristics in international scientific co-authorship relations. *Scientometrics* 51, 69–115.

Göthenberg, A., Pohl, H., Adler, N., 2012. *Strategic Measures for Competitive Internationalization of Higher Education and Research*. OECD, Paris.

Green, M.F., 2005. *The Challenge of Internationalizing Undergraduate Education: Global Learning for all*. Presented at the Global Challenges and U.S. Higher Education Conference, Duke University. Durham, NC, pp. 1–30.

Green, M.F., 2007. Internationalizing community colleges: barriers and strategies. *New Directions for Community Colleges* 138, 15–24.

Green, M.F., 2012a. *Global Citizenship: What are we Talking About and Why Does It Matter? Trends & Insights for International Education Leaders, January, 1–4* [WWW document]. URL: http://www.nafsa.org/Explore-International-Education/Trends/TI/Global-Citizenship-What-Are-We-Talking-About-and-Why-Does-It-Matter/

Green, M.F., 2012b. *Measuring and Assessing Internationalization*. NAFSA, the Association of International Educators, Washington, DC.

Green, M.F., Luu, D.T., Burris, B., 2008. *Mapping Internationalization on U.S. Campuses: 2008 edition*. American Council on Education, Washington, DC.

Green, M.F., Olson, C., 2003. *Internationalizing the Campus: A User's Guide*. American Council on Education, Washington, DC.

Green, M.F., Marmolejo, F., Egron-Polak, E., 2012. The internationalization of higher education: future prospects, in: Deardorff, D., de Wit, H., Heyl, J., Adams, T. (Eds.), *The SAGE Handbook of International Higher Education*. Sage, Thousand Oaks, CA, pp. 439–456.

Green, W., Mertova, P., 2009. *Internationalisation of Teaching and Learning at the University of Queensland: A Report on Current Perceptions and Practices*. The University of Queensland, Australia, Brisbane, Australia.

Green, W., Mertova, P., 2011. Enaging with the gatekeepers: faculty perspectives on developing curriculum for globally responsible citizenship, in: Clifford, V., Montgomery, C. (Eds.), *Internationalisation of the Curriculum for Global Citizenship: Policies, Practices and Pitfalls*. Oxford Centre for Staff and Learning Development (OCSLD) Press, Oxford, UK, pp. 69–91.

Group of Eight, 2014. *Group of Eight Australia* [WWW document]. URL: https://go8.edu.au/ (accessed 5.19.14).

Halpern, S., 1969. *The Institute of International Education* (doctoral dissertation). Columbia University, New York.

Hammer, M., 2012. The Intercultural Development Inventory: a new frontier in assessment and development of intercultural competence, in: Vande Berg, M., Paige, R.M., Lou, K.H. (Eds.), *Student Learning Abroad*. Sty, Sterling, VA, pp. 115–136.

Hanson, L., 2008. Global citizenship, global health, and the internationalization of curriculum: a study of transformative potential. *Journal of Studies* 14, 70–88.

Harden, N., 2012. *The End of the University as we Know It* [WWW document]. The American Interest. URL: http://www.the-american-interest.com/articles/2012/12/11/the-end-of-the-university-as-we-know-it/

Hatry, H.P., Winnie, R.E., Fisk, D.M., *The Urban Institute. Practical Program Evaluation for State and Local Government Officials (No. NCJ 014322)*. U.S. Department of Housing and Urban Development, Washington, DC.

Hazelkorn, E., 2011. *Rankings and the Reshaping of Higher Education: The Battle for World-Class Excellence*. Palgrave Macmillan, Houndmills, Basingstoke, UK.

Hearn, J.C., 1996. Transforming U.S. higher education: an organizational perspective. *Innovative Higher Education* 21, 141–154.

Hénard, F., Diamond, L., Roseveare, D., 2012. *Approaches to Internationalisation and Their Implications for Strategic Management and Institutional Practice: A Guide for Higher Education Institutions*. OECD Higher Education Programme (IMHE). OECD, Paris.

Heyl, J.D. (2007). *The Senior International Officer (SIO) as Change Agent* [Monograph]. Durham, NC: Association of International Education Administrators.

Heyl, J.D., Thullen, M., Heyl, J.D., Brownell, B.A., 2007. *The Senior International Officer (SIO) as Change Agent*. Association of International Education Administrators (AIEA), Durham, NC.

Hoffa, W.W., 2007. *A History of US Study Abroad: Beginnings to 1965*. A special edition of Frontiers: The Interdisciplinary Journal of Study Abroad.

Hudzik, J.K., 2011. *Comprehensive Internationalization: From Concept to Action*. NAFSA: Association of International Educators, Washington, DC.

Hudzik, J.K., 2012. *More Action, Not Just Talk, on Internationalization* [WWW document]. The Chronicle of Higher Education. URL: http://chronicle.com/blogs/worldwise/more-action-not-just-talk-on-higher-education-internationalization/29068 (accessed 4.23.14).

Hudzik, J.K., 2014. *Tripping Over or Reconciling the Words of Internationalization* [WWW document]. Trends and Insights for International Education Leaders. NAFSA, Washington DC. URL: http://www.nafsa.org/Explore_International_Education/Trends/TI/Tripping_Over_or_Reconciling_the_Words_of_Internationalization/ (accessed 10.16.14).

Hudzik, J.K., Pynes, P.J., 2014. *Developing Sustainable Resources for Internationalization*. NAFSA, Washington, DC. https://www.nafsa.org/sustainableIZN (accessed 10.16.14).

Hudzik, J.K., McCarthy, J.S., 2012. *Leading Comprehensive Internationalization: Strategy and Tactics for Action*. NAFSA, the Association of International Educators, Washington, DC.

Hudzik, J.K., Simon, L.K., 2012. From a land-grant to a world-grant ideal: Extending public higher education to a global frame, in: Fogel, D., Malson-Huddle, E. (Eds.), *Precipice or Crossroads? Where America's Great Public Universities Stand and Where They Are Going Midway Through Their Second Century*. SUNY Press, New York.

Hudzik, J.K., Stohl, M., 2009. Modeling assessment of outcomes and impacts from internationalization, in: de Wit, H. (Ed.), *Measuring Success in the*

Internationalization of Higher Education. European Association for International Education (EAIE), Amsterdam.

Hudzik, J.K., Stohl, M., 2012. Comprehensive and strategic internationalization of U.S. higher education, in: Deardorff, D., de Wit, H., Heyl, J., Adams, T. (Eds.), *The SAGE Handbook of International Higher Education.* Sage, Thousand Oaks, CA, pp. 61–80.

Hudzik, J.K., Wakeley, J.H., 1981. Evaluating court training programs. *Judicature* 64, 369–375.

Hunter, F., 2012. European universities: victims or agents of change?, in: Beelen, J., de Wit, H. (Eds.), *Internationalisation Revisited: New Dimensions in the Internationalisation of Higher Education.* Center for Applied Research on Economics and Management (CAREM), Amsterdam, pp. 113–124.

Institute of International Education (IIE), 2012. *U.S. Students Pursuing Degrees Overseas* [WWW document]. Institute of International Education. URL: http://www.iie.org/en/Who-We-Are/News-and-Events/Press-Center/Press-Releases/2012/2012-01-18-US-Students-Pursuing-Degrees-Overseas-Report (accessed 4.29.14).

International Association of Universities (IAU), 2009. *Initial Results: 2009 IAU Global Survey on Internationalization of Higher Education.* International Association of Universities, Paris.

International Association of Universities (IAU), 2012. *Affirming Academic Values in Internationalization of Higher Education: A Call for Action* [WWW document]. URL: http://www.iau-aiu.net/sites/all/files/Affirming_Academic_Values_in_ Internationalization_of_Higher_Education.pdf (accessed 10.16.14).

Ip, G., 2013. *The gated globe. The Economist,* October 12.

Ivarsson, V., Petochi, M., 2012. *What Will the University of the Future Look Like?* [WWW document]. World Economic Forum Blog. URL: http://forumblog.org/2012/06/what-will-the-successful-university-of-the-future-look-like/ (accessed 4.23.14).

Jensen, C., 2012. *Strategic Grants—Situation Report.* Lund University, Lund, Sweden.

Jeptoo, M.L., Razia, M., 2012. Internationalization of higher education: rationale, collaborations and its implications. *International Journal of Academic Research in Progressive Education and Development* 1, 365–372.

Jones, E., 2011. GLOBAL: Internationalisation—Aid, trade, pervade. *University World News* No. 195, October 30.

Jones, E., 2012. Challenging received wisdom: personal transformation through short-term international programmes, in: Beelen, J., de Wit, H. (Eds.), *Internationalisation Revisited: New Dimensions in the Internationalisation of Higher Education.* Center for Applied Research on Economics and Management (CAREM), Amsterdam.

Jones, E., 2013a. Internationalisation and student learning outcomes, in: de Wit, H. (Ed.), *An Introduction to Higher Education Internationalisation.* V & P, Milan, Italy, pp. 107–116.

Jones, E., 2013b. The global reach of universities: leading and engaging academic and support staff in the internationalization of higher education, in: Sugden, R., Valania, M., Wilson, J.R. (Eds.), *Leadership and Cooperation in Academia: Reflecting on the Roles and Responsibilities of University Faculty and Management.* Edward Elgar, Northampton, MA.

Jones, E., de Wit, H., 2012. Globalization of internationalization: thematic and regional reflections on a traditional concept. *AUDEM: The International Journal of Higher Education and Democracy* 3, 35–54.

Jones, E., de Wit, H. (Eds.), 2014. Globalized internationalization: from concept to action. *IIE Networker*, Spring, 28.

Jones, E.E., Kannouse, D.E., Kelley, H.H., Nisbett, R.E., Valins, S., Weiner, B., 1972. *Attribution: Perceiving the Causes of Behavior*. General Learning Press, Morristown, NJ.

Jooste, N., 2012. *Benchmarking Across Borders*. Colloquium Series Volume 5. Nelson Mandela Metropolitan University Port Elizabeth, South Africa.

Jooste, N., 2013. Towards a comprehensive internationalisation practice, in: Jooste, N. (Ed.) *Study South Africa. The Guide to South African Higher Education, 13th Edition*. IEASA.

Jowi, J.O., 2009. *Internationalization of Higher Education in Africa: Developments, Emerging Trends, Issues and Policy Implications*. African Network for Internationalization of Education (ANIE), Moi University, Kenya.

Jung, C.G., 1969. *Psychology and Religion: West and East*, 2nd ed., Bollingen series. Princeton University Press, Princeton, NJ.

Kearney, M.-L., Yelland, R., 2010. *Higher education in a world changed utterly— doing more with less*. Presented at the OECD/IMHE General Conference Institutional Management in Higher Education, Paris, France.

Kehm, B., 2011. *Research on internationalisation in higher education*. Presented at the The International Higher Education Congress: New Trends and Issues, Istanbul, Turkey.

Kehm, B.M., Teichler, U., 2007. Research on internationalisation in higher education. *Journal of Studies in International Education* 11, 260–273. doi:10.1177/1028315307303534

Kerr, C., 1987. A critical age in the university world: accumulated heritage versus modern imperatives. *European* 22, 183–193.

Kerr, C., 1994. *Higher Education Cannot Escape History: Issues for the Twenty-First Century*. State University of New York Press, Albany, NY.

Kezar, A., 2001. *Understanding and Facilitating Organizational Change in the 21st Century: Recent Research and Conceptualizations*. ASHE-ERIC Higher Education Report, Jossey-Bass Higher and Adult Education Series 28, iii–147.

Kezar, A., Eckel, P.D., 2004. Meeting today's governance challenges. *The Journal of Higher Education* 75, 371–398.

Kim, W.C., Mauborgne, R., 2005. *Blue Ocean Strategy: How to Create Uncontested Market Space and Make the Competition Irrelevant*. Harvard Business School Press, Boston, MA.

Kirkpatrick, D.L., 1977. Evaluating training programs: evidence vs. proof. *Training and Development Journal* 31, 9–12.

Klastorin, T., 2004. *Project Management: Tools and Tradeoffs*. John Wiley, Hoboken, NJ.

Knight, J., 1994. Internationalization: elements and checkpoints. *Canadian Bureau of International Education Research* 7, 1–15.

Knight, J., 2003. Updating the definition of internationalization. *International Higher Education* 33, 2.

Knight, J., 2004. Internationalization remodeled: definitions, rationales, and approaches. *Journal for Studies in International Education* 8, 5–31.

Knight, J., 2008. *Higher Education in Turmoil: The Changing World of Internationalization*. Sense Publishers, Rotterdam.

Knight, J., 2011a. Five myths about internationalization. *International Higher Education* 62, 14–15.

Knight, J., 2011b. Is internationalisation having an identity crisis? *IMHE Info*, August, 1.

Knight, J., 2012. Concepts, rationales, and interpretive frameworks in the internationalization of higher education, in: Deardorff, D., de Wit, H., Heyl, J., Adams, T. (Eds.), *The SAGE Handbook of International Higher Education*. Sage, Thousand Oaks, CA, pp. 27–42.

Knight, J., de Wit, H. (Eds.), 1997. *Internationalization of Higher Education in Asia Pacific Countries*. European Association for International Education, Amsterdam.

Knight, J., de Wit, H. (Eds.), 1999. Internationalization of higher education, in: *Quality and Internationalisation in Higher Education*. OECD, Paris.

Kotter, J.P., 2012. *Leading Change*. Harvard Business Review Press, Cambridge, MA.

Lane, J., Kinser, K., 2012. *What is the Role for Governments in Global Higher Education?* [WWW document]. The Chronicle of Higher Education. URL: http://chronicle. com/blogs/worldwise/what-is-the-role-for-governments-in-university-internationalization/29399 (accessed 4.23.14).

Lane, J., Kinser, K., 2013. *Looking Ahead: 5 International Trends for 2013* [WWW document]. Chronicle of Higher Education. URL: http://chronicle.com/blogs/ worldwise/looking-ahead-5-international-trends-for-2013 (accessed 7.28.14).

Leask, B., 2004. Internationalisation outcomes for all students using information and communication technologies (ICTs). *Journal of Studies in International Education* 8, 336-351.

Leask, B., 2009. Using formal and informal curricula to improve interactions between home and international students. *Journal of Studies in International Education* 13(2), pp. 205–221. Available at: http://jsi.sagepub.com/cgi/ doi/10.1177/1028315308329786 (accessed 10.16.14).

Leask, B., 2012a. *Internationalisation of the Curriculum in Action: A guide* [WWW document]. Australian Government Office for Teaching and Learning; University of South Australia. URL: http://www.ioc.net.au/main/file.php/2/V2_Internationalisation_of_curriculum_6pg_Brochure_Finale.pdf (accessed 1.31.13).

Leask, B., 2012b. Taking a holistic approach to internationalisation: connecting institutional policy with the everyday reality of student life, in: Beelen, J., Wit, H. de (Eds.), *Internationalisation Revisited: New Dimensions in the Internationalisation of Higher Education*. Centre for Applied Research on Economics and Management (CAREM), Amsterdam, pp. 73–88.

Leask, B., 2013. Internationalisation of the curriculum and staff engagement: an introduction, in: de Wit, H. (Ed.), *An Introduction to Higher Education Internationalisation*. V & P, Milan, Italy, pp. 91–106.

Leask, B., 2014. *'Blockers and Enablers' survey* [WWW document]. Internationalisation of the Curriculum in Action. URL: http://www.ioc.net.au/main/mod/ resource/view.php?id=87

Leeuw, F., Vaessen, J., 2009. *Impact Evaluations and Development: NONIE Guidance on Impact Evaluation*. The Network of Networks on Impact Evaluation, Washington, DC.

Leonard, D.C., 2002. *Learning Theories, A to Z*. Oryx Press, Westport, CT.

Loveland, E., 2011a. Place and promise: an interview with Stephen J. Toope, president and vice-chancellor of The University of British Columbia. *International Educator* 20, 22–28.

Loveland, E., 2011b. The emergence of the global network university: an interview with New York University President John Sexton. *International Educator* 16, 16–20.

Lund University, 2007. *Lund University Internationalisation Policy 2008–2011.* Lund University, Lund, Sweden.

Lund University, 2010. *Handlingsplan för internationalisering 2010–2011* [Action plan for internationalization 2010–2011]. Lund University, Lund, Sweden.

Lund University, 2012. *Strategic Plan: Lund University 2012–2016.* Lund University, Lund, Sweden.

Lund University, 2013. *Lund University 2013: Education, Research and Innovation since 1666.* Lund University, Lund, Sweden.

Malik, K., United Nations Development Programme, 2013. *Human Development Report 2013: The Rise of the South: Human Progress in a Diverse World.* United Nations Development Programme, New York.

Mandela, N., 1998. Address by President Nelson Mandela on Receiving an Honorary Doctorate from Harvard University.

Marginson, S., 2013. We are becoming more global, in: de Wit, H., Hunter, F., Johnson, L., van Liempd, H.-G. (Eds.), *Possible Futures: The Next 25 Years of the Internationalisation of Higher Education.* European Association for International Education (EAIE), Amsterdam, pp. 48–51.

Marginson, S., Considine, M., 2000. *The Enterprise University: Power, Governance, and Reinvention in Australia.* Cambridge University Press, Cambridge, UK.

Marginson, S., Rhoades, G., 2002. Beyond national states, markets, and systems of higher education: a glonacal agency heuristic. *Higher Education* 43, 281–309.

Marginson, S., van der Wende, M., 2007. *Globalisation and Higher Education* (OECD Education Working Papers No. 8).

Maringe, F., Foskett, N. (Eds.), 2010. *Globalization and Internationalization in Higher Education: Theoretical, Strategic and Management Perspectives.* Continuum, London.

Mazzarol, T., Soutar, G.N., Seng, M.S.Y., 2003. The third wave: future trends in international education. *International Journal of Educational Management* 17, 90–99. doi:10.1108/09513540310467778

McMaster, M., 2007. *Partnerships Between Administrative and Academic Managers: How Deans and Faculty Managers Work Together* [WWW document]. Association of Tertiary Education Management. URL: http://www.atem.org.au/downloads/doc/018_mcmaster.doc (accessed 5.10.07).

McPherson, P., Schulenburger, D.E., Gobstein, H., Keller, C., 2009. *Competitiveness of Public Research Universities and Consequences for the Country: Recommendations for Change*, in: National Association of State Universities and Land-Grant Colleges Discussion Paper Working Draft.

Mehaffy, G., 2012. Challenge and change. *EDUCAUSE Review* 47, 25–42.

Mestenhauser, J.A., 1998. Portraits of an international curriculum: an uncommon multidimensional perspective, in: Mestenhauser, J.A., Ellingboe, B. (Eds.), *Reforming the Higher Education Curriculum: Internationalizing the Campus.* The Oryx Press, Phoenix, AZ, pp. 3–39.

Mestenhauser, J.A., Ellingboe, B. (Eds.), 1998. *Reforming the Higher Education Curriculum: Internationalizing the Campus.* American Council on Education/Oryx Press Series on Higher Education, Phoenix, AZ.

Middlehurst, R., 2004. Changing internal governance: a discussion of leadership roles and management structures in UK universities. *Higher Education Quarterly* 58, 258–270.

Miller, C., 2006. *A Test of Leadership: Charting the Future of U.S. Higher Education.* Department of Education, Washington, DC.

Mintzberg, H., 1979. *The Structuring of Organizations: A Synthesis of the Research.* Prentice-Hall, Englewood Cliffs, NJ.

Moja, T., Cloete, N., 2001. Vanishing borders and new boundaries, in: Muller, J., Cloete, N., Badat, S. (Eds.), *Challenges of Globalisation: South African Debates with Manuel Castells.* Maskew Miller Longman, Pinelands, Cape Town.

Mueller, S.L., Thomas, A.S., 2001. Culture and entrepreneurial potential: a nine country study of locus of control and innovativeness. *Journal of Business Venturing* 16, 51–75.

Murray, D.A., 1960. *Proposal for the Inauguration of the Beloit College World Affairs Institute.* Morse Library Archives, Natick, MA.

Musil, C.M., 2006. *Assessing Global Learning: Matching Good Intentions with Good Practice.* American Association of Colleges and Universities, Washington, DC.

NACAC, 2013. *Report of the Commission on International Student Recruitment to the National Association for College Admission Counseling, May 2013.* National Association for College Admission Counseling (NACAC), Arlington, VA.

NAFSA: Association of International Educators, 2014. *Simon Award for Campus Internationalization: Selected institutions* [WWW document]. NAFSA: Association of International Educators. URL: http://www.nafsa.org/Explore_International_Education/Impact/Awards/Senator_Paul_Simon_Award/Simon_Award_for_Campus_Internationalization__Selected_Institutions/ (accessed 4.29.14).

NAFSA Task Force on Internationalization, 2008. *NAFSA's Contribution to Internationalization of Higher Education.* NAFSA: Association of International Educators, Washington, DC.

National Taiwan University, 2013. *2013 National Taiwan University Ranking (NTU Ranking)* [WWW document]. National Taiwan University Ranking: Performance Ranking of Scientific Papers for World Universities 2013. URL: http://nturanking.lis.ntu.edu.tw/ (accessed 5.19.13).

Neave, G., 1997. *The European dimension in higher education. An historical analysis.* Presented at the The Relationship Between Higher Education and the Nation-State, Enschede, the Netherlands.

Neave, G., 2002. Anything goes: or how the accommodation of Europe's universities to European integration integrates an inspiring number of contradictions. *Tertiary Education and Management* 8(2), 181–197.

Nilsson, B., Otten, M., 2003. Special issue: Internationalisation at home. *Journal of Studies in International Education* 7.

Nokkala, T., 2007. *Constructing the ideal university: The internationalisation of higher education in the competitive knowledge society* (Academic Dissertation). University of Tampere, Tampere, Finland.

NSB, 2010. *Science and Engineering Indicators: 2010.* National Science Foundation Board, Arlington, VA.

Nuffic, 2013. *Mapping Internationalisation* [WWW document]. Nuffic.nl. URL: http://www.nuffic.nl/en/expertise/quality-assurance-and-internationalisation/mapping-internationalisation-mint (accessed 5.9.14).

NVAO, 2011. *Frameworks for the Assessment of Internationalisation* [WWW document]. Netherlands Flemish Accrediting Association. URL: http://nvao.com/page/downloads/NVAO_Frameworks_for_the_Assessment_of_Internationalisation.pdf (accessed 4.23.14).

OBHE (Observatory on Borderless Higher Education)—Lawton, W., Ahmed, M., Angulo, T., Axel-Berg, A., Burrows, A., Katsomitros, A., 2013. *Horizon Scanning: What will Higher Education Look Like in 2020?* Research Series/12. The UK HE International Unit, London.

OECD, 2008. *OECD Feasibility Study for the International Assessment of Higher Education Learning Outcomes (AHELO)* [WWW document]. URL: http://www.oecd.org/edu/ahelo (accessed 4.29.14).

OECD, 2011. Education at a Glance 2011, *Education at a Glance.* OECD Publishing, Paris.

OECD, 2012. Education Today 2013, *Education Today.* OECD Publishing, Paris.

OECD, 2013a. Trends Shaping Education 2013, *Trends Shaping Education.* OECD Publishing, Paris.

OECD, 2013b. Education at a Glance 2013, *Education at a Glance.* OECD Publishing, Paris.

OECD, 2013c. Indicator C4: Who studies abroad and where?, in: *Education at a Glance 2013: OECD Indicators.* OECD Publishing, Paris.

OECD, 2013d. *OECD Skills Outlook 2013.* OECD Publishing, Paris.

Ogden, A., 2007. The view from the veranda: understanding today's colonial student. *Frontiers: The Interdisciplinary Journal of Study Abroad* 15, 35–56.

Olsen, A., 2013a. Outgoing International Mobility of Australian University Students 2012, Australian Universities International Directors Forum.

Olsen, A., 2013b. 2013 Research Agenda: Australian Universities International Directors' Forum Presentation to Australian International Education Conference, Canberra, October 2013. URL: http://www.spre.com.au/download/AIEC2013AUIDResearchPaper.pdf. (accessed 04.16.14)

Olson, C.L., Evans, R., Shoenberg, R.E., 2007. *At Home in the World: Bridging the Gap.* American Council on Education, Washington, DC.

Olson, C.L., Green, M.F., Hill, B.A., 2005. *Building a Strategic Framework for Comprehensive Institutionalization.* American Council on Education, Washington, DC.

Olson, C.L., Green, M.F., Hill, B.A., 2006. *A Handbook for Advancing Comprehensive Internationalization: What Institutions Can Do and What Students Should Learn.* Global Learning for All: The third in a series of working papers on internationalizing higher education in the United States. American Council on Education, Washington, DC.

Ota, H., 2012. Changes in internationalization of Japanese higher education. *IAU Horizons* 17, 26–27.

Pasternack, P., Bloch, R., Gellert, C., Holscher, M., Kreckel, R., Lewin, D., Lischka, I., Schildberg, A., 2006. *Current and Future Trends in Higher Education: Summary.* Federal Ministry for Education, Science and Culture, Vienna, Austria.

Pratt, B., Hailey, J., Gallo, M., Shadwick, R., Hayman, R., 2012. *Understanding Private Donors in International Development* (Policy briefing paper 31). INTRAC International NGO Training and Research Centre, Oxford, UK.

Project Management Institute, 2013. *A Guide to the Project Management Body of Knowledge, 5th edition.* Project Management Institute, Newtown Square, PA.

PROPHE, 2010. *Private and Public Higher Education Shares for 117 Countries* [WWW document]. Program for Research on Private Higher Education. URL: http://www.albany.edu/dept/eaps/prophe/data/international.htm   (accessed 6.15.11).

Quacquarelli Symonds Limited, 2014. *University Rankings—Top Universities* [WWW document]. QS Top Universities: Worldwide university rankings, guides & events. URL: http://www.topuniversities.com/university-rankings (accessed 5.19.14).

Rea, L., 2003. Responses and outcomes to international curricula offered off and on campus: two case studies at Hiram College. *International Education* 32, 40.

Redden, E., 2011. *"The end of internationalization"?* [WWW document]. Inside Higher Ed. URL: http://www.insidehighered.com/news/2011/06/03/international_educators_debate_the_why_behind_their_profession (accessed 10.16.14).

Rhoads, R., Szelényi, K., 2011. *Global Citizenship and the University: Advancing Social Life and Relations in an Interdependent World*. Stanford University Press, Palo Alto, CA.

Rindefjäll, T., 2010. *Halvtidsuppföljning av policy for internationalisering vid Lunds universitet 2008–2011: Slutrapport* [Mid-term evaluation of Lund University internationalization policy 2008–2011: Final report]. Lund University, Lund, Sweden.

Rodenberg, T.C., 2010. Measuring commitment to internationalizing the campus: an institutional fingerprint. *Journal of Applied Learning in Higher Education* 2, 39–53.

Rogers, P.J., 2008. Using programme theory to evaluate complicated and complex aspects of interventions. *Evaluation* 14, 29–48. doi:10.1177/1356389007084674

Ruby, A., 2010. *The Uncertain Future for International Higher Education in the Asia-Pacific Region*. NAFSA: Association of International Educators, Washington, DC.

Rumbley, L., Altbach, P., Reisberg, L., 2012. Internationalization within the higher education context, in: Deardorff, D., de Wit, H., Heyl, J., Adams, T. (Eds.), *The SAGE Handbook of International Higher Education*. Sage, Thousand Oaks, CA, pp. 3–26.

Russell, B.H., Ryan, G.W., 2010. *Analyzing Qualitative Data: Systematic Approaches*. Sage, Thousand Oaks, CA.

Samuelson, R.J., 2013. The new globalization. *The Washington Post*, October 16.

Schein, E.H., 2009. *The Corporate Culture Survival Guide, new and rev. ed.* Jossey-Bass, San Francisco, CA.

Schofer, E., Meyer, J.W., 2005. The worldwide expansion of higher education in the twentieth century. *American Sociological Review* 70, 898–920.

Scott, G., 2003. Effective change management in higher education. *EDU* 38, 64–80.

Scott, P., 1998a. Globalization and the university, in: Scott, P. (Ed.), *The Globalization of Higher Education*. SRHE and Open University Press, Buckingham, UK.

Scott, P. (Ed.), 1998b. *The Globalization of Higher Education*. Society for Research into Higher Education and Open University Press, Buckingham, UK.

Scott, P., 2013. Future trends in international education, in: de Wit, H., Hunter, F., Johnson, L., van Liempd, H.-G. (Eds.), *Possible Futures: The Next 25 Years of the Internationalisation of Higher Education*. European Association for International Education (EAIE), Amsterdam, pp. 52–57.

Shane, S., 1993. Cultural influences on national rates of innovation. *Journal of Business Venturing* 8, 59–73.

Shanghai Ranking Consultancy, 2013. *2013 World University Rankings* [WWW document]. Academic Ranking of World Universities since 2003. URL: http://www. shanghairanking.com/ (accessed 5.19.14).

Shealy, C.N., 2004. A model and method for "making" a combined-integrated psychologist: Equilintegration (EI) theory and the Beliefs, Events, and Values Inventory (BEVI). *Journal of Clinical Psychology* 60, 1065–1090. doi:10.1002/jclp.20035

Siegel, K., 1992. *No Longer the College on the Hill: Beloit's International Outlook from 1847–1924.* Beloit College Archives, Beloit, WI.

Simon, L.K., 2013. From land-grant to a "world-grant" university: musings of a state university president. *International Educator*, Sept–Oct, 48–51.

Slaughter, S., Leslie, L., 1999. *Academic Capitalism: Politics, Policies and the Entrepreneurial University.* Johns Hopkins University Press, Baltimore, MD.

Smith, M.K., 2003. *Learning Theory* [WWW document]. Infed. URL: http://www. infed.org/biblio/b-learn.htm (accessed 2.19.07).

Smithee, M.B., 2012. Finding leadership for the internationalization of U.S. higher education. *Journal of International Education and Leadership* 2, 1–29.

Soderqvist, M., 2002. *Internationalization and Its Management at Higher-Education Institutions: Applying Conceptual, Content and Discourse Analysis.* Helsinki School of Economics, Helsinki, Finland.

Sporn, B., 1999. Current issues and future priorities for European higher education systems, in: Altbach, P., Peterson, P.M. (Eds.), *Higher Education in the 21st Century: Global Challenge and National Response*, IIE Research Report 29. Institute of International Education and the Boston College Center for International Higher Education, Annapolis Junction, MD, pp. 67–77.

Sporn, B., 2003. *Convergence or Divergence in International Higher Education Policy: Lessons from Europe.* Publications from the Forum for the Future of Higher Education, Cambridge, MA.

Srivastava, R., Gendy, M., Narayanan, M., Arun, Y., Singh, J., 2012. *University of the Future: A Thousand Year Old Industry on the Cusp of Profound Change.* Ernst & Young, Australia.

Sternberger, L., Psyarchik, D.T., Yun, Z.-S., Deardorff, D.K., 2009. Designing a model for international learning assessment. *Diversity & Democracy: Civic Learning for Shared Futures* 12, 7–9.

Suchman, E.A., 1967. *Evaluation Research: Principles and Practices in Public Service and Social Action Programs.* Russell Sage Foundation, New York.

Swedish National Agency for Higher Education, 2011. Swedish Universities & Unversity Colleges: Short Version of Annual Report 2011. Report 2011:15 R. Swedish National Agency for Higher Education, Stockholm, Sweden.

Swedish National Agency for Higher Education, 2012. *Statistisk analys, Färre studenter från Asien efter avgiftsreformen* [Smaller number of students from Asia after the tuition fee reform]. Swedish National Agency for Higher Education, Stockholm, Sweden.

Sweeney, S., 2012. *Going Mobile: Internationalisation, Mobility and the European Higher Education Area.* The Higher Education Academy, York, UK.

Swinburne University of Technology, 2012. *Swinburne University of Technology 2020 Plan* [WWW document]. URL: http://www.swinburne.edu.au/chancellery/about/resources/documents/2020-plan.pdf (accessed 4.13.14).

Teichler, U., 1998. The role of the European Union in the internationalization of higher education, in: Scott, P. (Ed.), *The Globalization of Higher Education*. Open University Press, Buckingham, UK.

Teichler, U., 2004. The changing debate on internationalisation of higher education. *Higher Education* 48, 5–26. doi:10.1023/B:HIGH.0000033771.69078.41

Teichler, U., 2009. Internationalisation of higher education: European experiences. *Asia Pacific Education Review* 10, 93–106. doi:10.1007/s12564-009-9002-7

Teixeira, P., 2009. *Mass Higher Education and Private Institutions, Higher Education to 2030, Volume 2: Globalization*. OECD, Paris.

Times Higher Education, 2014. *World University Rankings* [WWW document]. *Times Higher Education*. URL: http://www.timeshighereducation.co.uk/world-university-rankings/ (accessed 5.19.14).

Toope, S.J., 2010. *Stephen Toope on Global Challenges and the Organizational-Ethical Dilemmas of Universities* [WWW document]. Inside Higher Ed. URL: http://www.insidehighered.com/blogs/globalhighered/stephen_toope_ubc_on_global_challenges_and_the_organizational_ethical_dilemmas_of_universities (accessed 4.20.14).

Trondal, J., Stensaker, B., Gornitzka, Å., Massen, P., 2001. *Internasjonalisering av høyere utdanning: Trender og utfordringer* (No. NIFU skriftserie nr. 28/2001). Norsk institutt for studier av forskning og utdanning (NIFU), Oslo.

Tucker, R., 2010. *Four Barriers to Innovation*. Comment on "In search of innovators" [WWW document]. Inside Higher Ed. URL: http://app3.insidehighered.com/news/2010/06/04/aei (accessed 10.16.14).

Twombly, S.D., Salisbury, M.H., Tumanut, S.D., Klute, P., 2013. Study abroad in a new global century: renewing the promise refining the purpose. *ASHE Higher Education Report* 38.

University of Queensland, 2013. *Vice-Chancellors' Awards for Internationalisation 2013* [WWW document]. UQ International. URL: http://www.uq.edu.au/international/vice-chancellors-awards-for-internationalisation-2013 (accessed 5.19.14).

University of Queensland, 2014a. *What is edX?* [WWW document]. UQx – The University of Queensland. URL: http://uqx.uq.edu.au (accessed 5.19.14).

University of Queensland, 2014b. Partner engagement framework [WWW document]. The University of Queensland: UQ International. URL: http://www.uq.edu.au/international/partner-engagement-framework (accessed 5.19.14).

U.S. Department of Education, 2012. *Succeeding Globally Through International Education Management (U.S. Department of Education International Strategy 2012–2016)*. USDE, Washington, DC.

U.S. News & World Report, 2014. *Top Public Schools: National Universities* [WWW document]. URL: http://colleges.usnews.rankingsandreviews.com/best-colleges/rankings/national-universities/top-public/page+2 (accessed 10.16.14).

Vaira, M., 2004. Globalization and higher education organizational change: a framework for analysis. *Higher Education* 48, 483–510. doi:10.1023/B:HIGH.0000046711.31908.e5

Van Damme, D., 2014. *The economics of international higher education*. Presented at the European Association for International Education, 25th Anniversary Event, Amsterdam.

Van der Water, J., 1997. Gaps in the bridge to the twenty-first century: the customer is always right. *International Educator* 6, 10–15.

Van der Wende, M., 2001. Internationalisation policies: about new trends and contrasting paradigms. *Higher Education Policy* 14, 249–259. doi:10.1016/S0952–8733(01)00018–6

Van Vught, F., van der Wende, M., Westerheidjen, D.F., 2002. Globalization and internationalization: policy agendas compared, in: Enders, J., Fulton, O. (Eds.), *Higher Education in a Globalizing World: International Trends and Mutual Observations. A Festschrift in Honor of Ulrich Teichler.* Kluwer Academic, Dordrecht, the Netherlands.

Vande Berg, M., Paige, R.M., Lou, K.H. (Eds.), 2012. *Student Learning Abroad: What Our Students are Learning, What They're Not, and What We Can Do About It, 1st edition.* Stylus Publishing, LLC, Sterling, Virginia.

Vickers, P., Bekhradnia, B., 2007. *The Economic Costs and Benefits of International Students. UK.* Higher Education Policy Institute, Oxford, UK.

Waechter, B., 2003. An introduction: internationalization at home in context. *Journal of Studies in International Education* 7, 5–11.

Waechter, B., 2013. *The drivers of mobility.* Presented at the ACA 20th Anniversary Conference, Academic Cooperation Association (ACA), The Hague, June 9–11, 2013.

Weick, K.E., 1991. Educational organizations as loosely coupled systems, in: Peterson, M.W., Chaffee, E.E., White, T.H. (Eds.), *Organization and Governance in Higher Education.* Ginn Press, Needham Heights, MA.

Weiler, H.N., 2008. Keyword: International research on higher education: Scholarship between policy and science. *Zeitschrift für Erziehungswissenschaft* 11, 516–541. doi:10.1007/s11618–008–0050–2

Wikipedia.org, 2014. *List of Development Aid Agencies* [WWW document]. Wikipedia, the free encyclopedia. URL: http://en.wikipedia.org/wiki/List_of_development_aid_agencies (accessed 2.27.14).

Wildavsky, B., 2010. *The Great Brain Race: How Global Universities Are Reshaping the World.* Princeton University Press, Princeton, NJ.

Wilson, L., 2013. The internationalisation of higher education and research: European policies and institutional strategies, in: de Wit, H., Hunter, F., Johnson, L., van Liempd, H.-G. (Eds.), *Possible Futures: The Next 25 Years of the Internationalisation of Higher Education.* European Association for International Education (EAIE), Amsterdam, pp. 28–33.

Winston, G., 1998. Creating the context for change, in: Meyerson, J. (Ed.), *New Thinking on Higher Education.* Anker, Bolton, MA, pp. 1–14.

Index

Note: *italic* page numbers indicate tables; **bold** indicate figures.